52

VOLUME **THREE**

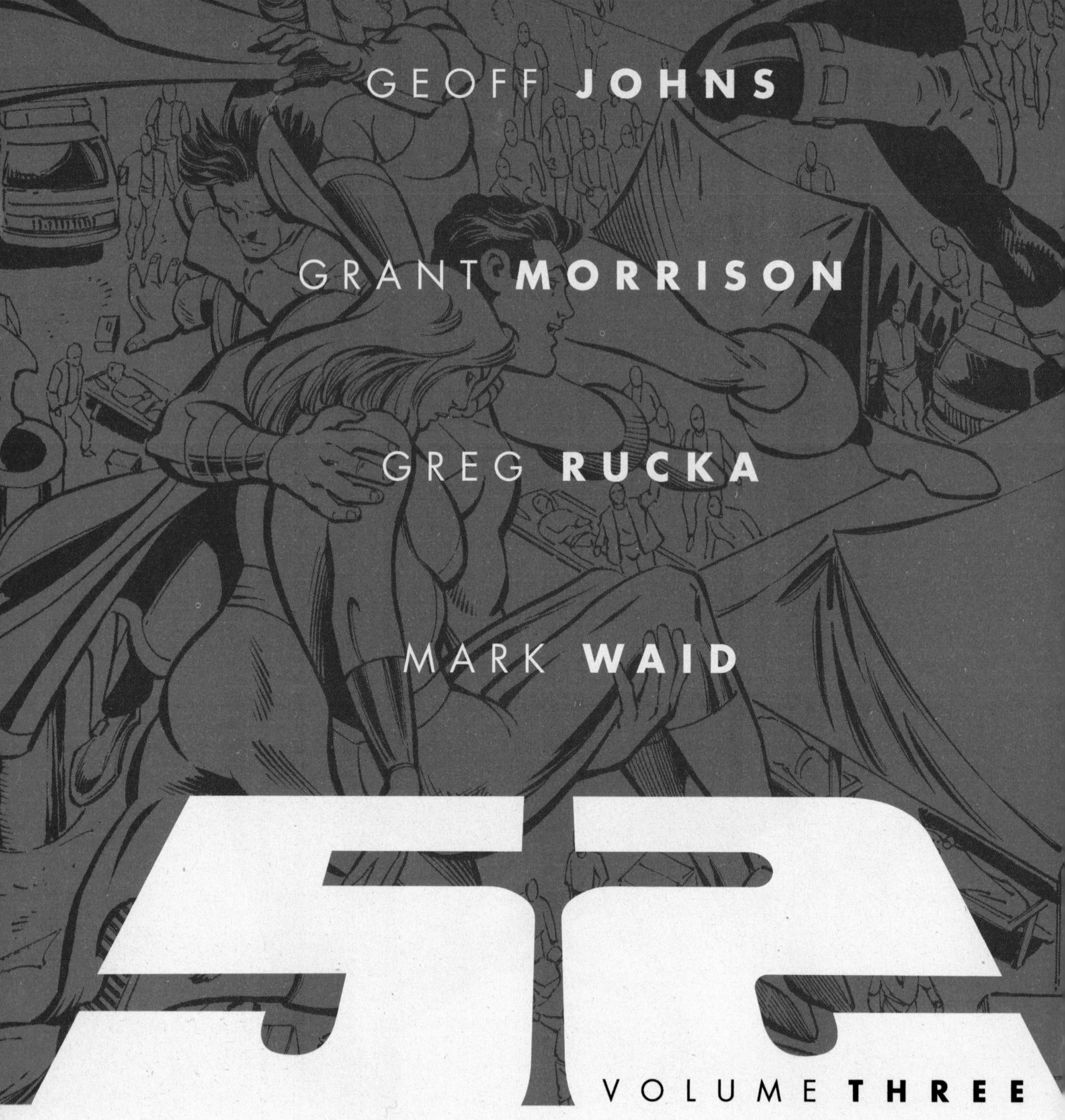

GEOFF **JOHNS**

GRANT **MORRISON**

GREG **RUCKA**

MARK **WAID**

52 VOLUME **THREE**

Dan DiDio Senior VP-Executive Editor **Stephen Wacker** **Michael Siglain** Editors-original series **Jeanine Schaefer** Associate Editor-original series **Harvey Richards** Assistant Editor-original series **Anton Kawasaki** Editor-collected edition **Robbin Brosterman** Senior Art Director **Paul Levitz** President & Publisher **Georg Brewer** VP-Design & DC Direct Creative **Richard Bruning** Senior VP-Creative Director **Patrick Caldon** Executive VP-Finance & Operations **Chris Caramalis** VP-Finance **John Cunningham** VP-Marketing **Terri Cunningham** VP-Managing Editor **Alison Gill** VP-Manufacturing **Hank Kanalz** VP-General Manager, WildStorm **Jim Lee** Editorial Director-WildStorm **Paula Lowitt** Senior VP-Business & Legal Affairs **MaryEllen McLaughlin** VP-Advertising & Custom Publishing **John Nee** VP-Business Development **Gregory Noveck** Senior VP-Creative Affairs **Sue Pohja** VP-Book Trade Sales **Cheryl Rubin** Senior VP-Brand Management **Jeff Trojan** VP-Business Development, DC Direct **Bob Wayne** VP-Sales

Cover by J.G. Jones with Alex Sinclair
Publication design by Robbie Biederman

52: VOLUME THREE

DC Comics, 1700 Broadway, New York, NY 10019. A Warner Bros. Entertainment Company. Printed in Canada. First Printing.
ISBN: 1-4012-1443-6 ISBN 13: 978-1-4012-1443-2

art breakdowns **KEITH GIFFEN** pencils **CHRIS BATISTA, JOE BENNETT TOM DERENICK, JAMAL IGLE, PHIL JIMENEZ, DREW JOHNSON, DAN JURGENS, SHAWN MOLL, PATRICK OLLIFFE, JOE PRADO, ANDY SMITH** inks **MARIAH BENES, JOE BENNETT, KEITH CHAMPAGNE, DREW GERACI, DAN GREEN, JACK JADSON, RUY JOSE, ANDY LANNING, JAY LEISTEN, DAVE MEIKIS, NELSON, RODNEY RAMOS, NORM RAPMUND, PRENTIS ROLLINS, RAY SNYDER** colors **DAVID BARON, HI-FI, PETE PANTAZIS, ALEX SINCLAIR** letters **PHIL BALSMAN, PAT BROSSEAU, JARED K. FLETCHER, ROB LEIGH, TRAVIS LANHAM**

original covers **J.G. JONES** with **ALEX SINCLAIR**

PREVIOUSLY . . .

In the wake of the INFINITE CRISIS, the DC Universe is left without its three biggest icons — Superman, Batman and Wonder Woman.

But it is *not* a world without heroes...

In Metropolis, fame-seeking Booster Gold takes advantage of Superman's absence — using his robot sidekick Skeets's knowledge of the future to help prevent crimes and catastrophes. But a new, mysterious hero known as Supernova has been stealing some of Booster's thunder. When both heroes try to stop a giant creature from causing a nuclear explosion in the middle of the city, Booster performs a courageous act...that proves to be his last.

Elsewhere in Metropolis, Lex Luthor's Everyman Program, which gives ordinary people super abilities, is in full swing. A newly powered Natasha Irons, niece of John Henry Irons (a.k.a. Steel), joins Luthor's new super-team: Infinity, Inc. — which has little in common with the former team, other than name. John Henry mourns the departure of Natasha, and suspects something sinister is going on behind the scenes with Luthor's team. When the group is deployed to take care of a rampaging Blockbuster, Luthor — watching from afar — takes the powers away from Infinity member Trajectory during a critical moment in the fight, causing her to be killed in action.

Ralph Dibny, the former hero known as Elongated Man, continues to search for a way to bring his dead wife Sue back to life by any means possible — exploring the realms of magic and the afterlife.

Noble scientist Will Magnus, creator of the Metal Men, find himself on Oolong Island — where a community of the smartest *criminal* minds of the world have been gathered to wield an unlimited budget and build earth-shattering weapons for the diabolical Chang Tzu.

With the low point of her Gotham City life behind her, former police officer Renee Montoya teams up with the enigmatic Vic Sage, a.k.a. The Question — and the two continue to track down the source of Intergang's deployment of powerful weapons into Gotham. Their quest leads them to Kahndaq, where they make unlikely allies with its leader...

Black Adam is happy for the first time in literally ages — having given a portion of his abilities to his new love Adrianna, transforming her into the powerful Isis. The two wed, and the ceremony is celebrated all throughout Kahndaq — though not everyone is happy with Black Adam's reign. An assassination attempt by a young girl is stopped when Renee is forced to shoot her. Later, Isis's missing brother is found, and he too is transformed — as Osiris, a powerful addition to the Black Marvel family. Yearning for friends, Osiris discovers one in the strange crocodile creature known as Sobek.

And in the farthest reaches of space, Adam Strange, Starfire and Animal Man are still stranded, trying to find their way home. Now in an unlikely alliance with Lobo, the space heroes are in the possession of the Emerald Eye of Ekron, and on the run from the Emerald *Head* of Ekron...

DC COMICS 52

WRITTEN BY GEOFF JOHNS, GRANT MORRISON, GREG RUCKA, MARK WAID

ART BREAKDOWNS BY KEITH GIFFEN • PENCILS BY SHAWN MOLL
INKS BY RUY JOSE, MARIAH BENES, RODNEY RAMOS, PRENTIS ROLLINS & NELSON

COLORS BY PETER PANTAZIS • LETTERING BY PAT BROSSEAU
COVER BY J.G. JONES & ALEX SINCLAIR

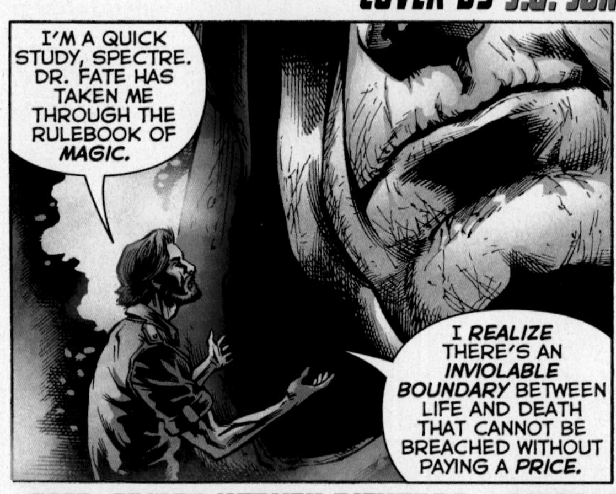

ASST. EDITOR HARVEY RICHARDS • ASSOC. EDITOR JEANINE SCHAEFER
EDITORS STEPHEN WACKER & MICHAEL SIGLAIN

Week 27

THE PAST BEST HOPE

DEEP SPACE. WHERE WOULD YOU HAVE US, SPECTRE?
WE STAND APPROXIMATELY 40 MILLION MILES FROM THE SUN.
MAGIC PROTECTS YOU BOTH FROM THE VOID.

AS IT DOES HER.
THE MAD GOD ECLIPSO. PLACED IN SOLAR ORBIT BY THE SHADOWPACT TO ETERNALLY NULLIFY HER SHADOW-FUELED SORCERY.

THANK YOU FOR THE EXPOSITION. WHAT DOES THIS HAVE TO DO WITH SUE?
TAKE A CLOSER LOOK AT THE BODY ECLIPSO NOW INHABITS, RALPH.
IT'S THE ONE VILLAIN YOU NEVER HAD A CHANCE TO CONFRONT.
OH, GOD.
OH, DEAR GOD.

IT'S JEAN LORING.
IT'S SUE'S MURDERER.

SHE USED THE ATOM'S SIZE-CHANGING BELT, RALPH.
LIKE A SKITTERING COCKROACH, SHE CRAWLED THROUGH A TELEPHONE INTO SUE'S HEAD.
SHE PULSED THROUGH YOUR WIFE'S BRAIN, LEAVING SUE TO DIE IN EPILEPTIC AGONY.
AND THEN SHE WENT ON TO MURDER AGAIN.
HER VICTIMS SCREAM FOR VENGEANCE, RALPH. YOU CANNOT FATHOM HOW DEEPLY I LONG TO PUNISH THIS HARRIDAN FOR ALL HER SINS.
BUT WITHOUT A HOST OF MY OWN, I'VE NO ABILITY TO DO SO.
TAKE MY POWER. USE IT AT YOUR DISCRETION.
AVENGE SUE SO THAT WE MAY BOTH BE FREE OF THE RAGE AND THE PAIN AND THE GRIEF JEAN LORING HAS WROUGHT UPON THE WORLD.
YOU CANNOT UNDO JEAN'S CRIMES. BUT EXACT FOR THEM A FITTING PUNISHMENT--
--AND I SWEAR BY ALL THAT IS HOLY THAT I WILL BRING SUE BACK TO YOU!
HSSSSSSS

I HAVE A BETTER IDEA!
WHY DON'T YOU JOIN HER!
YOU'RE GOING TO FIGHT BACK?
THAT'S A NICE CHANGE OF PACE! GOD KNOWS YOUR WIFE DIDN'T!
GO TO HELL.
ALREADY THERE.
YOU? NO. NOT BY A LONG SHOT YOU PSYCHO.
I'LL SHOW YOU HELL...

Week 27, Day 2

5:25:18 a.m.

TIK

5:25:19 a.m.

TIK

TIK

5:25:20 a.m.

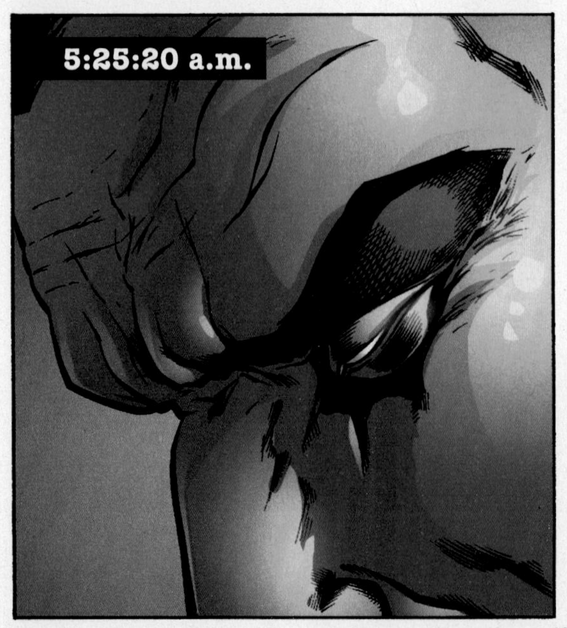

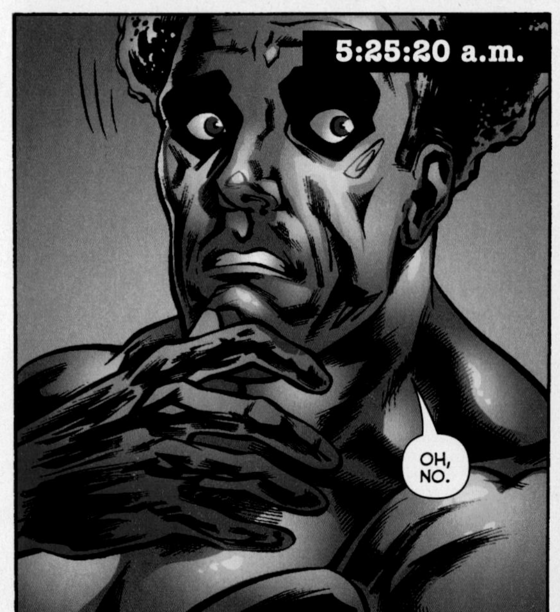

WHOOOOM

YOU *FOOL!* YOU *STUPID* FOOL!
TIME COMMANDER?!
WE WERE SUPPOSED TO BE THE NEW *TIME MASTERS!*

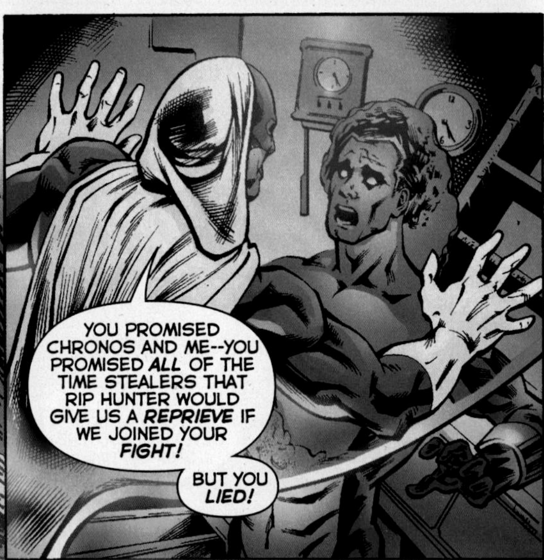
YOU PROMISED CHRONOS AND ME--YOU PROMISED *ALL* OF THE TIME STEALERS THAT RIP HUNTER WOULD GIVE US A *REPRIEVE* IF WE JOINED YOUR *FIGHT!*
BUT YOU *LIED!*

YOU L--
AIEEE!

HERE YOU ARE!
WAVERIDER. THE SEER OF HYPERTIME.
KEEPER OF DIVERGENT TIMELINES.
SKEETS?
BWOOM

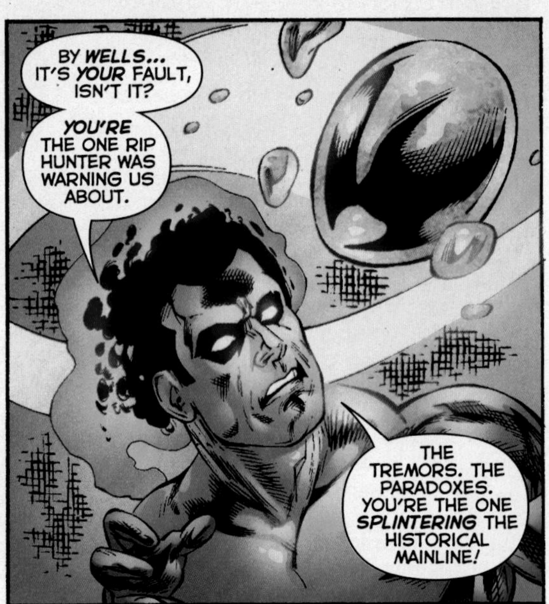
BY WELLS... IT'S YOUR FAULT, ISN'T IT?
YOU'RE THE ONE RIP HUNTER WAS WARNING US ABOUT.
THE TREMORS. THE PARADOXES. YOU'RE THE ONE SPLINTERING THE HISTORICAL MAINLINE!

NO. THE CATALYST WAS THE LUTHOR FROM THAT PARALLEL EARTH. BUT IN HIS WAKE... SOMETHING NEW...
...I CAN SMELL IT LIKE HONEY.
HISTORY'S FERTILE GROUND. THIS YEAR. LIKE WONDERFUL WET CEMENT.

WHEN IS RIP HUNTER, MATTHEW? TELL ME...

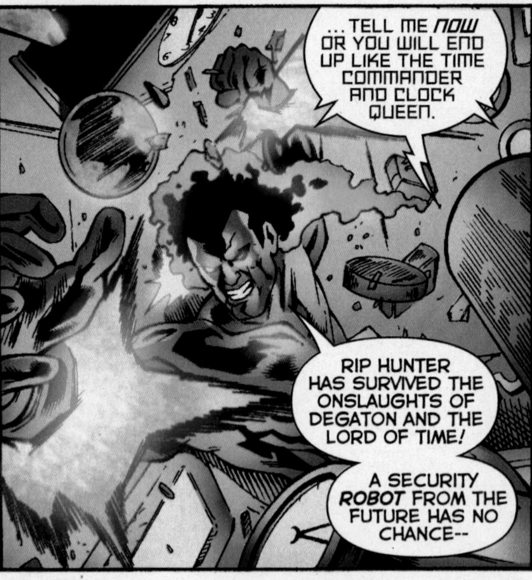
...TELL ME NOW OR YOU WILL END UP LIKE THE TIME COMMANDER AND CLOCK QUEEN.
RIP HUNTER HAS SURVIVED THE ONSLAUGHTS OF DEGATON AND THE LORD OF TIME!
A SECURITY ROBOT FROM THE FUTURE HAS NO CHANCE--

RIP HUNTER MAY BE THE PIONEER AND INVENTOR OF TIME TRAVEL, BUT HIS DEVICES AND WEAPONS ARE STICKS AND STONES COMPARED TO MY TWENTY-FIFTH CENTURY TECHNOLOGY!

AND YOU STILL CAN'T FIND HIM.
WANT TO KNOW WHY?

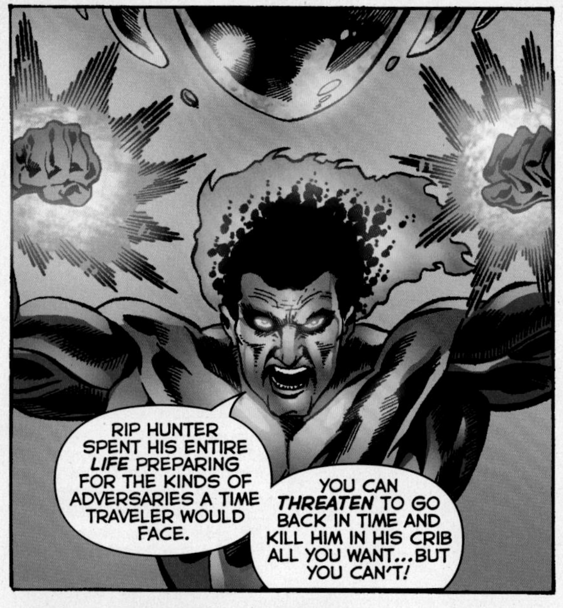
RIP HUNTER SPENT HIS ENTIRE LIFE PREPARING FOR THE KINDS OF ADVERSARIES A TIME TRAVELER WOULD FACE.
YOU CAN THREATEN TO GO BACK IN TIME AND KILL HIM IN HIS CRIB ALL YOU WANT...BUT YOU CAN'T!

RIP'S TRUE NAME IS A SECRET. WHERE AND WHEN HE WAS BORN AND RAISED IS A SECRET.
AND THEY'RE SECRETS I DON'T EVEN KNOW.

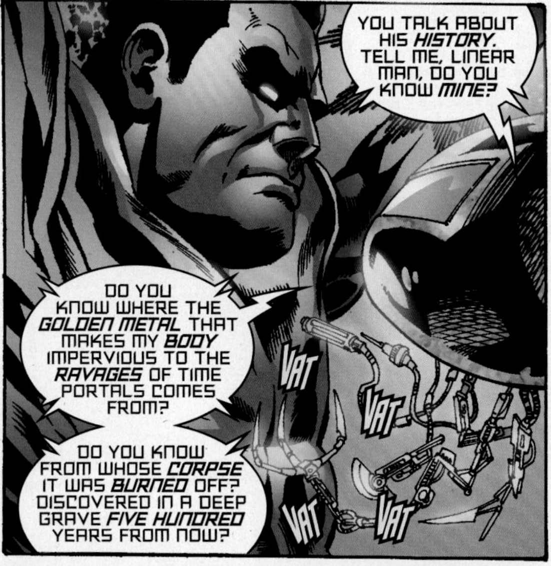
YOU TALK ABOUT HIS HISTORY. TELL ME, LINEAR MAN, DO YOU KNOW MINE?
DO YOU KNOW WHERE THE GOLDEN METAL THAT MAKES MY BODY IMPERVIOUS TO THE RAVAGES OF TIME PORTALS COMES FROM?
DO YOU KNOW FROM WHOSE CORPSE IT WAS BURNED OFF? DISCOVERED IN A DEEP GRAVE FIVE HUNDRED YEARS FROM NOW?
VAT
VAT
VAT
VAT

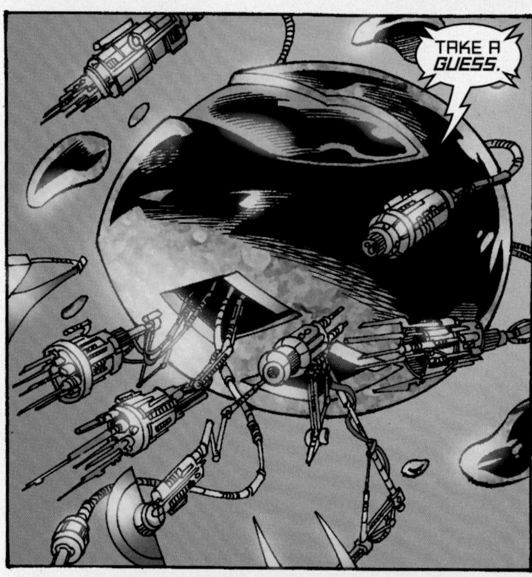
TAKE A GUESS.

FFZZZZAPP
AARGGHHH!

TIK
5:25:21 a.m.

Week 27, Day 5
Time stands still in Nanda Parbat.
Days, weeks, months... I can't tell. Life is defined by routines, not time.
When we arrived here, Charlie told me that Richard Dragon was a teacher, his teacher.
He told me class was now "in session."
So Richard's teaching me.
Just what, I don't know.
Richard says I have to stop running away, and learn to run with. He tells me I have to learn to let go.
When I ask him how I do that, he says "acceptance."
"Cherish it," Richard says. "The cold, the pain, the frustration, the heartache.
"Only when you want it to stay will you learn to release it."
IF I CHERISH IT, I WON'T WANT IT TO LEAVE.
SOMEONE ELSE ONCE SAID THE SAME THING. I'LL TELL YOU WHAT I TOLD HIM.
NOBODY SAID THIS WAS EASY.
Richard Dragon, ladies and gentlemen.

And then there's Charlie's friend "Tot"-- Doctor Aristotle Rodor.
He spends his days poring over the copy of the Book of Crime we stole from Intergang.

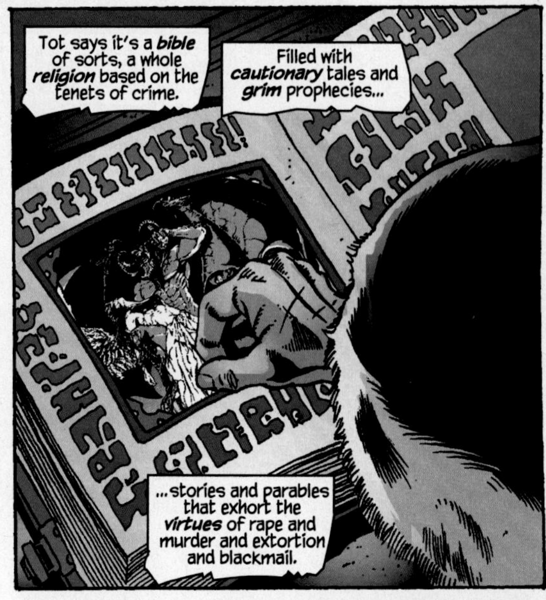
Tot says it's a bible of sorts, a whole religion based on the tenets of crime.
Filled with cautionary tales and grim prophecies...
...stories and parables that exhort the virtues of rape and murder and extortion and blackmail.

Light reading, obviously.

And Charlie?

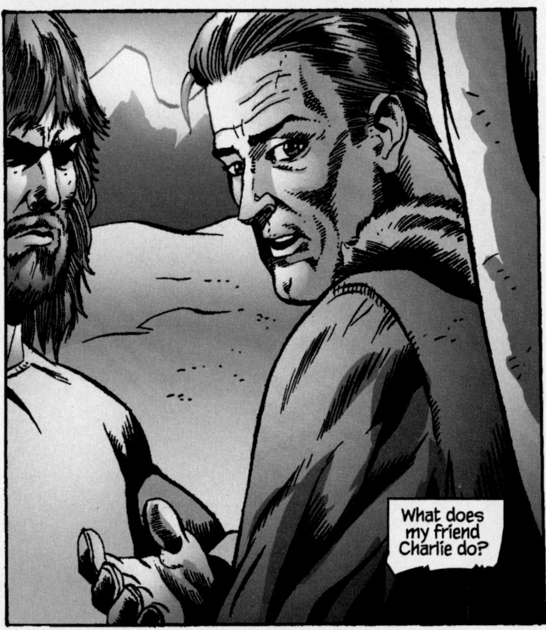
What does my friend Charlie do?

Charlie coughs.

It started just after we got here.

Charlie says it's the ***altitude,*** that he's having trouble ***acclimating.***

I was the pack-a-day smoker, but ***he's*** having trouble acclimating.

Richard makes him ***tea,*** uses ***acupuncture,*** massages ***pressure*** points.

Tot gives him the better part of a ***pharmacy*** in pills.

He's sick, and he's ***not*** getting better.
I'm beginning to wonder if he hasn't been sick for a while, and I've just been too wrapped up in myself to ***notice.***

And I'm ***scared*** for him.
SOUNDS ***WORSE*** THAN IT IS.
I'M WONDERING HOW THAT'S POSSIBLE.

WHEN'D YOU ***QUIT?***

NOT SOON ENOUGH.

HOW LONG HAVE YOU KNOWN?
ABOUT SEVEN MONTHS.
HOW LONG YOU HAVE?
NOT LONG.

TOT SAYS IT'S METASTASIZED.

WHY *ME*, CHARLIE?
EIGHT BILLION PEOPLE, WHY ME?

THAT'S THE QUESTION, ISN'T IT?

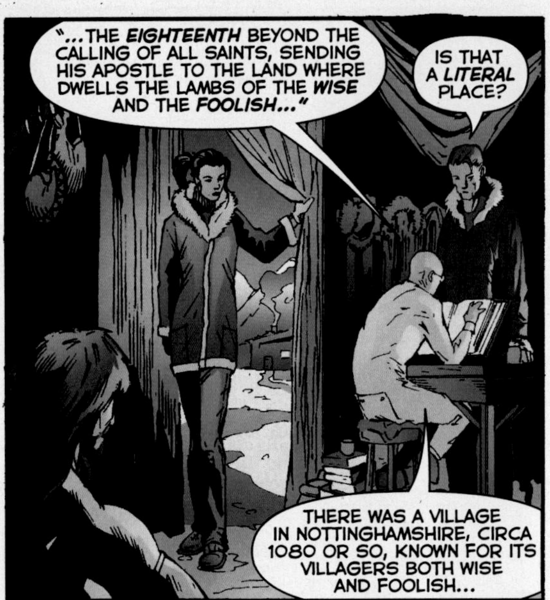
"...THE EIGHTEENTH BEYOND THE CALLING OF ALL SAINTS, SENDING HIS APOSTLE TO THE LAND WHERE DWELLS THE LAMBS OF THE WISE AND THE FOOLISH..."
IS THAT A LITERAL PLACE?
THERE WAS A VILLAGE IN NOTTINGHAMSHIRE, CIRCA 1080 OR SO, KNOWN FOR ITS VILLAGERS BOTH WISE AND FOOLISH...

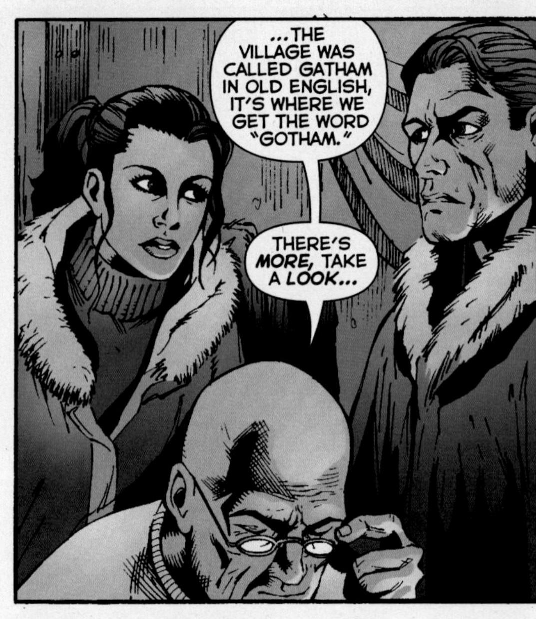
...THE VILLAGE WAS CALLED GATHAM IN OLD ENGLISH, IT'S WHERE WE GET THE WORD "GOTHAM."
THERE'S MORE, TAKE A LOOK...

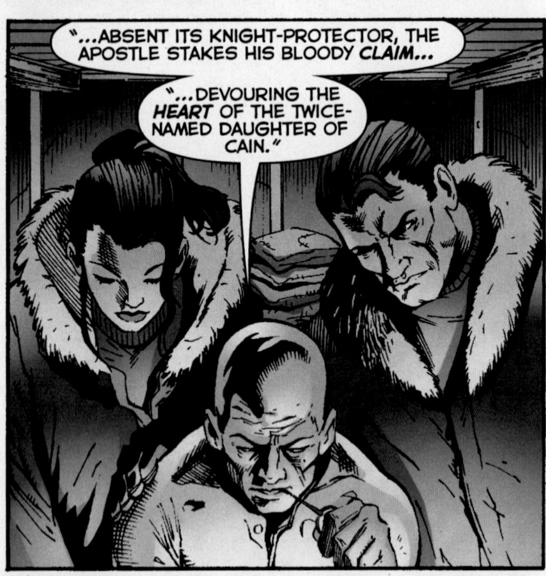
"...ABSENT ITS KNIGHT-PROTECTOR, THE APOSTLE STAKES HIS BLOODY CLAIM...
"...DEVOURING THE HEART OF THE TWICE-NAMED DAUGHTER OF CAIN."

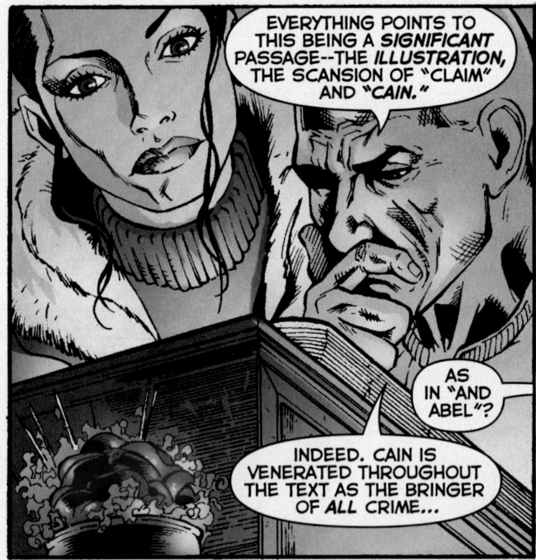
EVERYTHING POINTS TO THIS BEING A SIGNIFICANT PASSAGE--THE ILLUSTRATION, THE SCANSION OF "CLAIM" AND "CAIN."
AS IN "AND ABEL"?
INDEED. CAIN IS VENERATED THROUGHOUT THE TEXT AS THE BRINGER OF ALL CRIME...

...INCLUDING THE "MOST SACRED" ONE, THAT OF MURDER.
GOTHAM...

...OH NO, OH NO--
EASY, RENEE. WHAT'S--
I'VE GOT TO GET TO A PHONE, I HAVE TO CALL HOME, I HAVE TO--

THERE IS NO PHONE, RENEE.
IT'S NANDA PARBAT, MESSAGES COME VIA DREAMS AND TELEPATHY.
A SATELLITE PHONE, THEN. ANYTHING!

I'VE GOT TO CALL HER, CHARLIE!
WE HAVE TO WARN HER!
WHO? RENEE, YOU'RE NOT--

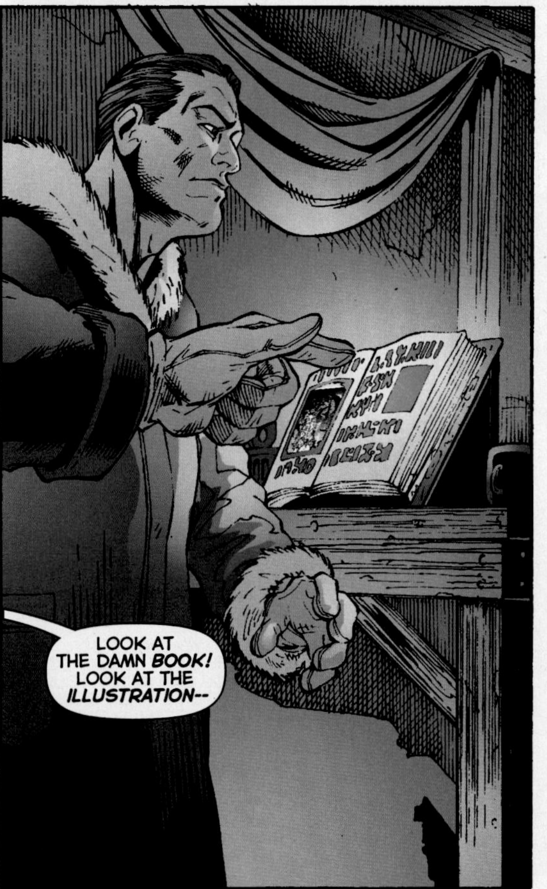
LOOK AT THE DAMN BOOK! LOOK AT THE ILLUSTRATION--

--IT'S NOT CAIN, CHARLIE--
--IT'S KANE, THE DAUGHTER OF KANE...

Week -84, Day -2
DIBNY
HOME OF THE JUSTICE LEAGUE'S WORLD-FAMOUS ELONGATED MAN, DUCTILE DETECTIVE
STRUGGLE ALL YOU WANT--
--WE'RE GHOSTING OUT.
YOU'RE NOT HERE TO TOUCH ANYTHING. YOU'RE NOT HERE TO BE SEEN OR BE HEARD.
YOU'RE HERE TO SUFFER, YOU HOMICIDAL BITCH.
TUNK
HELLO...?
OLLIE, IS THAT YOU...?
OH, GOOD GOD.
YOU BROUGHT US BACK IN TIME SO YOU CAN WATCH YOUR WIFE GET HER BRAIN STEPPED ON?
ARE WE BOTH NUTS?

ENOUGH EXCUSE FOR WHAT YOU *TOOK FROM ME!*
NO, JEAN...

...YOU DON'T GET TO PLAY THE *"MENTALLY UNBALANCED"* CARD THIS TIME.

I WANT YOU SANE FOR THIS.

...
R-RALPH...? RALPH, WHAT DID YOU JUST...
...I...I FEEL *DIFFERENT.* ALL THE *DARK* IS...
...IT'S *GONE...!*
YEAH. YOU KNOW *WHY?*

BECAUSE DAMNING A SOUL IS SO MUCH MORE *SATISFYING* WHEN THEY KNOW *RIGHT* FROM *WRONG.*

YOU CALLED IT. WE *ARE* HERE TO WATCH YOU MURDER *MY WIFE* IN THE SICKEST, MOST BRUTAL MANNER YOU COULD *IMAGINE.*
AND THE ONLY THING... THE *ONLY* THING... THAT'S GOING TO KEEP ME FROM *SUICIDE* ONCE THAT'S *OVER...*

...IS THE KNOWLEDGE THAT *I'M* LEAVING YOU *HERE,* IN A TINY LOOP OF *TIME,* TO WITNESS IT OVER AND OVER *AGAIN* FOR ALL *ETERNITY.*

RALPH, NO!
NOOOOO!
RALPH, I'M SORRY I'M SORRY DON'T MAKE ME DO THIS!
I LOVED HER TOO OH GOD RALPH I WAS CRAZY CRAZY GOD IT WASN'T ME DON'T PLEASE--!
...HAPPY BIRTHDAY, DEAR RA-ALPH...
I LOVED YOU SO MUCH, SUE...
RALPH! NONONONONONO!!
NO PLEASE GOD RALPH YOU KNOW THIS ISN'T RIGHT I'M SO SORRYYYYY FORGIVE ME DON'T

BREEP BREEP
BREEP BREEP
RALPH... LOOK AWAY...
...YOU'RE ONLY PUNISHING *YOURSELF*...
AAAAAH!!

I COULDN'T.
YOU TRICKED M--
I MADE NO FALSE CLAIMS. YOU SIMPLY FAILED TO UPHOLD YOUR END OF OUR BARGAIN.
WE ARE BOTH THE POORER FOR IT.

FATE, GET ME AWAY FROM HERE.
FROM HIM.
DO YOU HAVE A DESTINATION IN MIND?

YEAH.
I KNOW WHO CAN HELP ME NOW.

THE SPECTRE MAY BE REPUGNANT, BUT HE'S NOT A LIAR. AND HE TOLD ME SOMETHING CRUCIAL.
I CAN GET SUE BACK.
AND THERE'S A BETTER WAY THAN THROUGH HIM.
TAKE ME TO NANDA PARBAT.

NEXT IN 52

MARK WAID

Ralph Dibny's spiritual journey continues in a scene that was a moral nightmare both for Ralph and for me. Early in the planning, we decided that the Spectre — God's angel of vengeance — would naturally be someone to whom Ralph turned for answers about why he can't have his wife back. When I put Spectre on stage, however, I remembered what a sadistic, dark bastard he is and that Ralph approaching him would be like me asking Hannibal Lecter for advice. Still, their encounter underlined Ralph's theme perfectly: nothing comes without a price.

The scene timestamped "Week 84, Day 2" takes place in the middle of another storyline entirely — Brad Meltzer and Rags Morales' IDENTITY CRISIS #1, the 2004 DC comic in which Jean Loring murdered Sue Dibny. In the ongoing tradition of using these "notes" sections to remind you how clever we are, let me point out what great care I took to ensure that this scene fit seamlessly into Brad's original narrative. In fact, if you have a copy of IDENTITY CRISIS, you can go back and see that we tied up one of its loose ends, finally revealing what caused the downstairs noise that made Sue call out, "Hello...? Ollie, is that you...?"

The Waverider scene is all Geoff. The Time Commander was the mostly-since-forgotten villain in a pair of 1960s Batman/Green Lantern team-ups. I adore the Time Commander. But not enough not to offer him up to Geoff for liquidation. My love is fickle.

IDENTITY CRISIS #1

SCRIPT EXCERPT

(COMPARE WITH PAGE 23 OF THIS COLLECTION)

52 WEEK TWENTY-SEVEN   PAGE NINETEEN

PANEL ONE
In extreme foreground, the cordless phone receiver on the table as it rings. In background, Ralph and Jean look at it with silent dread.

PHONE SFX: brEEP brEEP

PANEL TWO
Likewise, Sue looks up from her table-arranging to glance at the phone.

PANEL THREE
Tighter on Ralph, forcing himself to keep his eyes open and his jaw tight, but seriously starting to break down despite his resolve.

PHONE SFX: brEEP brEEP

PANEL FOUR
Tighter on Jean, slightly calmer now, her head still held tight but she's straining to turn it ever so slightly so she can at least start to look up in Ralph's direction. She's not moving it very much.

JEAN: Ralph...look away...

PANEL FIVE
Tighter still on Ralph, his tear-filled eyes squeezed shut as he finally breaks.

JEAN (off-panel): ...you're only punishing YOURSELF...

PANEL SIX
Tight on Sue's hand picking up the phone.

PANEL SEVEN
Tighter still on Ralph, head thrown back, eyes shut, screaming in utter agony.

RALPH (huge): aaAAAH--!

THIS IS NOT GOING TO WORK.
IT'LL WORK.
NO, IT WON'T.
Week 28, Day 2

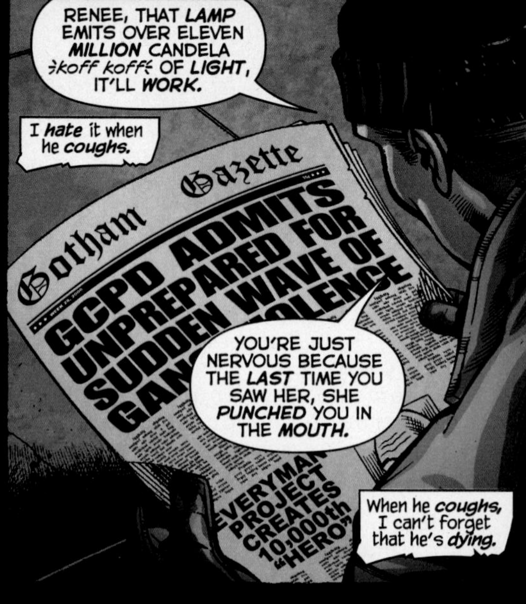
RENEE, THAT LAMP EMITS OVER ELEVEN MILLION CANDELA *koff koff* OF LIGHT, IT'LL WORK.
I hate it when he coughs.
Gotham Gazette
GCPD ADMITS UNPREPARED FOR SUDDEN WAVE OF GANG VIOLENCE
YOU'RE JUST NERVOUS BECAUSE THE LAST TIME YOU SAW HER, SHE PUNCHED YOU IN THE MOUTH.
EVERYMAN PROJECT CREATES 10,000th "HERO"
When he coughs, I can't forget that he's dying.

He shouldn't even be here.
I'M NERVOUS BECAUSE WE'RE THROWING A BAT SIGNAL AROUND IN GOTHAM CITY, CHARLIE...
...A GUARANTEED WAY TO BRING HALF THE GCPD AND ALL THE COSTUMED FREAKS RUNNING.
YOU GOT ANOTHER WAY TO REACH HER?
He should still be in Nanda Parbat.

He should be with his friends, with Richard and Tot...
NONE OF THE OTHER WAYS WORKED, AND YOU KNOW THAT.
BET THE DAMN BUTLER NEVER EVEN TOLD HER I CALLED.
...not with me trying to save someone he doesn't know from something we're not sure will happen.

MOAN MOAN MOAN.
OH, BITE ME.
HE CAN'T...

...HE DOESN'T HAVE A MOUTH.
NOW TURN THAT THING OFF.

WE'VE BEEN TRYING TO REACH YOU--
CONGRATULATIONS, YOU DID.
GOODBYE.
NOBODY HAS ANY CURIOSITY THESE DAYS, YOU NOTICE THAT?

SHE DOESN'T EVEN WANT TO KNOW WHY *kaff* WE'VE GONE TO THIS TROUBLE.
IT'S TOO BAD, REALLY. WE MIGHT HAVE IMPORTANT INFORMATION, MAYBE ABOUT INTERGANG.
OR HOW SHE'S PROPHESIED TO HAVE HER HEART RIPPED OUT THREE NIGHTS FROM NOW.

INTERGANG I ALREADY KNOW ABOUT.
LET'S HEAR THAT SECOND PART.
PICTURE'S WORTH A THOUSAND WORDS.
IT'S TAKEN FROM SOMETHING CALLED THE BOOK OF CRIME...

...AND I'M PRETTY DAMN SURE THAT'S SUPPOSED TO BE YOU DYING IN THAT PICTURE....
DC COMICS 52

Week 28, Day 2

RIDGE FERRICK

RIDGE-

WRITTEN BY GEOFF JOHNS, GRANT MORRISON, GREG RUCKA, MARK WAI

ART BREAKDOWNS BY KEITH GIFFEN • PENCILS BY DREW JOHNSON

INKS BY JACK JADSON, RODNEY RAMOS & RUY JOSÉ

COLORS BY DAVID BARON • LETTERING BY ROB LEIGH

ASSISTANT EDITOR HARVEY RICHARDS • ASSOCIATE EDITOR JEANINE SCHAEFER

EDITED BY STEPHEN WACKER & MICHAEL SIGLAIN COVER BY J.G. JONES & ALEX SINCLAIR

...OR I'LL SET MY #!$@! ROBOT ON YOU!
FACE THE POWER OF THE *TORNADO MAN!*
52!
52!
Ah, GIMME PEACE, SON!
AT EASE, FELLAS! IT'S ONLY SOME PILE OF OLD *JUNK* AND...

CLANNKK

52!
SNURRF
GAHH

THAT'S BLOODY *IT!*

BULLETS ARE BOUNCING OFF THE BLOODY THING!
NAH, *THAT'S* IT!
YOU *SHOW* 'EM, MATE!
52! 52!

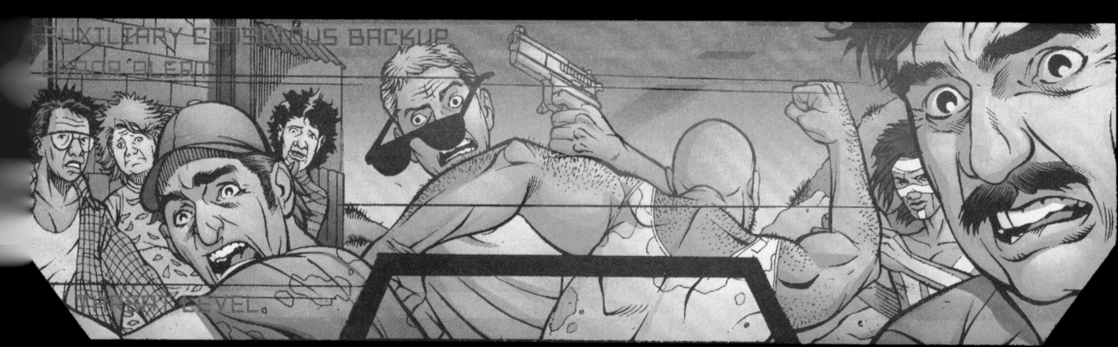
AUXILIARY CONSCIOUS BACKUP
THREAT LEVEL.

I TOLD YOU I COULD DO IT!
WHAT THE BLOODY HELL.
WHAT HAVE YOU DONE?
SOMETHING'S UP.

TORNADO DREAMING.

NOTICE OF EVICTION
52!

KLLANNGG

WHAT D'YA HAFTA DO THAT FOR?

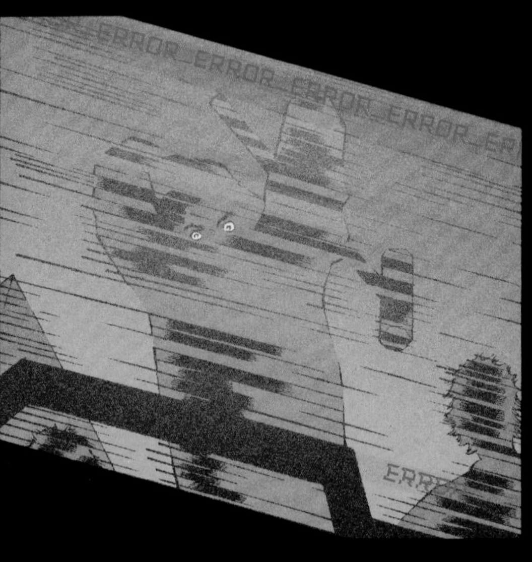
ERROR_ERROR_ERROR_ERROR_ERROR
ERR

IT AIN'T RIGHT.
YOU WANT THIS THING TO *KILL* SOMEONE?

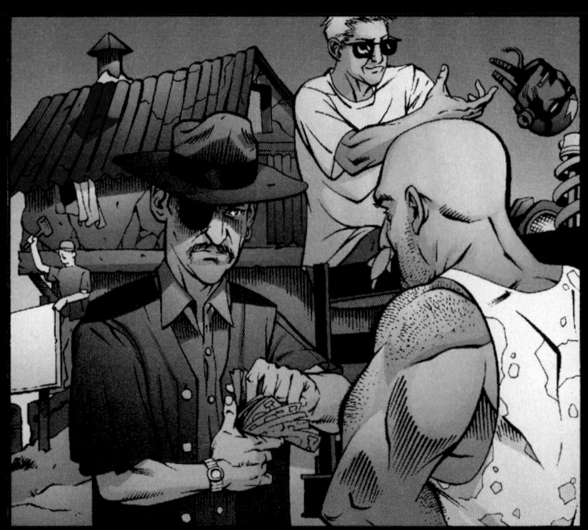

Week 28

BEYOND THE BLACK STUMP

Week 28, Day 2

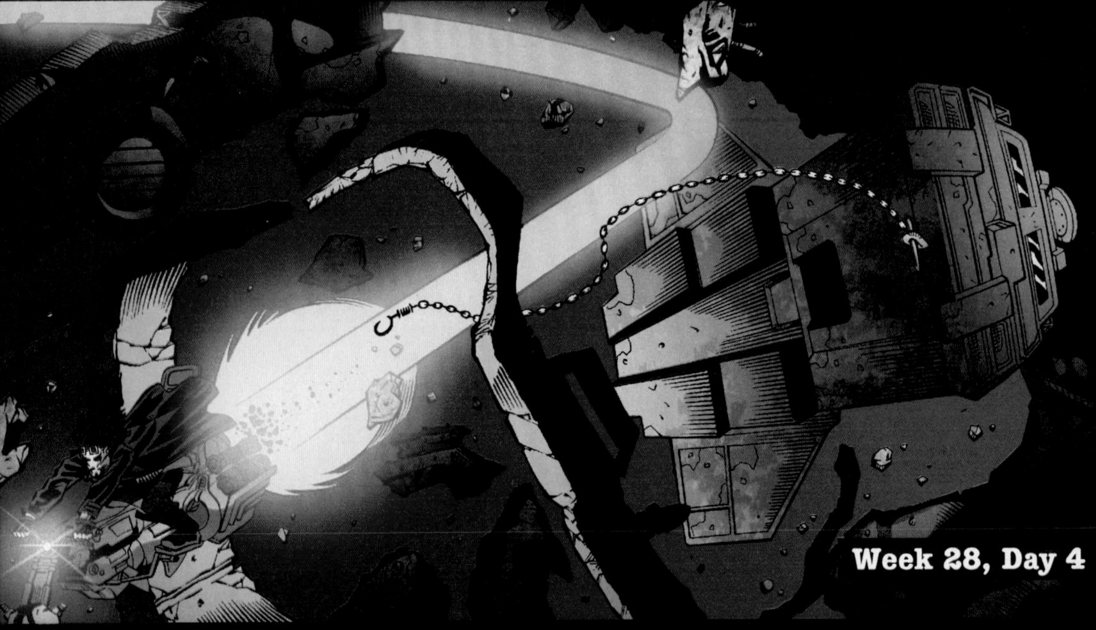
Week 28, Day 4

...ON EARTH, WHERE THE PLANET HAS A FUNCTIONING *MORPHOGENETIC FIELD* TO WORK WITH, I'M *THE MAN WITH ANIMAL POWERS*...
...OUT HERE, I'M A FAMILY GUY IN SOILED *PAJAMAS.*

I HAVE A WIFE AND TWO KIDS I HAVEN'T *SEEN* FOR SIX MONTHS.
I HAVE ALL KINDS OF STUPID RESPONSIBILITIES AND--

Week 28, Day 5
Gotham City.
SO MUCH FOR YOUR PROPHECY.
KRUNNCH
HNNNFFF!!!

UNGH!

I'VE ALWAYS FELT THAT PEOPLE SHOULD TAKE *RESPONSIBILITY* FOR THEIR *ACTIONS...*

...NOT *EXCUSE* THEM BY DENYING THERE WAS ANY *CHOICE* IN THE MATTER.
THEN YOU ARE A *FOOL...*

...BECAUSE THE *WORD* WILL *NOT* BE *DENIED!*
HNNNN!

PROPHECY IS *UPON* YOU...

...WITH YOUR DEATH, INTERGANG'S FEAST WILL TRULY BEGIN.
I SHALL DEVOUR YOU, JUST AS THE RED ROCK AND THE RAGE SHALL DEVOUR ALL OF GOTHAM...
...SO IT HAS BEEN WRITTEN, AND SO IT SHALL COME TO PASS.

TOO BAD FOR YOU WE'RE WORKING OFF A DIFFERENT TEXT.
"WE"?
SHE MEANS US...

...NOW PUT THE BATWOMAN DOWN, AND WE WON'T HAVE TO VAPORIZE YOUR UGLY ASS.
THE QUESTIONS...

...NO... NO, YOU CAN'T BE HERE, NOT YET...

--THE QUESTIONS HAVE NOT YET BEEN *ANSWERED!*
LOOK OUT--
DON'T MOVE, DON'T--

--STOP *HIM*, DON'T LET HIM GET--

...I *HATE* IT WHEN THEY DO *THAT*.
TELL ME ABOUT IT.

SO WE HAVE TO STAND AND FIGHT.

YA THINK I BROUGHT YA ALONG FER ANY *OTHER* REASON, MY SON!

I'DA DEALT WITH THIS *MYSELF* IF IT WASN'T FER TH' HOLY PACIFIST VOWS I'M SADDLED WITH...

Week 28, Day 7

LET ME GET THIS TRAIGHT...
THIS CREATURE WANTS ITS *EMERALD EYE* BACK.
WHICH *YOU* STOLE, LOBO.
THEY FOUND TH' *EMERALD HEAD* GUILTY OF BLASPHEMY AGAINST THE *TRIPLE FISH GOD,* SEE, SO TH' CHURCH SENT *ME* TO... LOOK, THIS IS A LONG AN' BORIN' STORY...

YOU NEVER HEARD OF *"AN EYE FOR AN EYE"*?
DARK, CONFINED SPACE.
GIANT MONSTER.
THIS WILL WORK.

YEAH, WELL, WE CAN USE THE *WORM-TUNNELS* IN THIS ASTEROID TO OUR *ADVANTAGE.*
THE HEAD'S GONNA FIND IT HARD TO *MANEUVER* DOWN HERE.
ALL WE NEED IS AN *HOUR* OR TWO TO LAY SOME *TRAPS.*

SO...
ANY QUESTIONS?

ADAM!

X'HAL!

EASY, FISHY!
AAAIIEEEEE

SEE NOW, IF I COULD ONLY RELAX MY VOW OF NON-VIOLENCE, I COULD DEAL WITH THIS IN ABOUT HOW MANY GORE AN' GIZZ ENCRUSTED SECONDS?
mmf

TRAPS?
HOW ABOUT HUNDREDS OF TONS OF BONES?
AND JUST AN OUNCE OF LUCK.

NNNAUUUU

MMMMNN ORTA YELLEC MOR
HEPP

IT'S NOT ATTACKING.
I HAVE A PECULIAR *FEELING* ABOUT ALL THIS.
THE HEAD DOESN'T SEEM PARTICULARLY FEROCIOUS AT ALL, AND THERE'S SOMETHING...

HELP.
HELP ME.

SEE?
THOSE *MARKINGS* ROUND THE COCKPIT... DON'T YOU *RECOGNIZE* THEM?

IT'S A *GREEN LANTERN* INSIGNIA.

PASSOVER HAS BEGUN!
TILL SHE CAME-- A DESTROYING FLAME.
QUIT WHININ'!
YA CAME TA THE WRONG CHURCH FER THE SYMPATHY VOTE!
HAKK!
FORGIVE MY ANGER, TRIPLE-BECOMING ONE.
KAK!
NOT SO TOUGH NOW, huh?
MAYBE IF YA HADN'T HACKED OFF TH' FISH GOD, YA MIGHT HAVE KEPT YER EYE AN' YER DIGNITY.
WAIT A MINUTE!
IF THIS THING'S A SPACE COP FROM THE LANTERN CORPS, WHAT DOES THAT MAKE YOU, LOBO?
TALL, DARK AN' HANDSOME!
YOU STOLE HIS PRIMARY WEAPON AND LEFT HIM DEFENSELESS AGAINST A POWER THAT DEVASTATED THE PLANETS UNDER HIS PROTECTION.
LEVEL WITH US, LOBO!
THE EYE DOESN'T BELONG TO YOU!
BITE ME, MY CHILD.

...SO WE'RE DEALING WITH AN UNHINGED GREEN LANTERN WHO WATCHED HIS SPACE SECTOR PROTECTORATE TRAMPLED TO DUST BY...WHAT?
"THE STYGIAN PASSOVER," HE CALLED IT, JUST LIKE THOSE REFUGEES WE MET A FEW WEEKS AGO.
IMAGINE THE KIND OF POWER IT MUST TAKE TO BREAK SOLAR SYSTEMS DOWN TO RUBBLE.

YOU KNOW, LIKE IT'S NOT ENOUGH TO BE BLIND!
IT'S NOT ENOUGH TO BE A THOUSAND LIGHT-YEARS FROM HOME!
ONE MORE THING YOU JUST DON'T NEED!

ONE MORE @$%?!$#& TWIST!

Tt
SORRY.
HAD TO BLOW OFF STEAM.

YOU'VE BEEN VERY BRAVE, ADAM STRANGE.
BUT WE MAY ALL HAVE TO BE BRAVER.
CAN'T WE JUST GO HOME?

WE ARE GOING HOME.
BUT OUR WAY LIES WITH LOBO-- AND THE "STYGIAN PASSOVER," WHATEVER IT IS, IS HEADING IN THE SAME DIRECTION.

THAT MAKES US POSSIBLY THE ONLY PEOPLE ALIVE WHO CAN STOP IT FROM REACHING VEGA, ALPHA CENTAURI...
...AND EARTH.

SO IT'S THREE OF US AGAINST SOMETHING THAT CAN TURN PLANETS TO POWDER?
AND IF WE DON'T STOP IT, EARTH'S NEXT?

GREAT.

MY WIFE ALWAYS WARNED ME SOMETHING LIKE THIS WOULD HAPPEN IF I DIDN'T WATCH OUT.

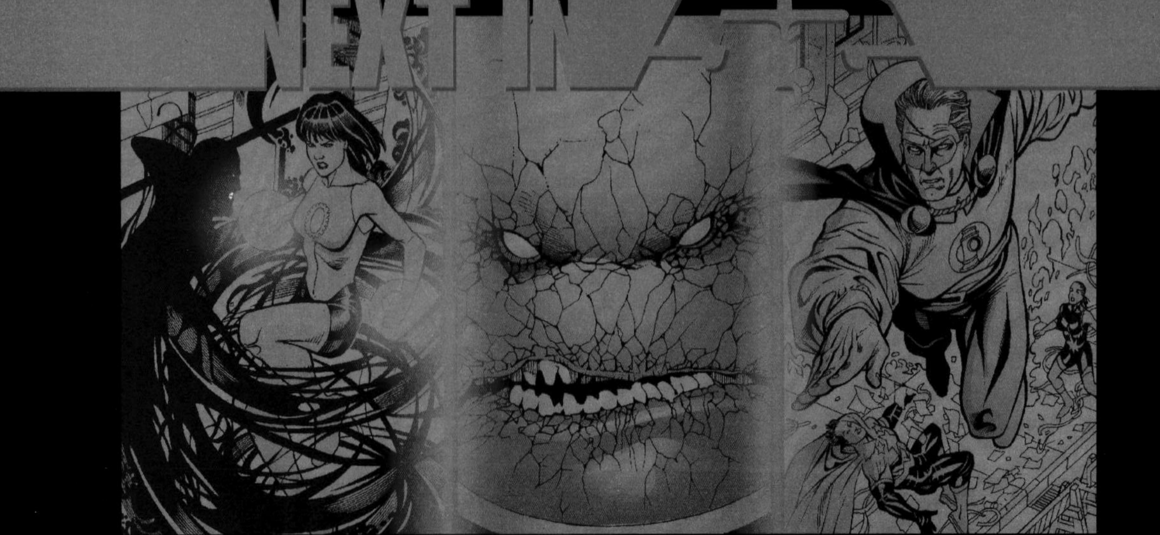
NEXT IN

WEEK TWENTY-EIGHT NOTES

GREG RUCKA

I have, apparently, not one, not two, not three, but four revisions of the script for this week, all marked in my bizarre filing code "52Week28 – Final Draft," all of them dated between July 11 and July 17 of 2006.

I was on vacation with my family from July 11 and July 17 of 2006.

I didn't vacate much, I'll tell you that for free.

The cover for this week was another of J.G.'s braingasms, whipped out on the sly while the four writers all went round and around on some story point or another during, I believe, the first of our face-to-face conferences. Grant had Red Tornado's journey mapped out (heh, see, I foreshadow without even meaning to – wait until Volume 4, you'll get it) pretty much from the start, and I think he mentioned "aborigine" and "Outback" and "Red Tornado's head," and that was all J.G. needed. It's one of the more poetic and beautiful covers of the series, I think, all the more so because of the relative serenity of the moment. Even if that is Red Tornado's decapitated head that Johnny's cradling in his arm.

Note, also, the Ridge-Ferrick sign on page 4 of the issue. That Intergang, they've got a very long reach...or is it, rather, the Religion of Crime that's been expanding its web?

The Religion of Crime (and I must confess at this point that I *loathe* that name – "Hey, buddy? Wanna join the Religion of Crime?" "Sure!" I mean, c'mon, seriously. It's a perfectly serviceable comic book thing to call it, yes, it tells you what it is and what it's about, but the fan of Lovecraft in me screams at it. Call it the Dark Faith. Call it the Way of Sin. Call it late for dinner, but, really, Religion of Crime? How's that going to win converts?) forms an (almost) unintentional spine for this week – Renee and Charlie fighting to save Kate from the prophecy held in the Crime Bible (and again, Crime Bible? Who does their marketing, for Pete's sake?), the "tornado dreaming," His Eminence Pope Lobo, the coming of Lady Styx – binding the issue with both spirituality, the lack thereof, and that Old Tyme Religion Favorite, impending doom.

There's a lot I'm fond of in this issue, perhaps self-servingly. I quite like the fact that Renee and Charlie are bickering at the start, and yet the moment Batwoman shows up, they present a united front. Over halfway through, and with Charlie's illness worsening, it's moments like that – to me – that illustrated the depth of their friendship.

While on the subject of Batwoman, here's another in the continuing examples of just how collaborative the process was. As scripted, the description for the splash of Week 28, Day 5, was quite vague: "Batwoman is finishing off the last two Intergangers with a devastating move that will have people saying "holy ****, she's cool!" but which, since I am not cool, cannot begin to describe, so I'll leave that to Keith."

Keith came through with glee. Note, please, Batwoman's *boot* in fish-faced crocodile creature's *mouth*, an injury that, I hasten to add, the Batman himself would think twice about before inflicting. The layout, I believe, had the added "KRRNCHH" sound effect, and a note that, yes, this was supposed to be a very mean thing to do to someone.

Keith worries me.

THE PROCESS

(COMPARE WITH PAGE 36 OF THIS COLLECTION)

Original Script

52 WEEK TWENTY-EIGHT – PAGE NINE

PANEL ONE (splash)
Cut to a full-page pic of intense action in space. LOBO on his bike is racing into foreground surrounded by flashes of green laser-like destructive energy. Behind him, towed on a chain, is the Warbird piloted by Adam Strange — swinging wildly as it rolls and yaws, also narrowly avoiding the tracer fire of green destruction. In hot pursuit through an environment of drifting rocks and skeletal spacecraft is the EMERALD HEAD OF EKRON, spraying deadly green rays into foreground. Big mad Heavy Metal space chase scene. Lobo, head down, teeth gritted.

Breakdown by Keith Giffen

Pencils by Drew Johnson

Final Page

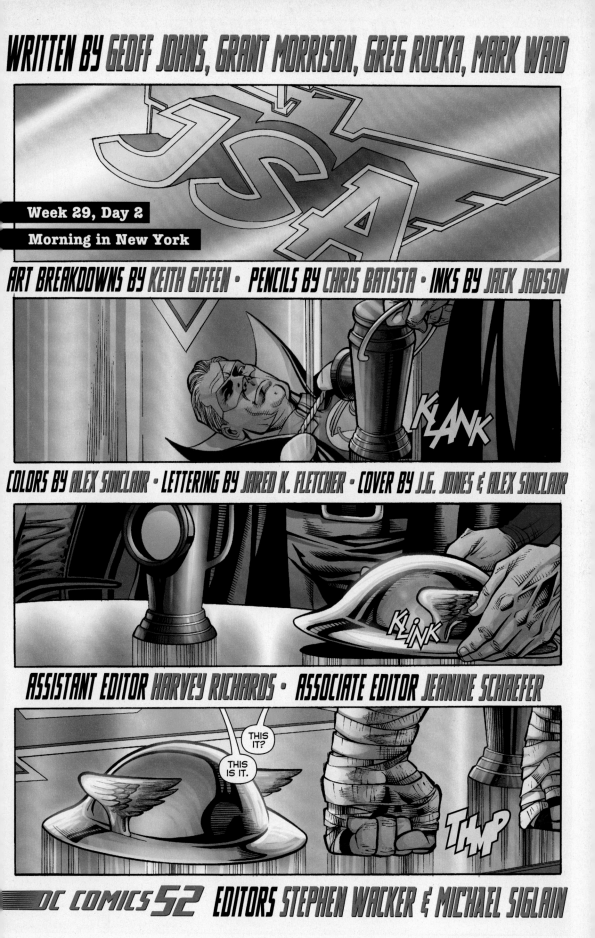

WRITTEN BY GEOFF JOHNS, GRANT MORRISON, GREG RUCKA, MARK WAID

ART BREAKDOWNS BY KEITH GIFFEN • PENCILS BY CHRIS BATISTA • INKS BY JACK JADSON

COLORS BY ALEX SINCLAIR • LETTERING BY JARED K. FLETCHER • COVER BY J.G. JONES & ALEX SINCLAIR

ASSISTANT EDITOR HARVEY RICHARDS • ASSOCIATE EDITOR JEANINE SCHAEFER

DC COMICS 52 EDITORS STEPHEN WACKER & MICHAEL SIGLAIN

NAME CALLING

WAS ONLY A YEAR AGO THE JUSTICE SOCIETY WAS HAVIN' ANOTHER TURKEY DAY WITH THE LEAGUE.
SEEMS LONGER.
ALWAYS THOUGHT THE END A' THIS TEAM WOULDA BEEN SOME KINDA LIFE-AND-DEATH BATTLE WITH THE ULTRA-HUMANITE. OR AT LEAST A REMATCH WITH EXTANT.

EXTANT IS *DEAD,* TED.

THE *IDEA* OF THE JSA IS DYIN' *TOO,* ALAN. WE SHOULD GO FIGHTIN' INTO THE NIGHT. SAVIN' THE WORLD ONE LAST TIME. SHOWIN' THESE *NEWBIES* HOW TO DO IT RIGHT.
INSTEAD IT FEELS LIKE THE WORLD'S FIRST SUPER-TEAM IS FADIN' AWAY LIKE THE OLD FARTS THEY'RE CALLIN' US.
JUSTICE SOCIETY OF AMERICA

I MEAN, LOOK'T THAT.

...IN THE SKY, KIDS! THEY AREN'T BIRDS! OR PLANES! THEY'RE BRAVE MEN AND WOMEN JUST... LIKE...
YOU!

WITH POWERS AND ABILITIES YOU COULD ONE DAY SHARE, THANKS TO LEX LUTHOR!
OUR SPONSORS, SUNDOLLER COFFEE AND LIT BEER, ARE NOW PROUD TO PRESENT--

--SKYMAN! STARLIGHT! MATRIX! NUKLON! EVERYMAN! AND EVERYONE'S FAAAAVORITE ANGRY GUY-- FURY!
...INFINITY, INC!
LEX

HAPPY TURKEY DAY, Y'ALL!

INFINITY INCORPORATED.
IT DOESN'T SIT WELL WITH ME EITHER, ALAN.
THOSE KIDS ARE USING NAMES THAT WERE BOUGHT AND PAID FOR BY LUTHOR.
IF SYLVESTER PEMBERTON WERE ALIVE, HE WOULD NEVER'VE ALLOWED THIS TO HAPPEN.
MR. TERRIFIC SPENT WEEKS TRYING TO UNTANGLE THE RED TAPE. BUT LEGALLY, THERE'S NOTHING WE CAN DO.
BECAUSE OF GIMMIX'S DISAPPEARANCE, THE PEMBERTON ESTATE WAS UP FOR GRABS.

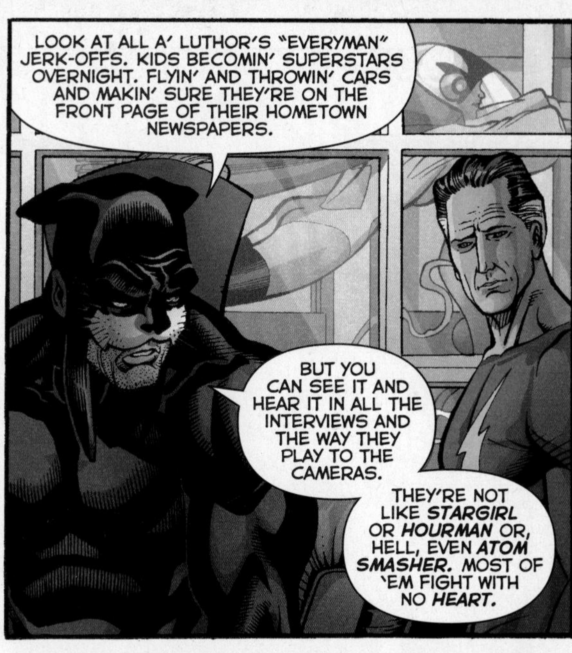
LOOK AT ALL A' LUTHOR'S "EVERYMAN" JERK-OFFS. KIDS BECOMIN' SUPERSTARS OVERNIGHT. FLYIN' AND THROWIN' CARS AND MAKIN' SURE THEY'RE ON THE FRONT PAGE OF THEIR HOMETOWN NEWSPAPERS.
BUT YOU CAN SEE IT AND HEAR IT IN ALL THE INTERVIEWS AND THE WAY THEY PLAY TO THE CAMERAS.
THEY'RE NOT LIKE STARGIRL OR HOURMAN OR, HELL, EVEN ATOM SMASHER. MOST OF 'EM FIGHT WITH NO HEART.

AND MORE IMPORTANT, NO MORAL COMPASS... NO MATTER WHAT LUTHOR WANTS THE PUBLIC TO BELIEVE.
SANDMAN UNCOVERED CHARGES BROUGHT AGAINST A DOZEN OF LUTHOR'S "HEROES" OVER THE LAST FEW MONTHS.
ASSAULT AND BATTERY. VANDALISM. EVEN ATTEMPTED MURDER.
BUT LUTHOR'S P.R. TEAM IS BURYING THE FACTS.

AND WHEN POWER GIRL TRIED TO EXPOSE THEM... YOU HEARD WHAT JACK RYDER CALLED US LAST NIGHT?

"A GROUP OF OLD MEN DESPERATE TO CONTROL THE NEXT GENERATION."

...EVERYBODY WHO CAME OUT SO EARLY ON THANKSGIVING DAY TO SEE US. WE'RE ALL VERY THANKFUL FOR YOUR SUPPORT. GOD BLESS AMERICA!
GOD BLESS LEX LUTHOR!
AND NOW I'D LIKE TO INTRODUCE YOU ALL TO THE NEWEST MEMBER OF INFINITY INCORPORATED!

SHE WAS A GRAPHIC ARTS STUDENT FROM THE SAN FRANCISCO ART INSTITUTE.

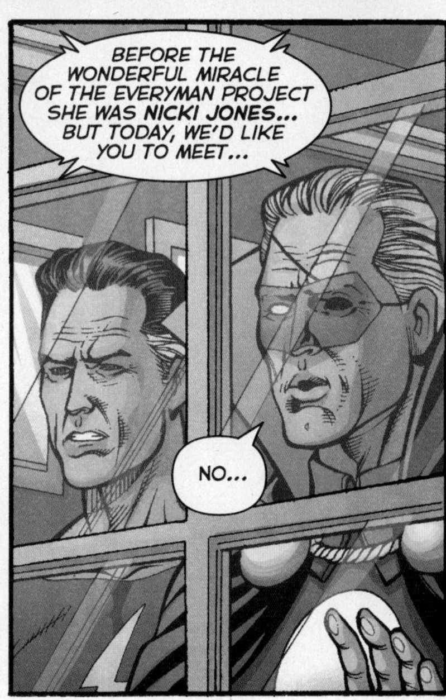
BEFORE THE WONDERFUL MIRACLE OF THE EVERYMAN PROJECT SHE WAS NICKI JONES... BUT TODAY, WE'D LIKE YOU TO MEET...
NO...

JADE!
GO LUTHOR

I CAN'T TELL YOU WHAT AN HONOR AND PLEASURE IT IS TO BE THE NEWEST MEMBER OF INFINITY INCORPORATED!
I'D LIKE TO SAY HI TO MY GRANDMA WHO HELPED ME GET WHERE I AM TODAY. THIS IS FOR YOU, GRANDMA! SAY YES TO PLANTS! SAY NO TO MEAT!

THIS ISN'T RIGHT, DAD.
TODD?

OBSIDIAN!
THIS ISN'T WHAT JENNY WOULD WANT.

I'VE ONLY BEEN ON THIS TEAM A FEW DAYS AND ALREADY I'VE MADE SO MANY FRIENDS. AND I'VE LEARNED SO MUCH.
FOR YEARS WE'VE WATCHED WONDER WOMAN, BATMAN AND SUPERMAN MAKE MISTAKES. AND WE COULDN'T DO ANYTHING BUT HOPE THEY'D GET BACK ON THE RIGHT PATH.
TODAY, LEX LUTHOR HAS PUT THAT HOPE IN OUR HANDS.

THEY TURNED INFINITY INC. INTO THE CORPORATE SYMBOL OF LEX LUTHOR. THEY TOOK SYLVESTER'S AND AL'S AND LYTA'S NAMES WITH NO RESPECT FOR WHAT CAME BEFORE.
AND NOW THEY USE MY SISTER'S NAME? THEY CAN'T SELL JENNY'S NAME!
CALM DOWN, SON.

WITH THE GIFTS WE'VE BEEN GIVEN, AND THE PERSPECTIVE OF REAL PEOPLE--
--WE'RE GOING TO DO THEIR JOB BETTER.

TODD!
SKRRAKKSH
I WON'T LET THEM REPLACE HER LIKE THIS, DAD!

AIEEE!
LOOK OUT!
FURY! NUKLON! GET THESE PEOPLE CLEAR!

WHAT IS THAT, STARLIGHT?
THAT'S THE ORIGINAL GREEN LANTERN'S SON-- OBSIDIAN.
I THOUGHT HE WAS A GOOD GUY AGAIN.
HE'S SUPPOSED TO BE!

TAKE OFF THAT UNIFORM.
COME ON NOW, HON, NOT IN FRONT OF THE KIDDIES.
'SIDES, I READ IN LAST WEEK'S "WORLD'S FINEST" THAT YOU GO THE OTHER WAY.

HAVE YOU EVER HAD NIGHT TERRORS? I DID. FOR YEARS.
THEY'RE VERY UNPLEASANT.

NOW I WON'T ASK AGAIN, "JADE."
TAKE. OFF. THAT. UNIFORM.
YOU WERE HER BROTHER, RIGHT? THE SCHIZO. YOU ALMOST SUCKED MILWAUKEE INTO A BLACK HOLE.
YOU'RE CRAZY.

I WAS.
I GOT BETTER.

BOOOOM

I DON'T WANT TO *HURT* YOU.

WHAT'S *WRONG* WITH HER? AND WHAT'S WRONG WITH OUR *SHADOWS?*
OBSIDIAN FUNNELS POWER FROM A DIMENSION CALLED THE SHADOW-LANDS. IT'S A PLACE WHERE NIGHT-MARES BECOME REALITY.
WELL, IT'S AFFECTING EVERYONE IN THE CROWD. WE NEED TO *STOP* HIM.

I'LL DO THAT.

LET THE GIRL GO, TODD.
FWOOOSH
BUT THIS IS WRONG, DAD.

SO IS STARTING A FIGHT IN THE MIDDLE OF THE THANKSGIVING DAY PARADE.
YOU'RE ENDANGERING PEOPLE AGAIN. YOU'RE SCARING THEM. IS THAT WHAT YOU WANT?
IS THAT WHAT YOUR SISTER WOULD WANT?

NO.

YOU ALL RIGHT, NICKI?
I THINK SO.
THIS IS OVER.

OVER? YOUR SON JUST ATTACKED ONE OF OUR TEAMMATES!
YOU'RE LUCKY THAT'S ALL HE DID, "SKYMAN." YOU DON'T HAVE ANY IDEA WHY YOU'VE UPSET MY SON--

HEY, HOLD ON A SECOND, GRANDPA!

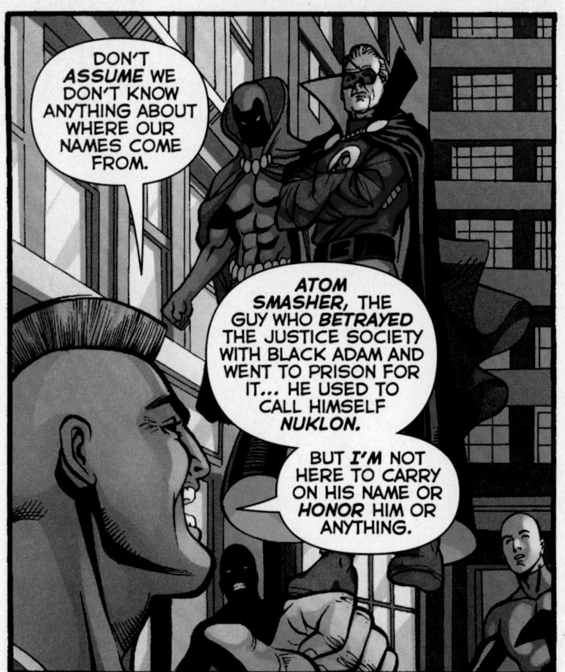
DON'T ASSUME WE DON'T KNOW ANYTHING ABOUT WHERE OUR NAMES COME FROM.
ATOM SMASHER, THE GUY WHO BETRAYED THE JUSTICE SOCIETY WITH BLACK ADAM AND WENT TO PRISON FOR IT... HE USED TO CALL HIMSELF NUKLON.
BUT I'M NOT HERE TO CARRY ON HIS NAME OR HONOR HIM OR ANYTHING.

LIKE JADE SAID, I'M HERE TO DO A BETTER JOB THAN HE EVER DID.
WE "GET" THAT YOU FOUNDED THE MASKS AND THE CAPES AND EVERYTHING, BUT YOU CAN'T TELL US HOW TO DO OUR JOBS FOREVER.
LEX LUTHOR HAS POISONED YOUR BODY AND MIND.
THAT'S WHY THE FIRST INFINITY INC. WAS FOUNDED. YOUR KIDS DIDN'T WANT TO LISTEN TO YOU ANYMORE.
YOU'RE LEAPING INTO A LIFE YOU'RE NOT READY FOR.

LISTEN, MAN. WHEN THE WORLD GOES TO HELL, WHEN EVERYTHING LOOKS LIKE IT'S GOING TO END, I PROMISE YOU--
--I'LL BE THE FIRST ONE RUNNING INTO BATTLE. WITH INFINITY INC. AT MY SIDE.
YOU NEED TO FINALLY FACE IT...

...THE WORLD DOESN'T NEED ANTIQUES WATCHING OUT FOR IT WHEN ITS GOT HUNDREDS OF KIDS LIKE US.

LET'S GO, SON.

STAND WELL CLEAR!
I'LL CARVE!
Week 29, Day 2
Afternoon on Oolong Island
AAAIIIEEEEEE!
EEEEHAHAHAHAHA!
HA HA HA HA HA HA HA HA HA HA HA HA HA HA HA

WILL?
YOU HAVE TO STAY!
CAN YOU HONESTLY SAY YOU'VE EVER EATEN PTERO-TURKEY BREAST ON THANKSGIVING IN PARADISE BEFORE?
EAT IT?
PROFESSOR MORROW, I'M DRENCHED IN IT.

FEAR NOT.
I'LL SAVE A CHOICE CUT FOR YOU, MY BOY.
MY WATCH!
WHO STOLE MY WATCH?!

MY GOLD WATCH!
IT WAS A GIFT FROM DEAR OLD NIKITA KHRUSHCHEV HIMSELF!
HOW COULD THEY!
IN THE NAME OF REASON, KRABB!
YOU'RE ON AN ISLAND FULL OF CRIMINAL SCIENTISTS!

...HOW COULD THEY NOT...
YOU CHASED HER AWAY.

NEAT WASHING UP LIQUID IS GOOD FOR GRAVY STAINS-- THE CHARDONNAY TASTES LIKE IT MIGHT ALMOST QUALIFY...
IT'S WILL, ISN'T IT?
DOCTOR WILL MAGNUS, CYBERNETICS GENIUS.

SMOKE?
I DON'T.
THE PIPE'S JUST TO... UH... TO CHEW ON.

FREUD WOULD CALL THAT AN ORAL FIXATION.
HMMM...
I DIDN'T REALIZE THEY'D KIDNAPPED FREUD TOO.

YOU'RE DIFFERENT FROM THESE GROPING, STUMBLING, SELF-CONSCIOUS, MAN-BOYS, THESE AUTISTIC MIDGET SAVANTS.
YOUNGER, TALLER, FOR A START.
HERE WITHOUT YOUR CONSENT, ON AN ISLAND POPULATED BY MADMEN.

I.Q.S LIKE TELEPHONE NUMBERS AND ALL THE GRACE OF GARDEN GNOMES!
THE ONLY TIME THEY SEE LIVE WOMEN IS IN THE SIGHTS OF THEIR DEATH RAYS OR THROUGH THE LENSES OF MICROSCOPES!

I JUST WANT TO GET OUT OF HERE.
BUT I KNOW TOO MUCH.
I KNOW YOU'VE ALL BEEN LET LOOSE WITH AN UNLIMITED BUDGET, TO CREATE WEAPONS FOR INTERGANG...

YES... SO WHAT DROVE YOU TO CRIME IN THE END, WILL?
I HEAR YOU BUILT A PLUTONIUM DEATH MACHINE FOR UNCLE SAM.

THAT'S NOT WHAT I'M KNOWN FOR!
AND I'M NOT A CROOK!
OF COURSE NOT.
WHAT KIND OF CROOK WOULD STEAL POOR, EVIL OLD KOMRADE KRABB'S PRECIOUS SOUVENIR OF THE COLD WAR?
HE DROPPED IT... I WAS GOING TO HAND IT BACK...

SO YOU MAKE ROBOTS THAT THINK AND ACT FOR THEM-SELVES?
I USED TO BE PRETTY GOOD AT IT.
NOT SO MUCH NOW.
AND YOU? THEY ASSIGNED YOU TO THE MYSTERIOUS PROJECT X UP ON THE HILL, RIGHT?

WHAT'S YOUR SPECIALITY?
TECHNOLOGY FROM ANOTHER WORLD-- A HIGHER, BRIGHTER, MORE TERRIBLE WORLD HAS FALLEN TO EARTH, DOCTOR MAGNUS.

"I SAW A STAR FROM THE SKY WHICH HAD FALLEN TO THE EARTH. THE KEY TO THE PIT OF ABYSS..."
OH, TO LIVE IN SUCH TIMES.
TO SEE THE WORLD CHANGED, FOREVER.

WELL, WELL, WELL...

NO ONE TOLD ME ABOUT THIS CELEBRATION.
WHY IS THAT, I WONDER?

PERHAPS CHUNG ZHU IS WAY TOO REPULSIVE TO SHARE A THANKSGIVING DINNER, EH?
TOO GROTESQUE AND RIDICULOUS!
GREAT ONE, PLEASE!
THANKSGIVING IS AN AMERICAN TRADITION, AND AS WE HAD ALREADY SERVED YOUR MACROBIOTIC SUPPER...

AND I HEAR SOME OF THE LOWER RANKS STILL CALL ME NAMES BEHIND MY BACK, IS THAT RIGHT?
IT MIGHT HAVE BEEN YOU!
SIR. NO, SIR.

YOU CALLED ME... "EGG FU," DIDN'T YOU?
WHAT'S FUNNY, EH?
WHAT'S SO FUNNY ABOUT THAT NOW?
SNNRT

IS THAT FUNNY?

IS A MUTANT FLESH-MACHINE-- AS FAR BEYOND THE CAPABILITIES OF YOUR PUNY VERMIN SPECIES AS YOU ARE BEYOND THE SWARMING PROTOZOA-- FUNNY?

WHAT ENTITLES YOU TO LAUGH AT ME?
I WASN'T LAUGHING.
KILLING PEOPLE WHO MAKE A WEIRD NOISE AT THE WRONG TIME ISN'T VERY FUNNY.
CHUNG TZU, I'D LIKE TO REPORT THE THEFT OF MY PRIZED GOLD WATCH!

SILENCE!
IF I HEAR OF ANYONE EVER CALLING ME ANY ONE OF NINE THOUSAND AND NINE DISGRACEFUL NAMES, I WILL ACT WITHOUT MERCY!
HEAR, HEAR!

IT'S THANKSGIVING!
WHY DON'T YOU JOIN US, CHUNG TZU, OLD PAL!
WE'LL TELL YOU ABOUT ALL THE HORRIFYING WEAPONS WE'VE INVENTED FOR YOU!

JUST ONE MOMENT, DOCTOR SIVANA!
YOU!
ONE MOMENT.

HOW IS MY PLUTONIUM MAN COMING ALONG!
UMM... SLOWLY...
LIAR!

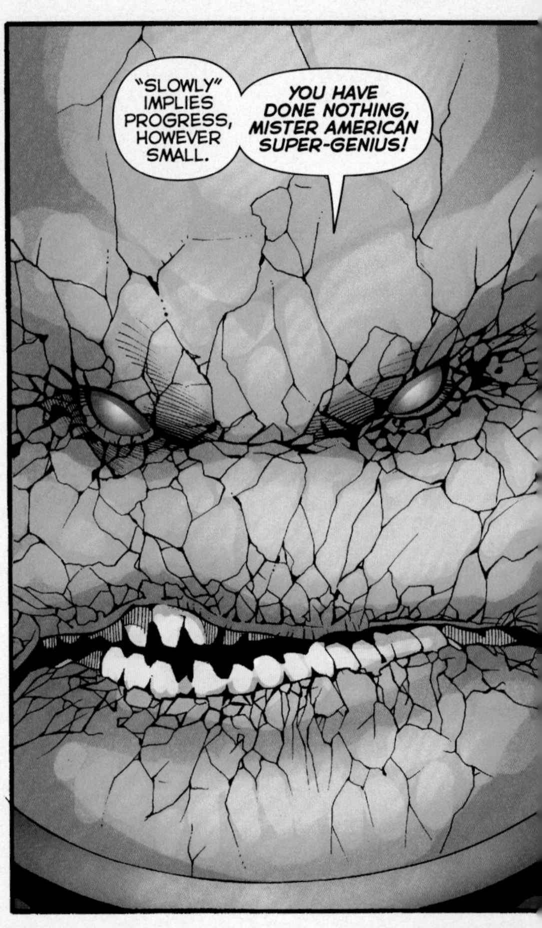
"SLOWLY" IMPLIES PROGRESS, HOWEVER SMALL.
YOU HAVE DONE NOTHING, MISTER AMERICAN SUPER-GENIUS!

PROFESSOR MORROW VOUCHED FOR YOU.
YOU ARE HERE, AND YOU ARE STILL ALIVE, ONLY BECAUSE OF HIM.

CHUNG TZU.
HE USES MEDICATION TO SUPPRESS MANIC/ DEPRESSIVE TENDENCIES.
NO!

HIS BEST WORK-- LIKE THE ORIGINAL, DEVASTATING *PLUTONIUM* ROBOT-- IS DONE DURING WILD, *MANIC* EPISODES.
TAKE HIS *MEDS* AWAY, THE CYCLE OF *HIGHS* AND *LOWS* WILL *RETURN,* AND WITH IT, THE WILD, DANGEROUS, *CREATIVE* STREAK HE'S BEEN *SUPPRESSING.*

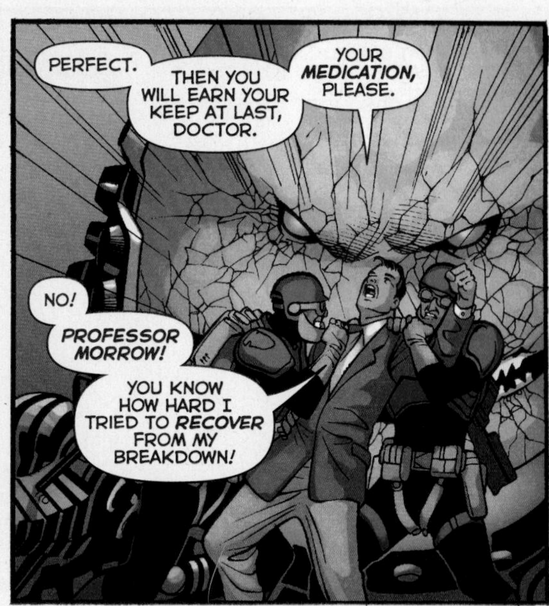
PERFECT.
THEN YOU WILL EARN YOUR KEEP AT LAST, DOCTOR.
YOUR *MEDICATION,* PLEASE.
NO!
PROFESSOR MORROW!
YOU KNOW HOW HARD I TRIED TO *RECOVER* FROM MY BREAKDOWN!

PROFESSOR, DON'T LET THEM DO THIS TO ME!
THEY'LL MAKE ME INSANE!

THANK GOD THERE'S STILL SOME REAL EVIL LEFT IN YOU, TOM.
THOUGHT YOU WERE TURNING PANSY.

WHY DON'T YOU TAKE WILL'S PLACE AT THE TABLE, CHUNG TZU?
LET'S ALL GIVE THANKS TO *INTERGANG...* AND THE GLORIOUS DAWN OF THE *GLOBAL CRIME STATE!*
I DO *LOVE* SEEING GOOD LITTLE BOYS TURN INTO EVIL *SUPER-CRIMINALS.*

I'M GOING TO ENJOY WORKING WITH *YOU,* WILL MAGNUS.

SO WHAT DO YOU THINK, JAY? YOU THE THINK THE JUSTICE SOCIETY IS OBSOLETE? YOU THINK WE'VE FINALLY HAD IT?

NOPE.
...YEAH. ME EITHER.
YOU SURE YOU GOT SOME-PLACE TO BE FOR DINNER? BART'S COMING. AND WE GOT PLENTY.

I GOT PLANS, THANKS. GIVE JOAN MY LOVE.
TAKE CARE.

YOU T--

--HM.

CLOSED

Week 29, Day 3
Metropolis: The Steelworks
...BACK TO THE QUESTION OF WHAT YOU PAID LUTHOR TO DO TO YOU, MISTER FERRY.

IT'S GABE, DOCTOR MID-NITE, CALL ME GABE.
AS FOR THE ANSWER TO YOUR QUESTION, I WANTED ELEMENTAL MASTERY. FIRE CONTROL, WATER CONTROL, LIKE THAT.
AND IT WORKED?
IT WAS LIMITED, BUT YEAH, IT WORKED, AT LEAST UNTIL HE TURNED IT OFF.

WHERE'D JOHN HENRY GO?
HEY, KALA. HE WENT UP TO THE APARTMENT TO LIE DOWN, SAID HE WASN'T FEELING WELL.
TOO MUCH LEFTOVER TURKEY, I THINK.

WOULD YOU BE WILLING TO SUBMIT TO MORE TESTING, GABRIEL?
IF IT'LL HELP NAIL LUTHOR, I'M WILLING TO DONATE ORGANS, DOCTOR.

JOHN?
I'M IN THE BEDROOM, KALA.

GAR SAID YOU WEREN'T FEELING WELL. IS EVERYTHING ALL RIGHT?
FERRY'S BEEN TELLING THE TRUTH, KALA...

...IT STARTED ≷NHN≶ PEELING OFF ABOUT AN HOUR AGO...
JOHN!
...WE KNEW LUTHOR COULD TAKE AWAY EVERYTHING HE GIVES...
...WE THOUGHT IT WAS A QUESTION OF PROCEDURE, THAT FERRY HAD A SECOND TREATMENT THAT TOOK HIS POWERS...
...BUT IF IT'S LIKE THIS, THEN THERE IS NO REVERSE THERAPY.
THERE'S AN EXPIRATION DATE.
NEXT IN 52

MICHAEL SIGLAIN

Thanksgiving in the DC Universe is not unlike Thanksgiving in the real world (or, for that matter, Thanksgiving in the DC offices... though, truth be told, in the DC offices, White Castle hamburgers have been served alongside the more commonplace cuisine of turkey and mashed potatoes, but I digress). In the DCU, Thanksgiving typically means the traditional shared dinner between the JLA and the JSA, our two most powerful super-hero teams. At this festive time of year, the heroes gather together, usually at the JSA headquarters, and break bread. But not this year. This is the year without Superman, Batman, and Wonder Woman. And, like the cover copy to this issue originally said, these are the "last days of the JSA."

The writers knew that they wanted the JSA to temporarily disband, and what better and more poignant time of year to do that than at Thanksgiving? We don't get to see the happy gathering of the two teams, but instead the writers give us three Golden Age heroes — The Flash (Jay Garrick), Green Lantern (Alan Scott), and Wildcat (Ted Grant) — discussing the current, depressing state of heroes in the DCU (and how Lex Luthor has artificially created super-heroes and bought old super-hero team names). The writers also bring another touch of poignancy to this scene by reminding readers of the death of the hero Jade, daughter of Green Lantern Alan Scott, and sister of Obsidian. (Incidentally, Jade fell during the RANN/THANAGAR WAR Special...not the JSA series.)

But this issue isn't without a turkey dinner. Thanks to the maniacal mind of Grant Morrison, we get a feast on Oolong Island, with a mutant bird and a giant egg. For those paying close attention, you'll notice that the turkey has two wings and six legs (three on each side), the logic being that the mad scientists would have genetically altered the turkey...'cause why not? And as for the giant egg, Grant brings back Wonder Woman foe Egg-Fu, and does so in such a weird, twisted, and dramatic way, that we actually fear him. Thus is the beauty Grant Morrison.

And because we can't celebrate Thanksgiving without a parade, here's a little tidbit for those paying extra close attention. See that white, panda-like balloon on pages 78-80? Notice anything familiar about its eyes? Here's a hint: they look remarkably similar to the eyes of a certain wall-crawler from our crosstown rivals. Here's why: breakdown artist Keith Giffen would frequently fill the backgrounds of the pages with many different characters, most of whom were Marvel characters. This was his way of keeping us all on our toes, and for making us laugh and smile (though I'm sure he'd never admit to the latter). The balloon was obviously changed for the actual issue, but the shape of the eyes was kept the same as a wink and a smile to those of us in the know. And now you know, and — as the saying goes — "knowing is half the battle!"

SCRIPT EXCERPT

(COMPARE WITH PAGE 62 OF THIS COLLECTION)

52 WEEK TWENTY-NINE PAGE TWELVE

PANEL ONE
Open with a big EC horror science image of Doctor Sivana poised as if to cut us up with a spinning laser chainsaw device of his own invention.

CAPTION: Week 29, Day 2

CAPTION: Afternoon on Oolong Island.

SILVANA: STAND ASIDE!

SILVANA: I'LL CARVE!

SILVANA: : AAAIIIEEEEEE

PANEL TWO
Sivana lowers his hellish outsize weapon with deranged relish and carves down into the horrific cadaver that lies in pride of place on the Thanksgiving table of the Mad Scientists on Oolong Island. It appears to be the cooked remains of a gigantic mutant ptero-turkey with eight legs — enough to feed a trestle table lined with dwarfish madmen.

As Sivana digs in with the spinning laser saw, grease sprays in all directions. The turkey is tied to a set of model train tracks. Any other warped Thanksgiving stuff any of you Colonials can add to the spirit of this (to me living in a land where the English WON) entirely alien festival will be appreciated!!!!

SILVANA: : EEEHAHAHAHA

PANEL THREE
And here's Doc Magnus glum as sprays of gravy hit his shirt and tweedy jacket. Next to him is his mentor T.O. Morrow, laughing at it all, gently drunk on cocktails with his girlie by his side.

And next to him is femme fatale CALE.

"EVERYTHING STARTED OUT SO *WELL*..."
DC COMICS 52

"...BUT ALFRED ALWAYS USED TO SAY BRUCE WOULD HAVE SELF-DESTRUCTED IF HE HADN'T MET ME AND LEARNED SOME RESPONSIBILITY."
"I GUESS WE BOTH WOULD HAVE.
"I MADE HIM LAUGH, AND HE WAS LIKE THE GREATEST BIG BROTHER YOU COULD EVER IMAGINE.
"THOSE WERE PRETTY COLORFUL YEARS IN GOTHAM, WHEN IT SEEMED LIKE ANYTHING COULD HAPPEN AND IT WAS OUR TOWN.
"THE JOKER GAVE UP BEING A MURDERER FOR A WHILE AND THERE WAS JUST THIS CRAZY, BRILLIANT CLOWN RUNNING AROUND.
I USED TO FEEL AS IF THOSE DAYS WOULD NEVER END.
"THEN, LITTLE BY LITTLE, EVERYTHING HE'D BUILT STARTED TO CRUMBLE.
"NOBODY NOTICED AT FIRST--HE'S THE BATMAN, THE SCARIEST GUY ON THE PLANET.
HUDSON U
"NONE OF US EVER WANTS TO THINK OF HIM HAVING MOMENTS OF DOUBT OR FEAR.
"WE DON'T LET HIM.
"BUT WHEN YOU THINK ABOUT THESE LAST FEW YEARS SINCE JASON BECAME THE SECOND ROBIN--
"WHEN YOU THINK ABOUT EVERYTHING THAT HAPPENED--
"IT'S TOO MUCH FOR ANY MAN.
"EVEN THE STRONGEST."

WRITTEN BY GEOFF JOHNS, GRANT MORRISON, GREG RUCKA, MARK WAID

ART BREAKDOWNS BY KEITH GIFFEN • PENCILS BY JOE BENNETT

INKS BY JOE BENNETT & RUY JOSE • COLORS BY DAVID BARON • LETTERS BY PHIL BALSMAN

COVER BY J.G. JONES & ALEX SINCLAIR • ASSISTANT EDITOR – HARVEY RICHARDS

ASSOCIATE EDITOR – JEANINE SCHAEFER • EDITORS – STEPHEN WACKER & MICHAEL SIGLAIN

AND THAT'S WHAT THIS IS ALL ABOUT.
WHY ELSE ARE WE HERE, PATIENTLY RECREATING THE JOURNEY THAT TURNED BRUCE WAYNE INTO BATMAN?
LOOK, I FIGURED ALL THIS OUT TOO.
IT'S JUST, WHY COULDN'T HE TELL US?
Week 30, Day 1
HE WANTS US TO BE THE NEW BATMAN AND ROBIN, RIGHT?
IT'S OBVIOUS.
I DON'T KNOW WHY NOBODY'S SAYING IT?
I CAN'T BELIEVE HE'D DO THIS TO ME.
FOUR BAD GUYS, JUST OFF THE PLANE, VERY SCARED.
HE'S BEEN HERE.

Week 30

DARK KNIGHT DOWN

I hate all of this.
SO DOES SHE MAKE HOUSE CALLS FOR ALL HER PATIENTS...
Gotham City
Week 30, Day 1
I hate that cancer is eating Charlie alive.
...OR IS THIS A SPECIAL ARRANGEMENT BETWEEN YOU AND MALLORY THERE?
I hate that even with my best friend dying, I can still be jealous.
I'M NOT SLEEPING WITH HER, IF THAT'S WHAT YOU'RE ASKING.
NO? THAT WASN'T THE IMPRESSION YOU GAVE ME BACK IN JULY.
I hate that all I have now is questions...
YOU'RE NOT THE ONLY ONE WHO WAS LOOKING TO SCORE POINTS THAT DAY.
DOESN'T MATTER. THIS YOU? HOW OLD ARE YOU IN THIS?
SIGH YES, THAT'S ME...
...and not one good answer.
KATE?
...I WAS NINETEEN.

Charlie and I left Gotham almost six months ago.
I GAVE HIM SOME **MORPHINE** TO HELP WITH THE **PAIN.**
YOU'RE GOING TO SEE THE ONSET OF BOUTS OF **DELIRIUM** SOON, WITH **DECLINING** MOMENTS OF **LUCIDITY.**
YOU SHOULD CONSIDER ADMITTING HIM TO A **HOSPITAL--**

We came back to save Kate's *life.*
WHY? SO HE CAN GO *IN* AND *NEVER* COME *OUT?*
RENEE--
We succeeded.
HE MIGHT BE **MORE** COMFORTABLE THERE, THAT'S ALL.

But it's costing Charlie **his.**
THEY'RE ***BOTH*** STAYING HERE FOR NOW.
THEN I'LL SEE WHAT I CAN DO ABOUT SETTING UP ***HOSPICE*** CARE.

I don't even know what it's going to cost **me.**

I'LL TAKE HIM TO THE *HOSPITAL* TOMORROW.
I ALREADY TOLD YOU, YOU AND CHARLIE CAN STAY FOR AS LONG AS YOU LIKE.
I'M NOT GOING TO *IMPOSE* MORE THAN I ALREADY *HAVE*--
YOU WERE *EVICTED* FROM YOUR *APARTMENT*, RENEE. YOU HADN'T PAID *RENT* IN *SIX* MONTHS!
WHERE ARE YOU TWO GOING TO *GO* IF YOU *LEAVE?*
YOU GOING TO LIVE OUT OF CHARLIE'S *VAN?*

STOP BEING SO DAMN *STUBBORN!*
JUST *ACCEPT* WHAT I'M *OFFERING,* ALL RIGHT?
PLEASE, RENEE.

OKAY.

I'VE GOT TO GO *OUT.*

I WON'T BE *BACK* UNTIL LATE.

DON'T WAIT UP.

SHE GOING OUT TO SEARCH FOR MANNHEIM AGAIN?

DIDN'T ASK.
SAYS THE GUY WHO NEVER ANSWERS ONE.
YOU SHOULD ALWAYS... ASK THE QUESTION.

YOU MIND IF I SIT WITH YOU FOR A WHILE?
I'M AFRAID I'M...NOT VERY CHATTY...RIGHT NOW.

IT'S ALL RIGHT, CHARLIE...

...I'M NOT EITHER.

IGNORE.
THESE GUYS MUST HAVE FLOWN IN FROM GOTHAM RIGHT AFTER HE STRUCK FOR THE DESERT.
THE EMPTY QUARTER, BLACK LIKE A SHADOW...
HAVE YOU SEEN WHAT'S IN THESE CRATES?
THIS STUFF COULD START WORLD WARS 3, 4 AND 5.
SO WHAT'S TH DEAL?
WHO SET YOU UP FLYING AIR APOCALYPSE OUT OF GOTHAM CITY?
TALK!
KRUNCH
CAIN OF THE ROCK AND THE RAGE, MAKER OF MARTYRS, GRANT ME SWIFT...SWIFT... RELEASE...
HEY!
HE JUST BIT DOWN ON A POISON CAPSULE.
WE COME LOOKING FOR BATMAN, WE FIND THIS.
WE WALK AWAY FOR HALF A YEAR AND INTERGANG'S RUNNING THE STREETS OF GOTHAM!
THE BIGGEST ORGANIZED CRIME NETWORK ON THE PLANET!

WE WALKED AWAY!
BRUCE CRACKED.
DO WE AGREE ON THAT NOW?
I'LL TALK TO HIM. WE'LL WORK IT OUT.

DO YOU WANT ME TO COME WITH YOU?

I HAVE G.P.S.
EUROPE WAS PRETTY COOL THOUGH, HUH?
WE HAD SOME FUN, TOO.
THE PARTY WITH THE MODELS IN CANNES WAS GOOD, I'LL ADMIT.

BUT VACATION'S OVER.
TELL BRUCE NOT TO WORRY, I HAVE IT COVERED.
TAKE AS LONG AS HE NEEDS TO REBUILD.

I'M GOING BACK TO WORK.

BRUCE WAYNNNNNE
Week 30, Day 3
UNNH?
WHO'S THERE?
YOU CALLED AND WE ANSWERED, BRUCE WAYNE.
JUST AS IT WAS WHEN LAST YOU VISITED US IN THE EMPTY QUARTER.
THAT WAS A LIFETIME AGO.
THE BLINK OF AN EYE.
WE TAUGHT YOU TO FIGHT AS GHOSTS FIGHT.
WHAT HAVE YOU LEARNED SINCE THEN?
THIS CEREMONY ALMOST KILLED YOU ALL THOSE YEARS AGO.
HA HA HA HA HA HA HA HA HA!

MY SOUL FEELS BLACK AND I FEEL SICK.
I'VE LOST MY RESOLVE.
BUT I CAN STILL TAKE YOU DOWN, UNARMED.

THEN DEFEAT ME AND THE TEN-EYED SURGEONS OF THE EMPTY QUARTER WILL COME TO SLICE OUT YOUR DEMONS.

BE STRONG.
THE WAY OF THE TEN-EYED BROTHERS MAKES USE OF SUBTLE SENSES.

GESTURES THAT REVEAL A WORLD OF MOTION AND PERSPECTIVE THE TWO-EYED MAN IS BLIND TO!
UNH!
FIND THE DEMON!

AND CUT!
SHNN!

HA HA HA
HA HA
HA HA HA HA HA HA HA!

DEFEAT ME OR DIE HERE!
WHAT GOOD ARE TEN EYES--

--WHEN NONE OF THEM CAN SEE?
AUUU!

UNNH!

I DIDN'T WALK ALL THIS WAY JUST TO *DIE.*
TEN EYES, *TWENTY*, A *HUNDRED*, GAZING IN JUDGMENT.
THE TEN-EYED TRIBES OF THE EMPTY QUARTER ARE *NUMBERLESS.*

IF YOU FLINCH.
IF YOU SHUDDER.
YOU WILL NOT SURVIVE.
DO IT.
BRUCE!
WRRRMMMMM
BRUCE?
YOU LOOK LIKE YOU NEED A HAND.
THE TEN-EYED MEN KILL DEMONS, TIM.
I ASKED THEM TO KILL MINE.
I ASKED THEM TO CUT OUT ALL THE DARK, FEARFUL, PARANOID URGES I'VE ALLOWED TO CORRUPT MY LIFE... AND THEY DID.
IT'S OVER.
BATMAN IS GONE.

Week 30, Day 7
KRUNCH
THIS IS ME ASKING YOU NICELY.
SNUFF
SNUFF
YAGHHH!
SHOULD I ASK THE REST OF YOU MEAN?
WHERE'S MANNHEIM?
KSHHH
HGGH!
HNNNH
RRMANNHEIM ISN'T YOUR PROBLEM.

THAT YOU CONTINUE TO LIVE DEFIES RRLLL THE WORD OF CAIN--

UNGH!
GRAARRR!
--AND THAT CANNOT BE ALLOWED!

MY MISTRESS HAS SENT ME TO GRRWWLL SET RIGHT WHAT YOU MADE WRONG!
THAT I'M ALIVE IS PROOF YOUR PROPHECY WAS WRONG IN THE FIRST PLACE, BRIGHT-EYES!

PERHAPS.

TAKE HER SNRRLLL HEART FOR THE APOSTLE.

YOU GOING TO LEND A HAND HERE, OR ARE YOU JUST PLANNING ON GETTING AN EYEFUL?

YOU HAVE TO ADMIT, IT'S QUITE AN EYEFUL.
WHAT CAN I SAY? I'VE GOT A THING FOR REDHEADS.
GFFFF
GRKK
UFFFF

TRUST ME, I'M *NOT* YOUR *TYPE.*
NHNN
THE *WOLF,* DON'T LET HIM--
--ESCAPE!
WHOA THERE.
YOU'LL GET *ANOTHER* CRACK AT HIM...
...BELIEVE ME, THERE'S *ALWAYS* A ROUND *TWO.*
AHEM.
NIGHTWING, PLEASED TO MEET YOU.
BATWOMAN.
YEAH, DEFINITELY *NOT* A BATGIRL.

GUESS WE SHOULD CALL THE COPS.
THESE ARE ALL INTERGANG, RIGHT?
YES.
THEY'RE LED BY A MAN NAMED MANNHEIM.
I'VE BEEN TRYING TO FIND HIM FOR THE LAST COUPLE OF WEEKS...
HNUUH
...HE'S GONE INTO HIDING.
KRAKK
I THINK I SCARED HIM.
IMAGINE THAT.
IF HE'S THE BIG BAD, WE'RE GOING TO HAVE TO FIND HIM.
I'LL START SEARCHING IN BURNLEY TOMORROW NIGHT, BEGIN WORKING MY WAY SOUTH.
AND I'LL TAKE TRI-CORNER AND BEGIN WORKING MY WAY NORTH?
UNLESS YOU HAVE AN OBJECTION.
PAF
NO.
NICE MEETING YOU, TOO.
NEXT IN

WEEK THIRTY NOTES

GREG RUCKA

All bats, all the time, this week.

Except for the part where Renee's watching her best friend die of a terminal illness.

Speaking as a guy who actually wrote DETECTIVE COMICS for a few years, Bruce Wayne's "conversion" was long, long, *long* overdue. Back when I'd been on the book and had the incredible Denny O'Neil editing, there had been much discussion about moving Batman away from the dour-faced humorless vigilante and bringing some light back into his life. There had even been a plan to do so, and a way to bring it to pass, but a change in group editors scuttled that, and shortly after, scuttled my own participation in all things Batman, at least for the time being. Personally, it was both vindicating and joyous to read "Batman is gone" and to know exactly what it was going to lead to.

The inevitable meeting between a member of the Bat Family and Batwoman occurs this week, as well, and of course, it had to be Nightwing, and of course, he had to start off with a flirt. We caught some grief for his "thing for redheads" line, but, c'mon, truth is an absolute defense, and he has a thing for redheads. The lightheartedness of the meeting, I think, served both characters well; imagine, for an instance, the same meeting with the "pre-surgery" Batman that Nightwing is describing at the start of the issue.

Yeah, that would've been a car crash.

This week also provided what was a much-needed insight into Kate Kane's life, via Renee and Charlie. Additionally, Renee's anger – her jealousy of Mallory, her argumentativeness, her goading of Kate – still comes across as very real to me. Helplessness is never a nice feeling.

The exchange between her and Charlie, as a note, is one of the most important they share in the entire series. It is also the last time Charlie is truly present with Renee until just before he dies. The smile he gives her in the last panel of the sequence, as she tries to "go inside" as he's taught her, is the most eloquent thing in the whole issue, in my opinion.

MARK WAID

Bruce Wayne's desert antagonists are Grant's nod to Phil Reardon, the Ten-Eyed Man, a Bat-foe from the 1970s whose optic nerves were in his fingertips. He gets a lot of grief among Batman aficionados, that Reardon — and it's true he's no Joker or Two-Face, but there nevertheless remains something compelling about the Ten-Eyed Man, as evidenced by the fact that I still know his real name off the top of my head.

HA HA HA HA HA HA HA HA HA!

BREAKDOWNS

BY **KEITH GIFFEN**

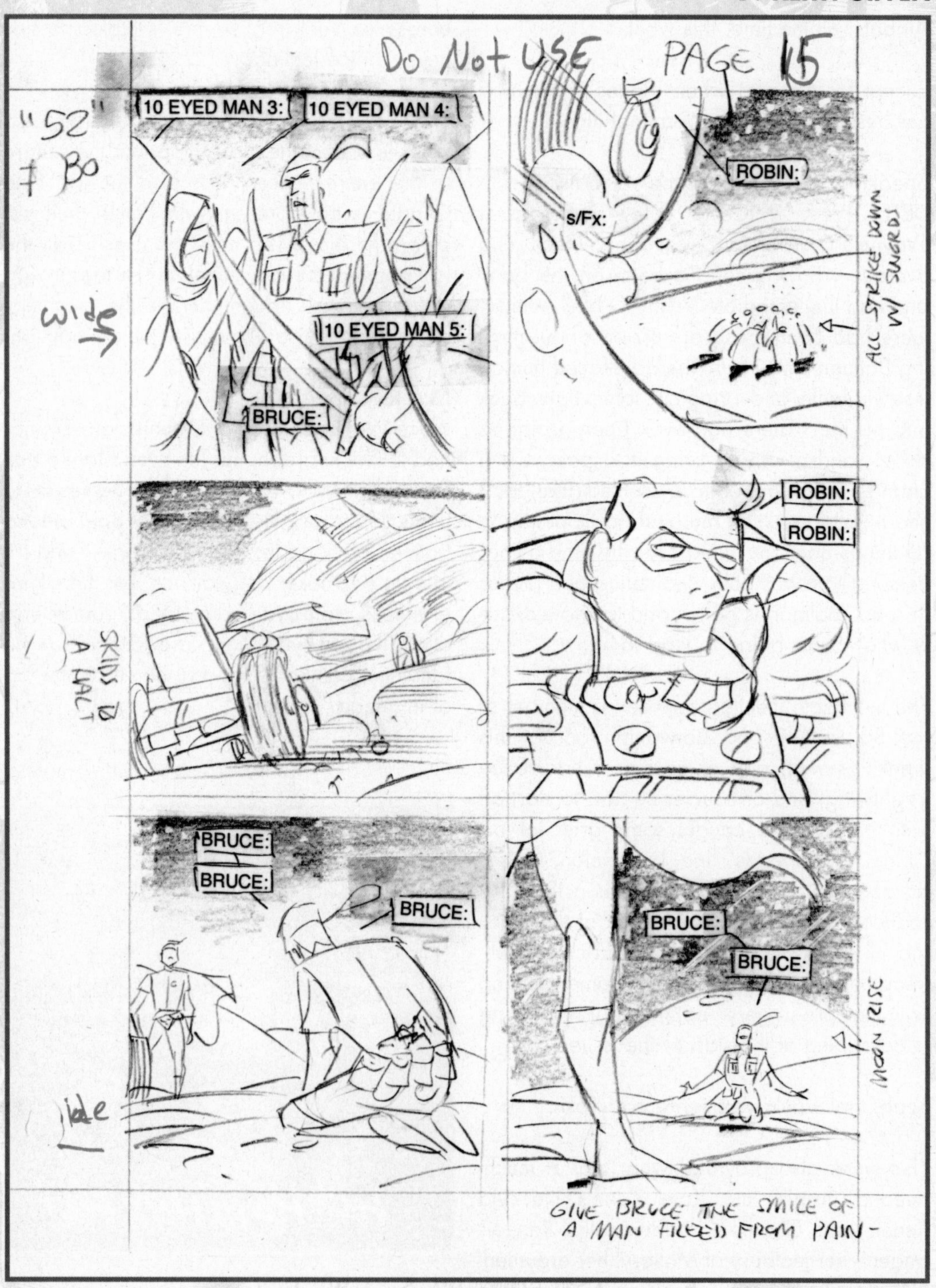

The original breakdown for Week 30 page 15 called for an even six-panel grid. But the layout was eventually changed to give the first and last panels a wider, more cinematic flair. Compare with the published version on page 89.

Week 31, Day 1

MY NAME IS ADAM BLAKE.

WRITTEN BY GEOFF JOHNS, GRANT MORRISON, GREG RUCKA, MARK WAID

A META, BORN TO HUMAN PARENTS, 100,000 YEARS AHEAD OF MY TIME.
THE VANGUARD OF THE WORLD-TO-COME.
MAN-PLUS IN BOTH AWARENESS AND PHYSICAL DEVELOPMENT.

MY TELE-THOUGHTS ARE RADIANT TO A DISTANCE OF FIVE LIGHT-YEARS.
ARE YOU RECEIVING ME?
IS THERE ANYONE THERE?

ART BREAKDOWNS BY KEITH GIFFEN • PENCILS BY CHRIS BATISTA • INKS BY RODNEY RAMOS, DAN GREEN, DAVE MEIKIS

COLORS BY ALEX SINCLAIR • LETTERING BY JARED K. FLETCHER • COVER BY J.G. JONES & ALEX SINCLAIR

ASSISTANT EDITOR HARVEY RICHARDS • ASSOCIATE EDITOR JEANINE SCHAEFER

DC COMICS 52 EDITORS STEPHEN WACKER & MICHAEL SIGLAIN

LEAVE HIM, JODD!
IN THE NAME OF O-DELL, LEAVE HIM!
HE SAVED OUR LIVES!
I WON'T LET HIM DIE LIKE AN ANIMAL, LURIBEL!

CAPTAIN COMET!

CAPTAIN COMET, SIR!
THIS WAY!
NO!
SAVE YOURSELF, INFANTRYMAN JODD!

SAVE YOURSELF.

THERE'S NOWHERE LEFT TO RUN, SIR.
SEE, THE SKY IS BURNING.

NO!
JODD!

GO TO HER!
TELL HER HOW MUCH YOU LOVE HER.

...BUT JODD WAS LOST.
WE WERE TO BE WED.
EVERYTHING IS LOST!
BE NOT AFRAID, CHILD OF VARDU, MY NAME IS THORMON TOX.

Week 31 Week 31 Week 31

HUMAN RESOURCES

I'M AN OFFICER IN THE INTERGALACTIC GREEN LANTERN CORPS.
MY PARTNER AND I WERE INVESTIGATING THE DISAPPEARANCE OF THE GREEN LANTERN OF VENGAR.
USZZ HEARD A VVOICZZE IN USZZ MIND, KALLING USZZ HERE.
TELL NOW... WHAT HAPPENED?

LET ME TAKE THE GIRL'S STATEMENT, LANTERN XAX.
AFFIRMATIVVE.
I'LL ALERT UZZZ ZZUPERIORSZZ ON OA.

...LANTERN XAX OF XAOSZZZ! SZZPACE SZZECTOR 3500 GONE, REPEAT, GONE.
BIG ZZOMETHING CHEWSZZ WAY ACROSSZ GALACTIC RIM TO VEGA ZZYSZZTEM.
REQUESZZT USZZ IMMEDIATE EMERGENCZZY ZZUPPORT!

HOW TO RESPOND?
THE THREAT HAS NO KNOWN CLASSIFICATION AND NO ENTRY IN OUR DATABASE.
AN ATTACK FROM OUTSIDE THE GALAXY, THEN?

NO, THIS MENACE ARISES FROM THE ETERNAL PIT BEYOND THE GATES OF SPACETIME ITSELF.
IT USES VOID TECHNOLOGY TO POWER ITS WEAPONS AND CONTAMINATES ALL FLESH IT ENCOUNTERS.
WE MUST RECALL OUR GREEN LANTERNS FROM THE OCCUPIED ZONES!

RECALL?
...THEY SZZZOUNDED... CHIRRUP FEARED.
GUARDIANSZZ OF UNIVERSZZE... RRRIKIT NEVER FEARED.
NO, NO, NO.

THEY'RE HERE!
THEY'RE EVERYWHERE!
I WITNESSED SEVEN MILLION MINDS FALL APART WHEN THE UNIMAGINABLE END ARRIVED.

I SAW MACHINES, THE SCALE OF WHICH THERE NO ADEQUATE WORDS TO DESCRIBE, AND ARMIES...
ARE YOU RECEIVING ME?
FIRST OF ALL, THE BELIEVER CUBES ANCHOR THEMSELVES TO A PLANET'S SURFACE AND SHATTER THE ECOSYSTEM IRREPARABLY.
THEN, THE GLORIFIERS EMERGE IN THEIR BILLIONS.

WALKING DEAD MEN, CHANTING HER CREED, UNSTOPPABLE.

WHERE SHE PASSES, HER ARMIES GROW, DEVOURING ALL IN THEIR PATH AS THEY SPREAD THE CONTAGION, THE LIVING WORD OF THE LADY.
THE LADY STYX.

"BELIEVE IN HER," THEY SAY.

"BELIEVE IN HER."

ARE YOU RECEIVING ME?

JOHN HENRY (today 9:48):
nat...please answer me.
JOHN HENRY (yesterday 10:12 pm):
very worried you are in danger. luthor lying about powers.
JOHN HENRY (yesterday 6:01 pm):
urgent. theory about trajectory. need to see you.
JOHN HENRY (yesterday 1:52 pm):
tried calling several times, no answer. plz call.
STARLIGHT?
Week 31, Day 2
Metropolis-- Infinity, Inc. Dormitory, LexCorp Tower.

UHM... I DIDN'T MEAN TO BOTHER YOU...
IT'S COOL. AND YOU DON'T HAVE TO CALL ME STARLIGHT WHEN WE'RE OUT OF COSTUME, SIERRA...
...NOT UNLESS YOU WANT ME TO CALL YOU JADE ALL THE TIME.

KINDA FEEL BAD ABOUT THE NAME ANYWAY, ESPECIALLY AFTER THAT THING ON THANKSGIVING.
LOOK, CAN I... CAN I ASK YOU SOMETHING? IT'S ABOUT EVERYMAN? I MEAN, HANNIBAL.
SURE.
I DON'T WANT TO MAKE ANY ACCUSATIONS OR ANYTHING...

...BUT I THINK HE WAS IN MY ROOM YESTERDAY, WHILE I WAS WORKING OUT...
HEY, JAKE!

HEY, BABE! BEEN LOOKING FOR YOU EVERYWHERE.
SIERRA AND I WERE ABOUT TO HAVE A CHAT ABOUT EVERYMAN...

...I THINK SIERRA'S CREEPED OUT BY HIM, THAT'S ALL.
NO KIDDING? HER, TOO?

IT'S NOT JUST ME?
NO, HE DOES IT TO ME AND JAKE, TOO. I THINK IT'S BECAUSE OF HOW HIS POWERS WORK.
HE JUST SHAPESHIFTS, RIGHT?

IT'S HOW HE ACQUIRES THE SHAPES HE SHIFTS TO THAT DOES IT, I THINK. SEE, HANNIBAL CAN ONLY TAKE THE SHAPE OF ORGANIC MATERIAL THAT HE'S DIGESTED.
HE DOESN'T HAVE TO EAT IT ALL, JUST A BIT. THAT'S WHY HE'S ALWAYS EATING WEIRD STUFF.
BUT? HE TURNED INTO A GORILLA LAST WEEK. THAT WOULD MEAN...

...OH, I THINK I'M GONNA BE SICK...

DID YOU SAY HE WAS IN YOUR ROOM?
YEAH... EWW, YOU DON'T THINK HE WAS LOOKING FOR SOMETHING OF MINE TO EAT?
WOULDN'T PUT IT PAST THE FREAK.

MAYBE HE WAS SCROUNGING FOR TOENAIL CLIPPINGS OR HAIR OR--
JAKE!

I'VE GOT TO GO--
SIERRA, WAIT!
I'M SORRY, IT WAS A JOKE!

A REALLY BAD JOKE...

THAT WAS REALLY UNCOOL, JAKE. WHAT GOT INTO YOU?
I KNOW, I KNOW, I SHOULDN'T HAVE SAID IT. I'LL GO APOLOGIZE.
NO... BETTER LET ME DO IT...

I REALLY AM SORRY.
I KNOW.

I'LL CATCH UP WITH YOU LATER, OKAY?
OKAY.
COLES
87

I'LL LOOK FORWARD TO IT.

Week 31, Day 3

Metropolis

MR. DIBNY?

MY BODYGUARD LIKES TO MAKE AN ENTRANCE.
HI, CASSIE. WE SHOULD TALK. FIGURED THIS'D BE THE BEST PLACE TO FIND YOU.

I SAY "BODYGUARD" IN CASE YOU'RE HOLDING A GRUDGE. HE'S ACTUALLY NOT MUCH GOOD IN A FIGHT.
...NO GRUDGE.
TURNS OUT YOU WERE RIGHT NOT TO TRUST US.

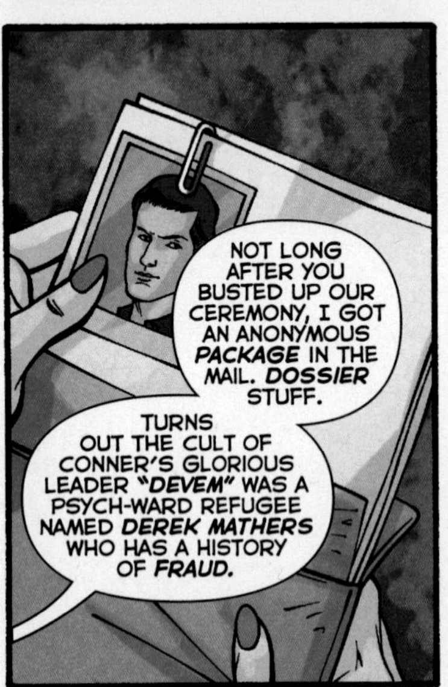
NOT LONG AFTER YOU BUSTED UP OUR CEREMONY, I GOT AN ANONYMOUS PACKAGE IN THE MAIL. DOSSIER STUFF.
TURNS OUT THE CULT OF CONNER'S GLORIOUS LEADER "DEVEM" WAS A PSYCH-WARD REFUGEE NAMED DEREK MATHERS WHO HAS A HISTORY OF FRAUD.

INTERESTING. YOU CARRY THIS AROUND?
TO SHOW OTHERS WHO GRAVITATE HERE, MAYBE GET HELP FINDING HIM.

HE SPLIT ONCE I CONFRONTED HIM, AND... YOU WERE RIGHT, MR. DIBNY. I GOT SUCKED INTO A SCAM.
I APOLOGIZE FOR WHAT I PUT YOU THROUGH.

SNIFF
EEEW. NO.
I'M JUST GLAD CALLING IT THE "CULT OF CONNER" WAS STRICTLY BETWEEN YOU AND ME. HANDING OUT SUPERBOY'S CIVILIAN NAME COULD HAVE CAUSED EVEN MORE DAMAGE.

WHERE DID YOU GO AFTER THE FIRE?
MARSEILLES, EVENTUALLY. WHICH SPARKED A NEW SEARCH. MEET MY SPIRIT GUIDE, DR. FATE. HE'S CHARMED, I'M SURE.

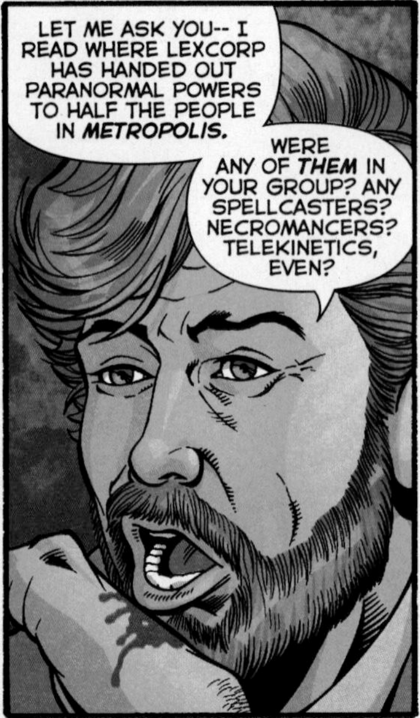
LET ME ASK YOU-- I READ WHERE LEXCORP HAS HANDED OUT PARANORMAL POWERS TO HALF THE PEOPLE IN METROPOLIS.
WERE ANY OF THEM IN YOUR GROUP? ANY SPELLCASTERS? NECROMANCERS? TELEKINETICS, EVEN?

JUST ORDINARY KIDS. LUTHOR'S EVERYMAN PROJECT DIDN'T KICK INTO OVERDRIVE UNTIL *AFTER. WHY?*
PROCEDURE. WANTED TO MAKE ABSOLUTELY CERTAIN BEFORE I REQUESTED AN AUDIENCE WITH... WELL... NEVER MIND.

SEE, SOMETHING *DID HAPPEN* DURING THE CEREMONY, CASSIE. DESPITE YOURSELVES, YOU WERE *ON* TO SOMETHING.
MY WIFE DID LIVE AGAIN, IF ONLY FOR A SECOND. I'M SURE OF IT. THE RESURRECTION?

--WAS *LEGIT.*
YOU DON'T SOUND *SHOCKED.*
I SAID *DEVEM* WAS A CON, MR. DIBNY. I DIDN'T SAY THE CHURCH'S *BELIEFS* WERE. RESURRECTION IS *POSSIBLE.*

SUPERBOY *IS BACK,* MR. DIBNY.
HE CALLS HIMSELF *SUPERNOVA.*

I... SEE. THAT'S...
...THAT'S GREAT, CASSIE. THANK YOU.
MR. DIBNY, WAIT! DON'T GO! MR. *DIBNY...!*

...MARSEILLES...

MARSEILLES, FRANCE
DONNA PRINCE
52 BEE ST APT. 322
PHILADELPHIA, PA

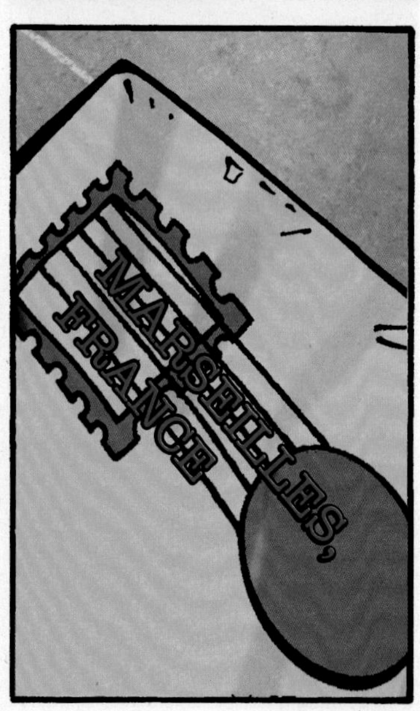
MARSEILLES, FRANCE

Week 31, Day 4
Metropolis
I SHOULDN'T BE OFF-ROUTE LIKE THIS. I SENT DR. FATE ON AHEAD BECAUSE WE HAVE THINGS TO DO... URGENT THINGS.
AND I DON'T OWE THAT GIRL ANYTHING.

BUT SHE'S CONVINCED HERSELF THAT SUPERNOVA IS SECRETLY THE BOY SHE LOVES COME BACK TO LIFE...
DAILY PLANET

...AND IT WOULD BE CRUEL TO LET THAT STAND.
WHY DIDN'T YOU TELL HER THE TRUTH?

BECAUSE THERE'S ONLY SO MANY TIMES I CAN BRING MYSELF TO RAIN ON HER PARADE.
THAT'S WHY I CAME LOOKING FOR YOU.
SOMEONE'S GOT TO TELL HER THAT IT'S NOT KON-EL UNDER THAT MASK, BUT RATHER--

DON'T SAY IT AGAIN. NEVER OUT LOUD. JUST GIVE ME THIS:

HOW DID YOU FIGURE IT *OUT?*
THE CLUES WERE THERE. ONCE I USED MY HEAD, THE *WHO* MADE PERFECT SENSE.
THE *POWERS* THREW ME, BUT WHEN I SAW THEM FROM THE PROPER *ANGLE,* I SUSSED OUT THE ONE DEVICE THAT COULD TIE THEM ALL *TOGETHER.*
SUPERMAN BEING OUT OF THE *PICTURE* WAS THE *KEY.* ONE OF *TWO* KEYS, IF YOU WANT TO BE *CUTE* ABOUT IT.

MIND TELLING ME THE *WHY?*
I CAN'T. YOU CAN NEVER BE SURE WHO'S--

I'M GOING TO GO. DON'T CONTACT ME AGAIN. WE SHOULDN'T BE MEETING AT *ALL.*
CAN YOU AT LEAST CLEAR THINGS WITH THE GIRL?

IF... CASSIE, IS IT?... IF CASSIE'S SO SURE I'M HER LOST LOVE, WHY ISN'T *SHE* TAKING THE INITIATIVE?
MY GUESS IS THAT, DEEP DOWN, SHE KNOWS IT'S A FANTASY. WAITING FOR YOU TO *UNMASK* KEEPS THAT *ALIVE.*

THEN SHE'LL JUST HAVE TO *KEEP* WAITING. THERE'S TOO MUCH AT STAKE.
GOODBYE, RALPH. AND GOOD LUCK.

Week 31, Day 6

LANTERN THORMON TOXZZ HELD THEM AT BAY FOR FIVE DAYZZ!
USZZ MOMENTSSS POWER LEFT IN GREEN RING!
REQUESTING IMMEDIATE BACKUP!

REQUEST DENIED, WITH HONORS.
I'M SORRY, LANTERN XAX.
WE CANNOT TAKE THE RISK OF EXPOSING OUR OFFICERS TO AN UNKNOWN EXTRA-UNIVERSAL CONTAMINANT AT THIS TIME.

END TRANSMISSION.
THEY'VE SHUT DOWN MY RING...

ADAM BLAKE WILL SAVE US.

ADAM BLAKE IS DEAD.
BELIEVE IN HER.
JODD?

OH NO, NOT YOU!

BELIEVE IN HER.
BELIEVE IN HER.
BELIEVE IN HER!
BELIEVE IN HER.
NOT YOU TOOOOO!

ARE YOU... ARE YOU RECEIVING ME?

...PREPARING... TO... JETTISON... PRIMARY... CONSCIOUSNESS...
ADAM BLAKE.
OUT.

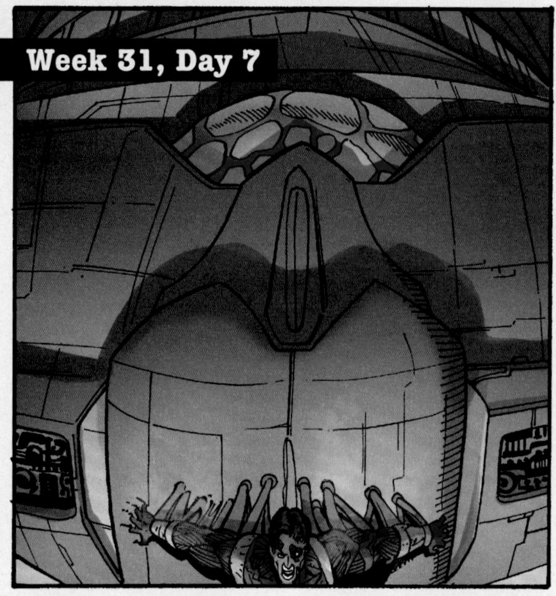
Week 31, Day 7

KRUNCH

LADIES AND GENTLEMEN...
LADY STYX.
UH-OH.
NEXT IN

WEEK THIRTY-ONE NOTES

KEITH GIFFEN

A lot happening in this issue. The forces of Lady Styx destroy a world, Ralph on the skids but still showing compassion, Everyman as pervert of the month...

Like I said, a lot happening.

Lady Styx was specifically created to pump up DC's cosmic menace index. I mean, Darkseid's a great character and all, but geez...he was being passed around the office like a bong. So enter Lady Styx and her undead hordes, exit...

Say, what was that world's name anyway?

The whole world-rending sequence has Grant written all over it and, if forced to make a call, I'd go with Grant but, as it turns out, I'd already miscalled a few who-wrote-whats, attributing to Mark what Geoff had written, to Grant what Mark had written...you get the point. To me, this was almost as fascinating as the story being told.

The Big Four were, at this point, in sync, to the point where, were it not for the different fonts used in their scripts, I couldn't pinpoint exactly who was responsible for what. The grasshopper Green Lantern earring that Lady Styx was wearing when she chowed down on the power rings? Dunno. Captain Comet flayed and mounted to a starship's bow? You got me. Ralph's having figured out who Supernova is? Okay, that's got to be Mark but only because it's a major plot point in Ralph's story and Mark...he do love himself some Elongated Man.

Ego set aside in favor of story. Not too shabby and all too rare in a comic book market that seems, at times, to thrive on, "Look! Over here! Look at me!" Much like I'm doing by writing this piece.

Chris Batista deserves special mention, if only because he knows where I live. Chris nailed it. Period. The action beats, the character bits, nailed them all. Hell, he even made Captain Comet look good. That alone is worth the price of admission.

All in all, a fun issue, one that I had a ball laying out. Huh... Thirty-one issues in and I'm still having fun...

Go figure.

SCRIPT EXCERPT

(COMPARE WITH PAGES 114 AND 115 OF THIS COLLECTION)

52 WEEK THIRTY-ONE PAGE 18

PANEL ONE
Horrible full-page image of Captain Comet's body lashed to the prow of Lady Styx's flagship — dead, screaming, flayed alive in the tatters of his costume. His head is split open, the skull shattered to reveal his four-lobed mutant brain, seething with maggots!

COMET CAPTION: ...preparing...to...jettison...primary.... consciousness...

PANEL TWO
Long horizontal insert at the bottom of the page. Close-up on his suffering eyes, steely in the midst of appalling pain and mutilation. He prepares to project.

COMET CAPTION: Adam Blake.

PANEL THREE
Then darkness. A black panel.

COMET CAPTION: Out.

52 WEEK THIRTY-ONE PAGE 19

PANEL ONE
Cut to the personal chamber of Lady Styx — horrible, drippy, spidery hell of bacterial machinery, wires and gelatinous hollows.

CAPTION: WEEK 31, DAY 7

PANEL TWO
A Necroton enters the chamber — it's the GIRL, Luribel, now made into a soldier of the undead army. In her hands she has two Green Lantern rings.

PANEL THREE
Close as the green rings are dropped into Lady Styx's outstretched claw.

PANEL FOUR
The terrible eyes of Lady Styx as she looks down towards the glow of the emerald treasures she holds in her articulate claw. She's wearing Xax of Xaos — now limbless and without his antennae — as an earring or some other jewelry.

PANEL FIVE
Then, backlit by hideous red light, she drops the Green Lantern rings towards her OPEN MOUTH!!!

PANEL SIX
Just letters across white space along the bottom of the page.

SFX (big): KRUNCH

DC COMICS 52

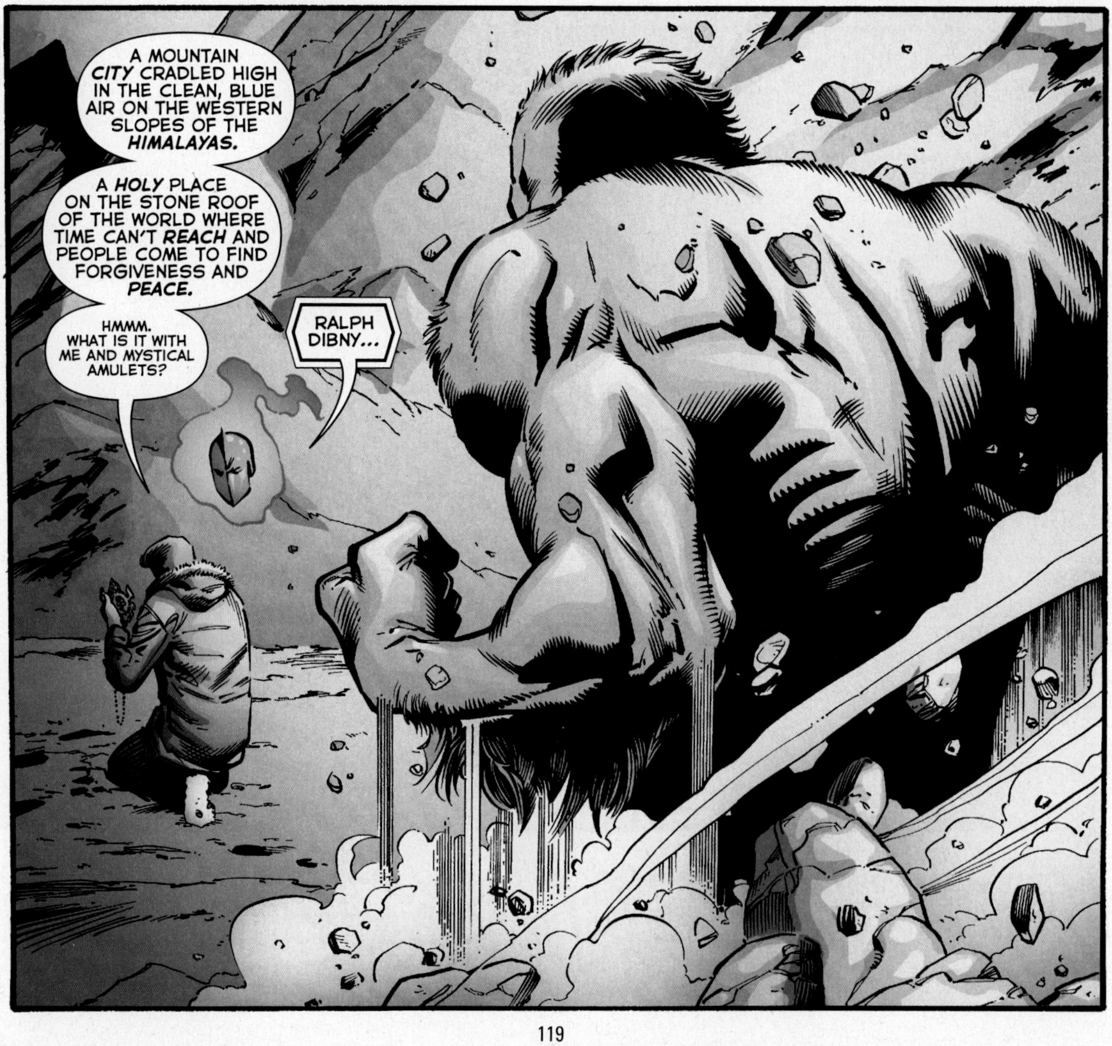

A MOUNTAIN *CITY* CRADLED HIGH IN THE CLEAN, BLUE AIR ON THE WESTERN SLOPES OF THE *HIMALAYAS.*

A *HOLY* PLACE ON THE STONE ROOF OF THE WORLD WHERE TIME CAN'T *REACH* AND PEOPLE COME TO FIND FORGIVENESS AND *PEACE.*

HMMM. WHAT IS IT WITH ME AND MYSTICAL AMULETS?

RALPH DIBNY...

WRITTEN BY GEOFF JOHNS, GRANT MORRISON, GREG RUCKA, MARK WAID

ART BREAKDOWNS BY KEITH GIFFEN • PENCILS BY PAT OLLIFFE • INKS BY DREW GERACI
COLORS BY DAVID BARON • LETTERING BY TRAVIS LANHAM

ASSISTANT ED. HARVEY RICHARDS • ASSOCIATE ED. JEANINE SCHAEFER
EDITORS STEPHEN WACKER & MICHAEL SIGLAIN
COVER BY J.G. JONES & ALEX SINCLAIR

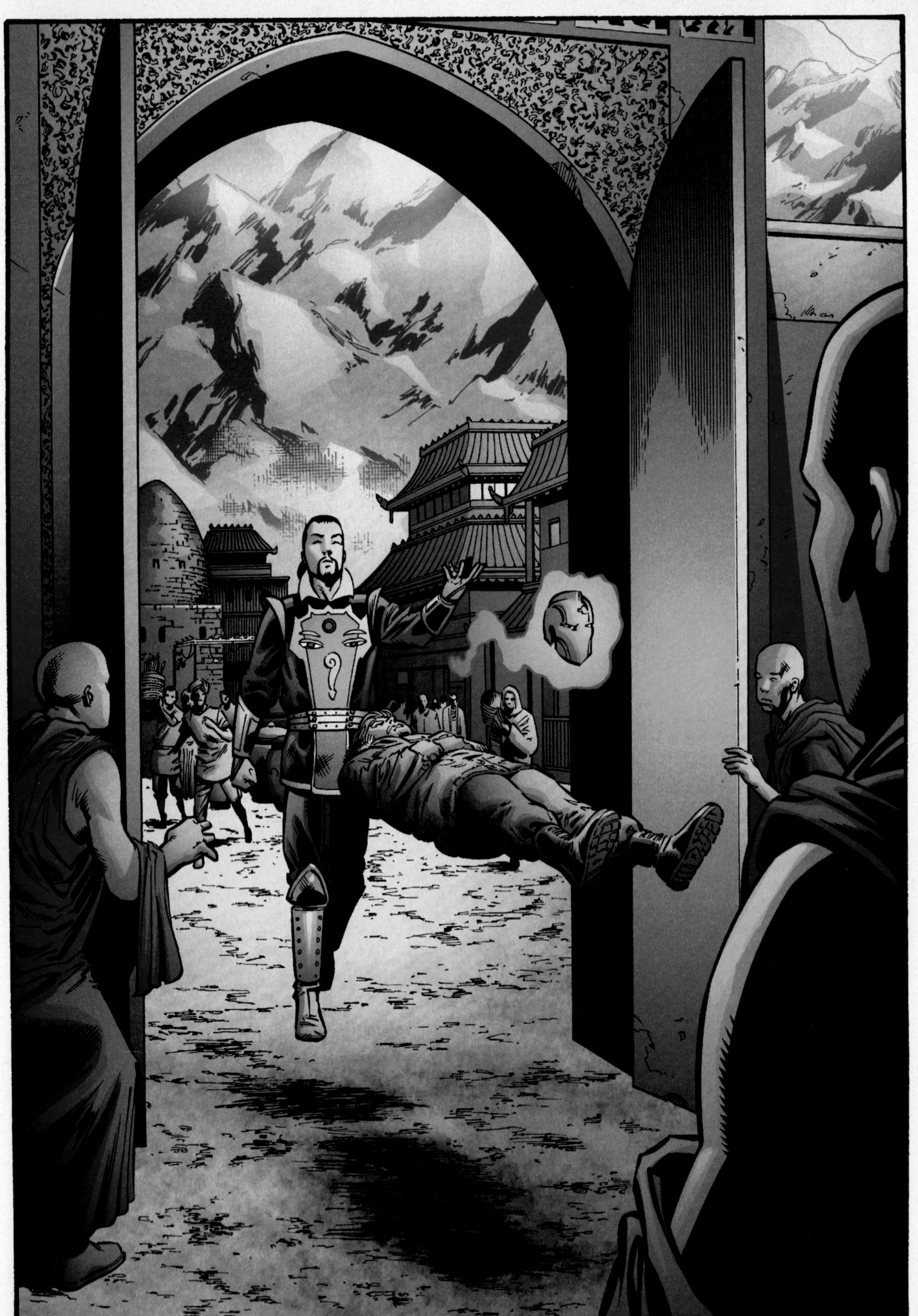

SEVEN DAYS IN NANDA PARBAT

Week 32

San Francisco. Titans Tower.
I KNOW WE ARE IN NEED OF MORE MEMBERS SINCE HAWK AND DOVE LEFT, GARFIELD, BUT...
...I CAN FEEL THE LUST FOR FAME AND POWER WITHIN SO MANY OUT HERE. AND HALF OF THEM ARE PRODUCTS OF LEX LUTHOR'S EVERYMAN PROJECT.
THAT'S WHAT WE WANT, RAVEN. DRAFTING ONE OF LUTHOR'S SIDEKICKS INTO THE TITANS WAS STEEL'S IDEA.
THOUGH I WAS HOPING WONDER GIRL WOULD'VE SHOWN UP FOR THIS.
CASSIE'S STILL LOOKING FOR SUPERBOY.
AREN'T WE ALL?
Week 32, Day 2

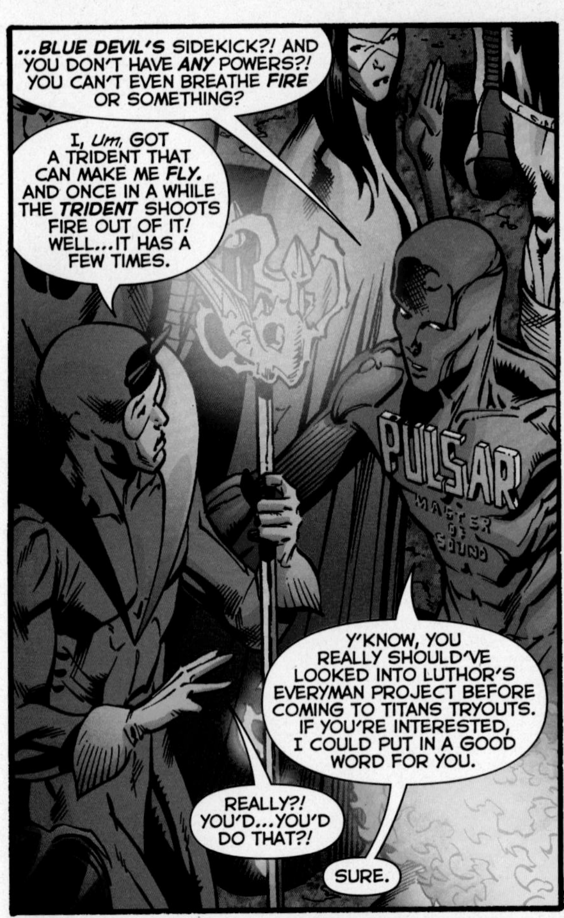

...BLUE DEVIL'S SIDEKICK?! AND YOU DON'T HAVE ANY POWERS?! YOU CAN'T EVEN BREATHE FIRE OR SOMETHING?
I, Um, GOT A TRIDENT THAT CAN MAKE ME FLY. AND ONCE IN A WHILE THE TRIDENT SHOOTS FIRE OUT OF IT! WELL...IT HAS A FEW TIMES.
PULSAR MASTER OF SOUND
Y'KNOW, YOU REALLY SHOULD'VE LOOKED INTO LUTHOR'S EVERYMAN PROJECT BEFORE COMING TO TITANS TRYOUTS. IF YOU'RE INTERESTED, I COULD PUT IN A GOOD WORD FOR YOU.
REALLY?! YOU'D...YOU'D DO THAT?!
SURE.

KRAKOOM
CHECK IT OUT, TONI! UP IN THE SKY!
I SEE HIM. ALL THAT GOLD...
THAT'S THAT ANTI-AMERICAN FROM KAHNDAQ!
Pfft. THAT KID WOULD GET HIS ASS KICKED ON MY EARTH.

IT'S THAT KID! BLACK ADAM JUNIOR!
HELLO, BEAST BOY. MY NAME IS OSIRIS.
I HAVE COME TO JOIN THE TEEN TITANS.
C-C-CAN WE LAND NOW?
EVERYONE STEP BACK!
DO YOU SEE THAT? THE MONSTER SPOKE?!

OH, DON'T BE AFRAID! THIS IS JUST SOBEK--THE TALKING CROCODILE!
HE'S MY BEST FRIEND!
THEY'RE STILL SCARED OF ME, OSIRIS.

THEY'RE THE TEEN TITANS, SOBEK. THEY'RE NOT SCARED OF ANYTHING.
YES, THEY ARE.

THEY'RE SCARED OF YOU.
ME?! THAT'S FUNNY.
CAPTAIN MARVEL JUNIOR. MY SISTER SPEAKS VERY HIGHLY OF YOU AND THE REST OF THE MARVELS. I SUPPOSE YOU ARE JOKING--

I'M...I'M SORRY ABOUT THIS, OSIRIS. BUT I'M AFRAID WE'RE GOING TO HAVE TO ASK YOU TO LEAVE.
LEAVE? BUT I WAS HOPING I COULD TRY OUT FOR YOUR TEAM.
I WAS HOPING SOBEK AND I COULD MEET SOME MORE FRIENDS. I WAS HOPING YOU AND I--

I KNOW THE CHANGES BLACK ADAM HAS GONE THROUGH. AND I KNOW A LOT OF THAT HAS TO DO WITH YOU AND YOUR SISTER.
I WAS AT ISIS' WEDDING. I SAW YOUR FAMILY TAKE DOWN SABBAC.
BUT THAT DOESN'T CHANGE THE FACT--

"--THAT THE "FATHER" OF YOUR FAMILY RIPPED A MAN IN HALF ON LIVE TELEVISION IN THE NAME OF HIS OLD-SCHOOL BRAND OF JUSTICE."

BUT I HAVEN'T DONE ANYTHING WRONG. I'VE ONLY HELPED PEOPLE. MY WHOLE FAMILY HELPS PEOPLE EVERY DAY!
WHY JUST YESTERDAY OSIRIS BUILT A HOSPITAL FOR EVERY VILLAGE IN SOUTHERN MODORA! AND HE PAINTED THEM A BEAUTIFUL GREEN TOO!

WE'RE ONLY TRYING TO MAKE THIS WORLD A *BETTER* PLACE.

CONVINCE THE *REST* OF THE WORLD OF THAT...
...AND I'LL HELP YOU JOIN THE TEEN TITANS.

RAVEN, WHAT EMOTIONS ARE YOU PICKING UP FROM OSIRIS?
JUST ONE.
HOPE.

Week 32, Day 3

YOU DON'T *HAVE* TO DO THIS, BUDDY.

WE CAN FIND A WAY TO GET YOU HOME.
YOU KNOW, YOU CAN GO ON AHEAD, PREPARE OUR *DEFENSES* WHILE WE GATHER *INTELLIGENCE.*

GATHER INTELLIGENCE?
ADAM, WE HAVE TO *STOP* THEM.
STOP THEM?
THERE ARE *MILLIONS* OF THEM.
WE NEED TO ALERT EVERY DAMN SUPERHERO IN THE *GALAXY!*

THEY'RE HEADING TOWARD OUR WIVES AND CHILDREN, ADAM.
NO MATTER HOW MANY THERE ARE, NO MATTER WHAT IT TAKES, WE'RE THE FRONT LINE!

WE HAVE TO STOP THEM. RIGHT HERE.
AND YEAH...I'M SCARED.
SO WHAT?

HELL, WE DON'T HAVE MUCH CHOICE OTHER THAN TO GO THROUGH 'EM, ANYWAY.
PRINCESS.
YOU STILL IN?

I LOST MY HOME WORLD.
AS INFURIATING AS BOTH OF YOU ARE SOMETIMES...
...I WON'T LOSE MY FRIENDS.

SO LET ME GET THIS STRAIGHT: IT'S US AGAINST A GENOCIDAL ALIEN WAR MACHINE.
WE HAVE A BOUNTY ON OUR HEADS AND WE HAVE LOBO AND THE EMERALD HEAD OF EKRON ON OUR SIDE.

MAY FORTUNE FAVOR THE CRAZY.
SADDLE UP!
NEXT STOP, HELL.

Week 32, Day 4
FATE...?

HOW LONG HAVE I BEEN *OUT?*

THREE DAYS.
YOU WERE *EXHAUSTED.*
YOU'VE COME A *LONG* WAY, BEARING A *HEAVY* BURDEN.

I GUESS YOU COULD SAY THAT.
THREE DAYS...
WAS THAT THE *YETI?*

HAHAHA
WHAT *BRINGS* YOU AND YOUR COMPANION HERE, TO *NANDA PARBAT,* MISTER DIBNY, AT SUCH AN AUSPICIOUS TIME?

RAMA KUSHNA.
I'M TOLD YOUR GOD *MANIFESTS* TO *PILGRIMS* WHO CLIMB THE *9999 STAIRS,* AND ANSWERS THEIR *QUESTIONS* ABOUT DEATH, AND DYING...
...AND THE *DEAD.*

HMM.
UNDERSTAND, RAMA KUSHNA IS NOT A GOD, NOT AN ORACLE.
RAMA KUSHNA IS THE LIVING *VOICE* OF ALL THAT IS AND IS *NOT,* THE PERFECT *COUNTENANCE* SMILING UPON US ALL, FOREVER.

WOULD YOU CARE TO MEET THE MAN WHO SAVED YOUR *LIFE* ON THE MOUNTAIN?
MISTER RALPH DIBNY, I'M HONORED.
I'M *YAO FEI:* ALSO KNOWN AS *ACCOMPLISHED PERFECT PHYSICIAN,* A SUPER-FUNCTIONARY OF THE *GREAT TEN* OF THE *CHINESE PEOPLE'S REPUBLIC.*

THANKS.
I *HEARD* ABOUT YOU GUYS.
WHAT'S YOUR CONNECTION TO *BIG UGLY* UP ON THE GLACIER? HE ONE OF *YOURS?*

THE *YETI* IS A MAN NAMED *HU WEI,* A *RESERVE* MEMBER OF THE GREAT TEN WHO DISCOVERED THE *ATAVISTIC TRIGGER GENE* WHICH TRANSFORMS *MEN* INTO *MONSTERS.*
AS YOU SAW, HE IS *IMMENSELY* POWERFUL IN THAT FORM.

THIS *CHARM* YOU FOUND IS AN ELECTRONIC DEVICE TO *INHIBIT* HIS RAGE.
HE DELIBERATELY DISCARDED IT AND RAN *WILD.*
THIRTY PEOPLE *DIED* IN THE VALLEYS BELOW UNTIL *I* ELECTED TO *END* HIS RAMPAGE AND RETURN HIM TO THE *GREAT WALL.*

CHINESE SUPERHEROES, HUH?
I GUESS IT HAD TO HAPPEN.
HEROES? NO. *SERVANTS* OF THE *PEOPLE.*
AS I SAY, *FUNCTIONARIES.*

I HEARD WEIRD MUSIC.
WHISTLING...
THAT WAS YOU?

I WAS TAUGHT HOW TO USE CERTAIN SOUNDS TO HEAL, AND SOMETIMES TO DESTROY.

WITH A SINGLE HUM I CAN SHATTER SOLID OBJECTS OR KNIT FLESH, MAKE AN EARTHQUAKE HAPPEN BY GROWLING, AND KILL CANCERS WITH A TONGUE CLICK.

I WAS A MEMBER OF THE RED ARMY, ONCE.
I WAS WITNESS TO ATROCITY. I WAS A KILLER, UNTIL I CAME TO ACCEPT THE OFFICE AND RESPONSIBILITIES OF THE ACCOMPLISHED PERFECT PHYSICIAN.

YOU DON'T NEED TO TELL ME ANY OF THIS.

I KNOW.
I WAS AN OUTLAW IN CHINA FOR A LONG TIME, BUT FIGHTING WAS COSTLY FOR THEM AND FOR ME.

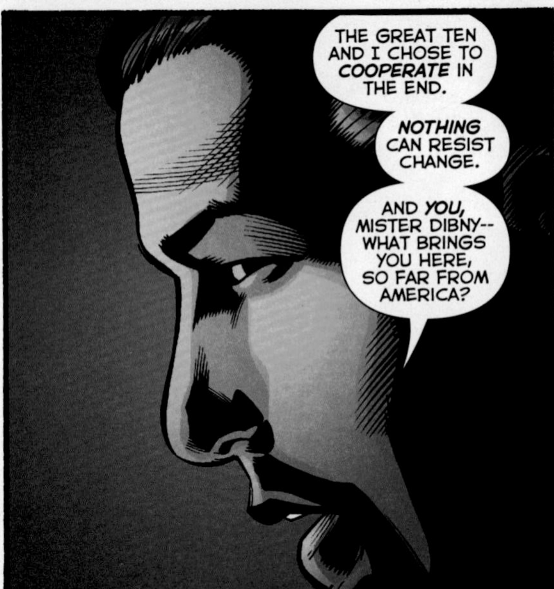
THE GREAT TEN AND I CHOSE TO COOPERATE IN THE END.
NOTHING CAN RESIST CHANGE.
AND YOU, MISTER DIBNY-- WHAT BRINGS YOU HERE, SO FAR FROM AMERICA?

IN THIS YEAR OF THE PIG THEY SAY NANDA PARBAT STANDS AT THE CROSSROADS OF LIFE AND DEATH, TIME, SPACE AND THE VOID.

ALL WHO COME HERE ARE TRANSFORMED.
YOU LOOK VERY HAPPY TOGETHER...

WE WERE.
SHE DIED A TERRIBLE DEATH.
MAY YOU FIND...EQUANIMITY, MISTER DIBNY.

NOW, IT WILL TAKE TWO GOOD MEN TO CAPTURE HU WEI IN HIS BEAST FORM. YOUR SPIRIT GUIDE CAN REMAIN BEHIND.
YOU DO HAVE SOME EXPERIENCE IN THE ART OF MONSTER HUNTING, I BELIEVE.
WAIT A MINUTE! I'M NOT A SUPERHERO ANYMORE, IF THAT'S WHAT YOU MEAN...
AND ANYWAY, I'M WAITING FOR AN AUDIENCE WITH RAMA KUSHNA.
IN FACT, THIS MIGHT JUST BE IT...

MISTER DIBNY--
--I'M AFRAID RAMA KUSHNA CANNOT SEE YOU.
WHAT?
I'LL DISTRACT HIM.
YOU CAN BELL THE BEAST.

Week 32, Day 5
THE THINGS OF THIS WORLD ARE ALL IMPERMANENT.
LOVE WILL OUTLIVE THEM.
I WAS ALWAYS THERE FOR HER.
EXCEPT FOR THE ONE TIME I NEEDED TO BE.

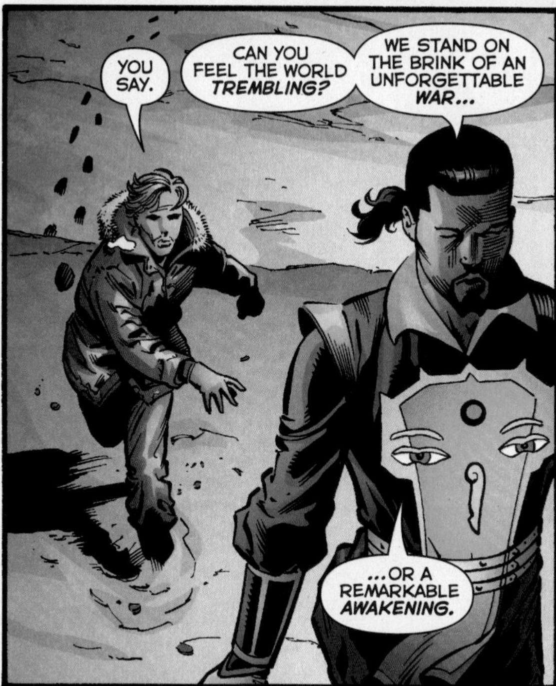
YOU SAY.
CAN YOU FEEL THE WORLD TREMBLING?
WE STAND ON THE BRINK OF AN UNFORGETTABLE WAR...
...OR A REMARKABLE AWAKENING.

WAR?
PERHAPS YOU'VE MISSED THE NEWS FROM THE MIDDLE EAST IN YOUR TRAVELS...

DOWN!

SNNAAAURR
GAAAAUR

CAREFUL, MISTER DIBNY, HE'S FASTER THAN HE...

HHNNN!
UKK...

GOTCHA!

RRRAAAAUUU

I'M VERY GLAD I MET YOU TODAY.
I OWE YOU MY LIFE, MISTER DIBNY.
THEY WANTED ME TO HAVE NO CONSCIENCE...
...LIKE AN ANIMAL... NO GUILT...A SOLDIER...

RALPH DIBNY.
HUH?

RAMA KUSHNA WILL *SEE* YOU NOW.

Week 32, Day 6
UNDERSTAND.
ONLY MEN OF SPECIAL DESTINY ARE PERMITTED TO ENTER AND TO SEE WHAT YOU WILL SEE.
RAMA KUSHNA AWAITS.
BUT...
BUT IT'S EMPTY.
THERE'S NOTHING HERE!
NO.
RAMA KUSHNA IS HERE.
EVERYTHING IS RAMA KUSHNA.
WHERE?

HERE IS THE SECRET.

THERE IS NO DEATH.

DEATH IS AN ILLUSION OF BEING IN TIME.

A TRICK OF THE LIGHT.

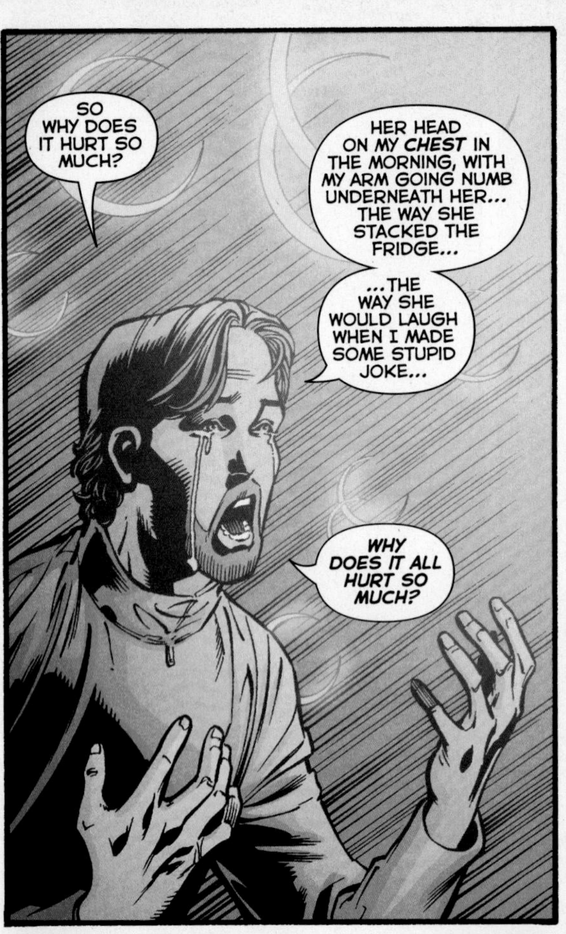
SO WHY DOES IT HURT SO MUCH?
HER HEAD ON MY CHEST IN THE MORNING, WITH MY ARM GOING NUMB UNDERNEATH HER... THE WAY SHE STACKED THE FRIDGE...
...THE WAY SHE WOULD LAUGH WHEN I MADE SOME STUPID JOKE...
WHY DOES IT ALL HURT SO MUCH?

NO LOVE IS WASTED.
NO LOVE IS LOST IN TIME.
THEN WHERE IS SHE?
WHERE'S THE ESSENCE YOU ALL TALK ABOUT? WHERE'S THE SOUL? THIS THING IN US THAT LIVES ON AND NEVER DIES?
WHY CAN'T I TALK TO HER?

YOU WISHED TO BE WITH HER AGAIN.
COME CLOSER, I WILL SHOW YOU HOW.

TELL ME...
DID YOU SEE?

Week 32, Day 7

YAO FEI. AT LEAST YOU GOT WHAT YOU CAME FOR, I SEE.
AND YOU DID NOT?

I DON'T KNOW.
I HEARD A WOMAN'S VOICE TELLING ME THINGS I ALREADY *KNEW.*
"THE END IS ALREADY WRITTEN."
AND THEY CALL *ME* CRYPTIC!

AND IF THIS END IS WRITTEN, WHO WAS THE *WRITER,* MISTER DIBNY?
IT WAS *ME.*
BACK IN *MAY,* AT THE END OF THE *CRISIS,* IN THE AMBASSADOR HOTEL.

BE CAREFUL, YAO FEI.
BE CAREFUL WHAT YOU *WISH* FOR.

NEXT IN

MARK WAID

As we've said before in interviews, while each member of the writing team took point on a different 52 character, we all still traded off from time to time. The Ralph scenes in this issue were written by Grant at our mutual insistence. I bow to no one on this team in my ability to write about guys with super-powers solving impossible crimes, but when it comes to transcendental matters of faith, I have the spirituality of a filing cabinet.

Eastern theology and mysticism are way, way, way out of my wheelhouse, whereas Grant hangs out with Deepak Chopra on a regular basis. Point, Morrison.

Nanda Parbat — an Asian mountain haven based on the Buddhist legends of Shambhala — first appeared in DC's 1960s DEADMAN series, about a circus aerialist who was murdered and whose ghost lived on to track down his killer. Artist/writer Neal Adams was the first to show us the goddess Rama Kushna, and if you look at the bottom of page 160 while slanting the top of the page away from you, you'll see artist Pat Olliffe's shout-out.

In Nanda Parbat, there is no death, which is why it's going to be so important in Volume Four of this series. If you've been paying attention so far to our other storylines, you'll see why.

Week 33, Day 4

The Flash Museum

Central City

BEST CHRISTMAS PRESENT HE EVER GOT ME?

ELONGATED MAN ROOM

ARRANGED A TIME-TRAVEL TRIP. EDGAR ALLAN POE AND I TEAMED UP TO CATCH JACK THE RIPPER. BIG HISTORICAL SECRET. DON'T TELL ANYBODY.

FLASH-- *BARRY--THERE* WAS A REAL *FRIEND.* IF HE WERE STILL ALIVE, THIS WOULD BE A *WING,* NOT A *CLOSET.*

HAVE A *CARE,* RALPH. INTOXICATION WILL INTERFERE WITH THE *GATEWAY SPELLS.*
I'M FINE. WE'LL 'PORT OUT AS SNEAKILY AS WE 'PORTED IN. FELLA COULD GET ACCUSTOMED TO THIS SORCERY STUFF.

JUST BEFORE YOU AND I HOOKED UP, I DONATED EVERYTHING SUE AND I *OWNED* TO THIS MUSEUM. WISH A LITTLE LESS OF IT WERE IN *STORAGE.*
STORAGE

DID YOU FIND THE ITEM YOU WERE *SEARCHING* FOR? SOME PERSONAL EFFECT, I PRESUME?
NOTHING YOU NEED TO WORRY ABOUT. I HAVE IT. LET'S ROLL.

DC COMICS 52

THE MOST WONDERFUL TIME OF THE YEAR

Week 33 Week 33 Week 33 Week 33 Week 33 Week 33 Week 33 Week 33 Week 33 Week 33 W

Gotham City, Cathedral Square.

Week 33, Day 5

DASHING THROUGH THE SNOW, IN A ONE HORSE OPEN SLEIGH, O'ER THE FIELDS WE GO, LAUGHING ALL THE WAY!

BELLS ON BOB TAILS RING, MAKING SPIRITS BRIGHT, WHAT FUN IT IS TO LAUGH AND SING A SLEIGHING SONG TONIGHT!

...OH, JINGLE BELLS, JINGLE BELLS JINGLE ALL THE WAY! OH, WHAT FUN IT IS TO RIDE, IN A ONE HORSE OPEN SLEIGH!

EXCELLENT, EVERYONE! VERY WELL DONE!

MISTER PENNYWORTH! DAN BLEW OUT MY *CANDLE*, HE DID IT BECAUSE HE'S *MEAN!*

NO TEARS NOW, JEANINE. WE SHAN'T HAVE *CRYING* ON CHRISTMAS.

AND YOU TELL YOUNG DANIEL THAT, SHOULD HE DO IT AGAIN, HE'LL BE DEALING WITH *ME.*

JOY TO THE WORLD, EVERYONE. ON THREE.

A-ONE AND A-TWO AND A-THREE--

MERRY CHRISTMAS.

JOY TO THE WORLD, THE LORD IS COME!

LOOKS LIKE SOMEONE WAS LACKING THE SPIRIT OF THE SEASON.
I THINK THE SPIRIT IS UPON HIM NOW.
LET EARTH RECEIVE HER KING!

SOMEHOW I DOUBT IT'S VISIONS OF SUGAR PLUMS HE'S SEEING AT THE MOMENT.
FOR THE BAT WHO HAS EVERYTHING.
LET EVERY HEART PREPARE HIM ROOM...

MANNHEIM'S ADDRESS?
STILL WORKING ON THAT ONE. GO ON, OPEN IT.
...AND HEAVEN AND NATURE SING! AND HEAVEN AND NATURE SING...

...AND HEAVEN AND HEAVEN AND NATURE SING!

ANOTHER BATARANG...
...HOW... NICE...
JOY TO THE WORLD THE SAVIOR REIGNS!

THIS ISN'T ANOTHER BATARANG, THIS IS A REAL BATARANG. NOT ONE OF THOSE HOMEMADE MODELS YOU'VE BEEN TOSSING ABOUT.
IT'S LOVELY, I DON'T MEAN--
HERE, GIVE ME.
LET MEN THEIR SONGS EMPLOY! WHILE FIELDS AND FLOODS, ROCKS, HILLS AND PLAINS REPEAT THE SOUNDING JOY!

DEAR SANTA,
THIS YEAR PLEASE
BRING ME:

GEOFF JOHNS,
GRANT MORRISON,
GREG RUCKA,
MARK WAID
WRITERS

KEITH GIFFEN
BREAKDOWNS
JOE PRADO,
TOM DERENICK
PENCILS

JAY LEISTEN,
RODNEY RAMOS
INKS
DAVID BARON
COLORS
PAT BROSSEAU
LETTERS

HARVEY RICHARDS
ASST. EDITOR
JEANINE SCHAEFER
ASSOC. EDITOR
JG JONES &
ALEX SINCLAIR
COVER

THANKS, SANTA! LOVE,
STEPHEN WACKER &
MICHAEL SIGLAIN
EDITORS

Week 33 Week 33
Week 33 Week 33
Week 33 Week 33

HE COULD DIE AT ANY MOMENT, MR. LUTHOR.
Week 33, Day 5 Metropolis.

OF THE THOUSANDS WHO HAVE UNDERGONE OUR EVERYMAN PROCESS, YOUNG DOMINERO IS THE ONLY ONE WHOSE BODY IS ACTIVELY FIGHTING AGAINST IT.
HE'S A MILLION-TO-ONE GENETIC FLUKE. DESPITE GETTING A THUMBS-UP ALL THROUGH SCREENING, LUIS DROPPED INTO A COMA THE FIRST TIME HE POWERED UP.
LUIS DOMINERO
EVERYMAN
SUBJECT 72126
ENERGY READINGS
INTELLIGENCE
POWER
SPEED
AGILITY
OTHER

OUR DOCTORS SAY HE'S HANGING ON BY A THREAD AND THAT HE PROBABLY WON'T LIVE ANOTHER NIGHT. THOUGHT YOU'D WANT TO KNOW.
ALL OF US CONNECTED WITH THE PROJECT ARE PULLING FOR HIM, SIR. HE WAS A GOOD KID.
THEN FLY HIS FAMILY IN, AND TELL THEM THEY ARE IN LEXCORP'S PRAYERS.

PARTICULARLY THE PUBLICITY DEPARTMENT'S.
PARDON?
NOTHING. KEEP ME APPRISED. I'LL BE IN THE INFINITY SUITE...

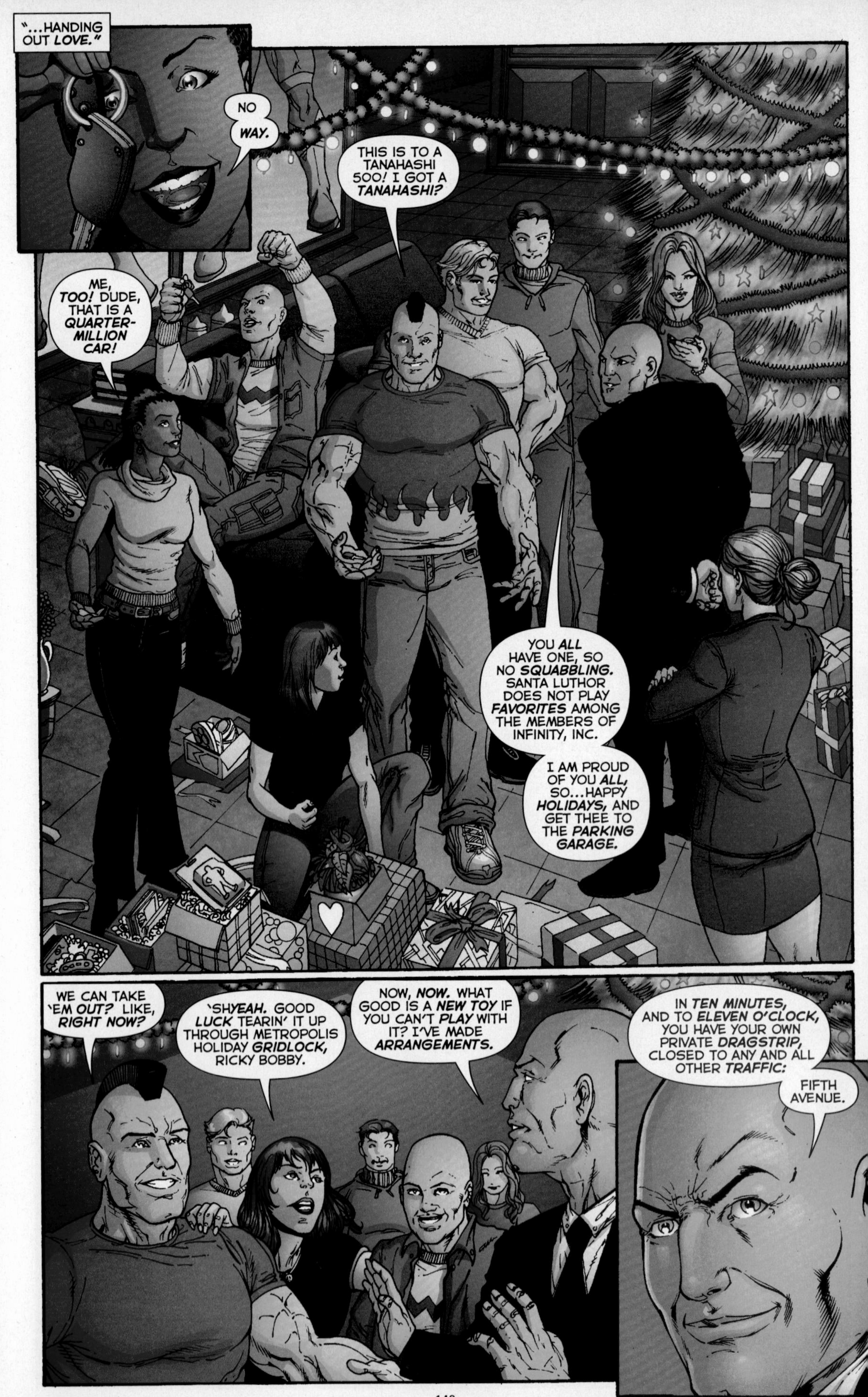
"...HANDING OUT LOVE."
NO WAY.
THIS IS TO A TANAHASHI 500! I GOT A TANAHASHI?
ME, TOO! DUDE, THAT IS A QUARTER-MILLION CAR!
YOU ALL HAVE ONE, SO NO SQUABBLING. SANTA LUTHOR DOES NOT PLAY FAVORITES AMONG THE MEMBERS OF INFINITY, INC.
I AM PROUD OF YOU ALL, SO...HAPPY HOLIDAYS, AND GET THEE TO THE PARKING GARAGE.
WE CAN TAKE 'EM OUT? LIKE, RIGHT NOW?
'SHYEAH. GOOD LUCK TEARIN' IT UP THROUGH METROPOLIS HOLIDAY GRIDLOCK, RICKY BOBBY.
NOW, NOW. WHAT GOOD IS A NEW TOY IF YOU CAN'T PLAY WITH IT? I'VE MADE ARRANGEMENTS.
IN TEN MINUTES, AND TO ELEVEN O'CLOCK, YOU HAVE YOUR OWN PRIVATE DRAGSTRIP, CLOSED TO ANY AND ALL OTHER TRAFFIC:
FIFTH AVENUE.

UNTIL THEN, IF YOU HAVE ANYTHING YOU'D LIKE TO, OH, SAY OR PERHAPS PRESENT--
HNNFFF!
RACE YOU!
QUIT SHOVIN'!
ONE SIDE!

LIKE MAYBE A SIMPLE "THANK YOU, BOSS." PUNK-ASS INGRATES. THEY DIDN'T GET YOU ANYTHING?
I LIVE A LITTLE BEYOND THEIR MEANS, MERCY.
IS THAT ENVELOPE FOR ME?

ONE OF YOUR TECHNOS ASKED ME TO DELIVER IT FOR SOME REASON.
EVERYMAN
FEASIBILITY STUDY
Subject: LEX LUTHOR
Prognosis: NEGATIVE
ENERGY READINGS
INTELLIGENCE
POWER
SPEED
AGILITY
OTHER
THEY FEARED I'D SHOOT THE MESSENGER.

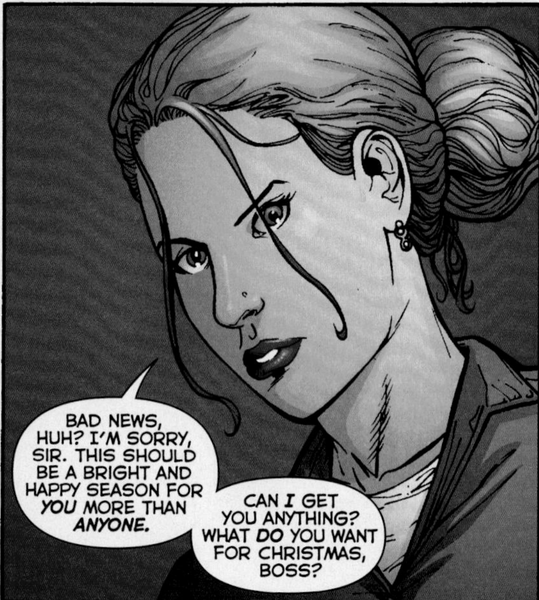
BAD NEWS, HUH? I'M SORRY, SIR. THIS SHOULD BE A BRIGHT AND HAPPY SEASON FOR YOU MORE THAN ANYONE.
CAN I GET YOU ANYTHING? WHAT DO YOU WANT FOR CHRISTMAS, BOSS?

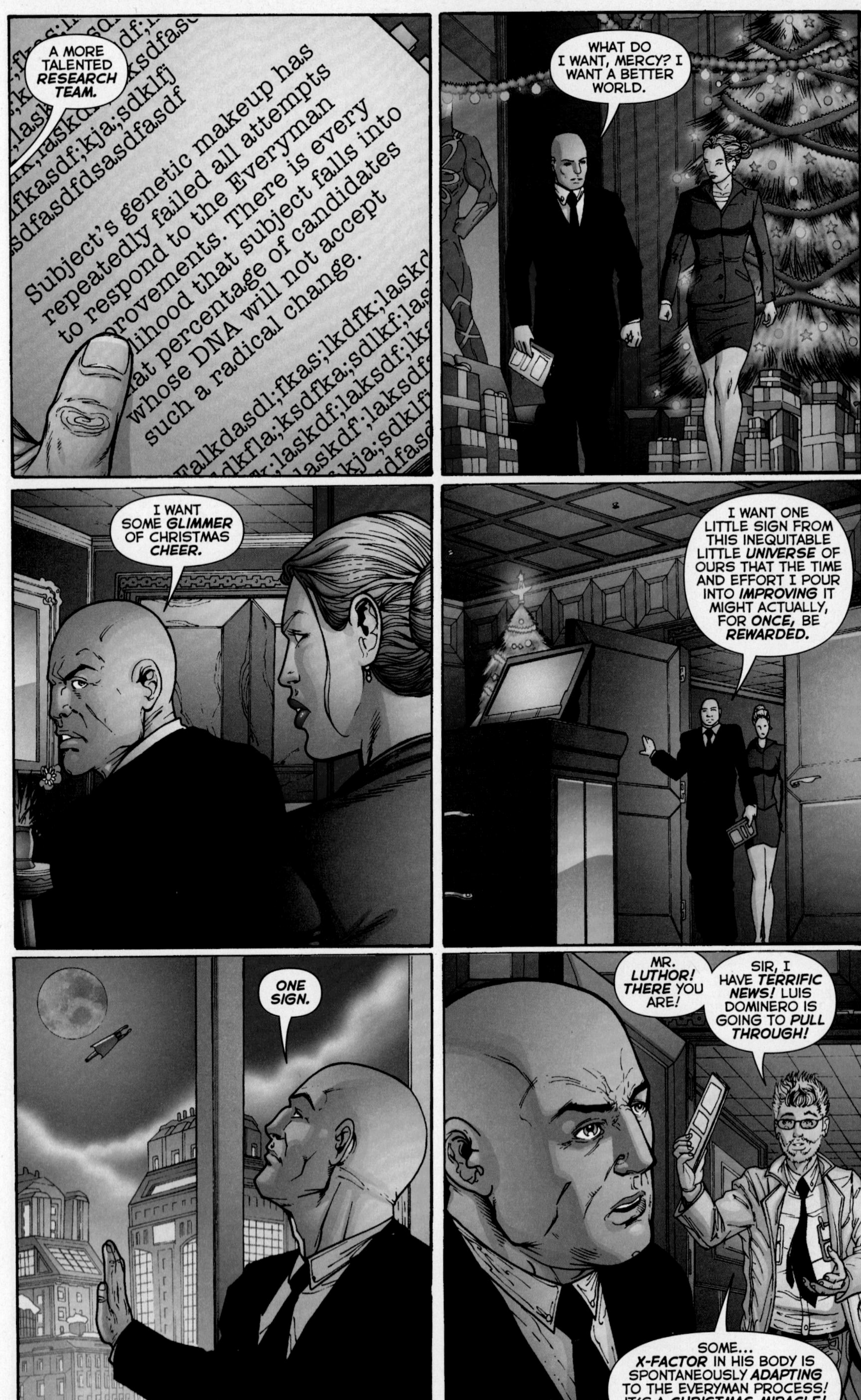
A MORE TALENTED RESEARCH TEAM.
Subject's genetic makeup has
repeatedly failed all attempts
to respond to the Everyman
provements. There is every
lihood that subject falls into
at percentage of candidates
whose DNA will not accept
such a radical change.
WHAT DO I WANT, MERCY? I WANT A BETTER WORLD.
I WANT SOME GLIMMER OF CHRISTMAS CHEER.
I WANT ONE LITTLE SIGN FROM THIS INEQUITABLE LITTLE UNIVERSE OF OURS THAT THE TIME AND EFFORT I POUR INTO IMPROVING IT MIGHT ACTUALLY, FOR ONCE, BE REWARDED.
ONE SIGN.
MR. LUTHOR! THERE YOU ARE!
SIR, I HAVE TERRIFIC NEWS! LUIS DOMINERO IS GOING TO PULL THROUGH!
SOME... X-FACTOR IN HIS BODY IS SPONTANEOUSLY ADAPTING TO THE EVERYMAN PROCESS! IT'S A CHRISTMAS MIRACLE!

THAT'S WONDERFUL, DR. LAUGHLIN.
I KNOW. THE WAY HE *SURVIVED*--
OH, NOT *THAT* PART.
ENERGY READINGS
THE PART WHERE SOMETHING *INSIDE* THE BOY OPENED THE DOOR TO THE POSSIBILITY OF GENETIC *ADAPTATION.*
DO A FULL ORGAN HARVEST AND SPINAL DRAIN ON LUIS, DRAFT A GLOWING OBITUARY, AND HAVE HIS PARENTS COMPENSATED FOR THEIR *TRAGIC LOSS.*
...O...OBITUARY...?
TONIGHT.
OH, AND *DENNIS?*
MERRY *CHRISTMAS.*
TINK

Hanukkah ended last night.
Kate made a big deal out of it. Cooked latkes and even laid out jelly doughnuts for dessert.

Charlie was actually *lucid* for most of the meal, but he couldn't keep *any* of it *down*.
Kate said she did it because that's how *her* family celebrated Hanukkah, at least before her father *remarried*.
That's probably true, but that's not why she did it.

Hanukkah is the *celebration* of a miracle.
...UPON THE *STAIR*, I MET A MAN WHO WAS NOT *THERE*...

...HE WAS NOT THERE AGAIN *TODAY*, I WISH TO GOSH HE'D GO *AWAY*.
CHARLIE...?
And she and I both know a *miracle* is the only thing that can *save* him.

I'VE GOT THE *ANSWER*, MYRA. THE ANSWER FOR *BOTH* OF US. IT'S BEEN SO SIMPLE, SO OBVIOUS--
CHARLIE--
--*LEAVE* HUB CITY...

...I *KNOW* THAT'S WHAT WE SHOULD DO...

...MOMMY TOLD ME.

He's delirious.
...MADE OUT OF PSEUDODERM...

He spends most of his time delirious, now.
...BINDER... TOXIC UNDER CERTAIN CONDITIONS... BLOOD POISONING...

It's the only way he can escape the pain.
CHARLIE...
...TOT...
...DID YOU KNOW THIS WOULD HAPPEN, TOT...?

...SON, CAN YOU HEAR ME?

...GET YOU BACK INTO BED.
WHAT'S YOUR NAME? I DIDN'T EVER HEAR YOUR NAME...
IT'S RENEE, CHARLIE. I'M RIGHT HERE, I'M STILL WITH YOU.

I'M SORRY, I TRIED, I REALLY TRIED...

...I'M SO SORRY ABOUT JACKIE...

...I LOVED HER LIKE SHE WAS OURS, MYRA...
...I LOVED HER LIKE I LOVED YOU...

...I COULDN'T SAY IT, YOU COULD SAY IT, BUT I NEVER SAID IT...

...I LOVE YOU...

I LOVE YOU, TOO.

GOING TO PLAY IN THE SNOW...

...AFTER LAST NIGHT, I SHOULD HOPE SO...

...SOME HOT CIDER, MIGHT MAKE YOU FEEL BETTER.
ONLY IF YOU ADDED SOME BOURBON TO IT.
I DIDN'T, BUT I CAN, IF YOU LIKE.

NO.
SEEMS THAT ALL THE PROBLEMS I HAVE WHEN I START DRINKING ARE STILL THERE WHEN I STOP.

YOU GIVE HIM PEACE. YOU SHOULD BE GLAD FOR THAT.
I AM.
I JUST WISH I COULD GET A LITTLE FOR MYSELF.

IT STOPPED SNOWING.

MERRY CHRISTMAS, RENEE.

HAPPY CHRISTMAS, BUDDY.
COME HOME.
SAN DIEGO, CALIFORNIA

TUNA
TUNA
TUNA
TUNA

Welcome back
Commissioner
Gordon!!

THAT STAR...
ALPHA LYRAE, BUDDY BAKER.
VEGA.

WEEK 33, Day 6
CHRISTMAS.

<YOU SHOULD'VE SEEN THE WAY THE TEEN TITANS WERE STARING AT ME AND SOBEK.>
<THEY WERE *AFRAID* OF US!>
<THEN CAPTAIN MARVEL JUNIOR TOLD ME AND SOBEK WHAT THE PEOPLE OUTSIDE OF KAHNDAQ *THINK* ABOUT US! IT'S AWFUL!>
<I THOUGHT SOBEK WAS GOING TO *CRY!*>
<A CROCODILE'S TEARS ARE NOTHING TO IGNORE, ADAM.>
<*PLEASE,* ADAM.>
<CAPTAIN MARVEL JUNIOR SAID IF WE CAN CONVINCE THE *WORLD* YOU'VE CHANGED, I CAN JOIN THE TEEN TITANS.>

KAHNDAQ
I ♥ ISIS

<WHO INVITED THE JUSTICE SOCIETY?>
<ISIS -->
<I DID.>
<YOU SERVED WITH THEM. YOU BEFRIENDED THEM. AND, IN THEIR EYES, EVEN BETRAYED THEM. YET, STILL, THEY ARE WILLING TO HEAR YOU OUT.>
<THE WORLD WILL SEE US ALL AS MONSTERS UNLESS WE SHOW THEM OTHERWISE.>

<FOR OSIRIS, ADAM.>
<THIS WILL CAUSE HIM GREAT PAIN.>

<IT'S OKAY. I'M READY, ADAM!>
<I'M READY TO SHOW THE WORLD!>

<AND YET HE STILL DOES IT WITH A SMILE.>
<SO CAN WE.>

I HAVE COME HERE TODAY...

...I HAVE BROUGHT MY FAMILY HERE TODAY...
...TO SHOW TO YOU THAT UNDERNEATH THE POWERS OF GODS LONG DEAD...

BLACK ADAM!
SHAZAM!
OH, MIGHTY ISIS!
KRAKOOM

...WE ARE AS HUMAN AS THE REST OF YOU.

I REALIZE IT WILL BE VERY DIFFICULT FOR MOST OF YOU TO LOOK BEYOND MY ACTIONS ON THESE GROUNDS SIX MONTHS AGO...
LISTEN TO HIM, WALLER.
Belle Reve Federal Prison.

HE'S CHANGED.
BECAUSE HE'S "SETTLING DOWN," ATOM SMASHER?
DO YOU REALLY BELIEVE A WIFE, A KID AND A TALKING REPTILE HAS TURNED THIS MAGICAL DICTATOR INTO A PEACE-LOVING PREACHER?
YOU WERE THERE WHEN HE LIBERATED KAHNDAQ.
AND BACK THEN BLACK ADAM WOULD NEVER LET ANYONE SEE HIM IN HIS HUMAN FORM.

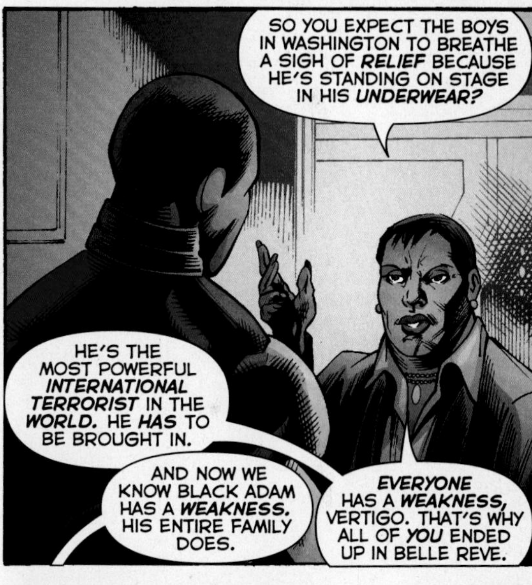
SO YOU EXPECT THE BOYS IN WASHINGTON TO BREATHE A SIGH OF RELIEF BECAUSE HE'S STANDING ON STAGE IN HIS UNDERWEAR?
HE'S THE MOST POWERFUL INTERNATIONAL TERRORIST IN THE WORLD. HE HAS TO BE BROUGHT IN.
AND NOW WE KNOW BLACK ADAM HAS A WEAKNESS. HIS ENTIRE FAMILY DOES.
EVERYONE HAS A WEAKNESS, VERTIGO. THAT'S WHY ALL OF YOU ENDED UP IN BELLE REVE.

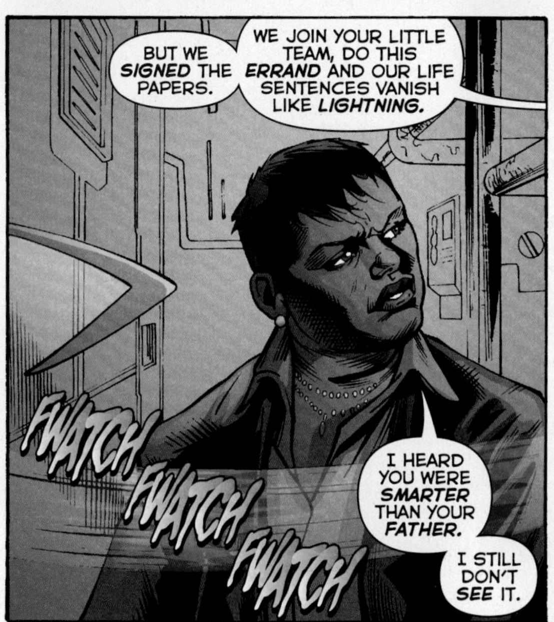
BUT WE SIGNED THE PAPERS.
WE JOIN YOUR LITTLE TEAM, DO THIS ERRAND AND OUR LIFE SENTENCES VANISH LIKE LIGHTNING.
FWATCH
FWATCH
FWATCH
I HEARD YOU WERE SMARTER THAN YOUR FATHER.
I STILL DON'T SEE IT.

SNATCH
YOU WILL, GORGEOUS.

AS SOON AS THE SUICIDE SQUAD WISH THE BLACK MARVEL FAMILY A HAPPY $#%@ING HOLIDAY.
NEXT IN 52

WEEK THIRTY-THREE NOTES

GREG RUCKA

Merry Christmas.

Mark did the Luthor/Mercy bit. Brilliant, and if you don't think so, wait until Week Thirty-Five.

The girl in tears standing before Alfred is named after Jeanine Schaefer, an editor at DC. Dan, who is mean, is, of course, Dan DiDio. This is called an "in-joke." It's not a terribly good one.

I wrote my pages for this issue in August of 2006, during a second, feeble attempt at taking some time off. While my family played on the beach, I sat in a frankly decrepit and unfinished rental house, surrounded by exposed drywall, and reread every single issue that Denny O'Neil had written of THE QUESTION. Why did I do this?

Here's something that most people don't know, and if Keith didn't want shared, he probably shouldn't have told me. Keith lost both his father and his father-in-law to lung cancer, and, as he once shared with me, he saw them go "both ways, easy and hard." His description of the dementia and hallucinations that arose once the cancer reached the brain were profoundly affecting to me, and became something that I couldn't let go of, no matter how hard I tried. It, honestly, broke my heart to think about it.

The reason I made a point of rereading every issue that Denny had written of THE QUESTION was that it was Denny who introduced me to the Question, and it was his interpretation of the character that had the most resonance for me, and the most influence. That was the character's history.

Almost every word Charlie speaks during this week is a line from Denny O'Neil's run. The lines about Jackie were mine; the rest were his.

On a much lighter note – though there was nothing light about it at the time – this issue was marked by transition, the departure of original editor Steve Wacker and the arrival of new editor Michael Siglain, and Siglain immediately took it on the chin. The menorah seen in Kate's apartment after she and Renee share a holiday kiss, and which has been corrected for this edition, initially had only seven candle holders, as opposed to the more crucial nine used by Jews around the world during Chanukah.

I still remember Siglain's scream of anguish when I pointed out the error to him. It was louder than mine had been, which was no mean feat. That was when I knew he and I would get along fine.

MARK WAID

The label on Ralph's gun — "The Anselmo Case" — is a wink to the 1980s show *Moonlighting*. You want more modern in-jokes? Go write your own comics.

PENCILS & INKS

BY **SHAWN MOLL** & **JAY LEISTEN**

The "holiday vignette" scenes went through three different pencillers before publishing. Some of the panels were altered in order to incorporate changes made to the DC Universe during its "One Year Later" phase. Here are the pages from original artists Shawn Moll and Jay Leisten — compare with the final version by artists Tom Derenick and Rodney Ramos on pages 154-155.

THAT STAR...
ALPHA LYRAE, BUDDY BAKER.
VEGA.

I SEE THE BLACK MARVEL FAMILY.
INTEL WAS RIGHT. THEY'RE COMING TO MEET OSIRIS AFTER HIS FIRST DAY AT THE TOWER AND THEY'RE...
THEY'RE WHAT, VERTIGO?
Week 34, Day 1
THEY'RE HOLDING HANDS.
DO YOU HAVE A VISUAL ON THE BOY AND HIS PET YET, BOOMERBUTT?
QUIT CALLIN' ME THAT, WALLER.
'CAUSE CAPTAIN BOOMERANG IS SO MUCH CLASSIER.
$#%@ OFF, PERSUADER.
WUSS.
THUNK
OSIRIS AND SOBEK LEFT TITANS TOWER FIVE MINUTES AGO. THEY'RE STILL IN RANGE...
...BUT AN ELECTROMAGNETIC BOOMERANG WILL JAM THEIR TITANS COMMUNICATORS.
THEN IT'S UP TO PLASTIQUE AND THE ELECTROCUTIONER TO START THE FIRE AND GIVE ATOM SMASHER HIS OPENING.
THE BOMB SQUAD'S ON IT, WALLER. WE BRING IN THE BLACK MARVELS AND OUR RECORDS GO CLEAN.
SO WHAT ARE YOU WAITING FOR, LESTER? I'M THE EXPLOSIVE. YOU'RE THE DETONATOR.
TICKLE ME.
KRRRAKKKLL
YEAH, BABY.

<I THINK ARGENT LIKES YOU. WHY ELSE WOULD SHE WEAR SUCH REVEALING CLOTHING? AND THAT BELLY RING. SHE PLAYED WITH IT THE ENTIRE TIME YOU WERE SPEAKING WITH HER!>
<THAT'S WHAT THEY DO IN AMERICA, SOBEK. THEY'RE JUST FRIENDLY. BESIDES, FREDDY SAID SHE WAS STILL GETTING OVER MOLECULE. THEY WENT THROUGH AN AWFUL BREAK-UP.>
<THAT'S TOO BAD.>
<OSIRIS!>
<ADAM! ISIS!>
<HOW WAS YOUR FIRST DAY?>
<IT WAS UNBELIEVABLE! BEAST BOY GAVE US A TOUR. I HAVE MY OWN LOCKER AND MY OWN TITANS COMMUNICATOR!>
<AND AFTER WE HELPED KID ETERNITY STOP THE KEEPER'S PLANS FOR CONTROLLING THE DEAD, ZATARA CONJURED UP SOME WONDERFUL HAM AND CHEESE SANDWICHES FOR LUNCH!>
<SOBEK ATE TWELVE.>
< OH, SOBEK.>
<DESPITE OUR SPEECH LAST WEEK, MANY ARE STILL CONDEMNING MY ACTIONS IN AND OUT OF KAHNDAQ.>
<YOUR SPEECH WAS GOOD ENOUGH FOR THE TITANS TO GIVE ME A SHOT, ADAM.>
<THE WORLD WILL COME AROUND. THEY'LL SEE THE GOOD WE'RE GOING TO DO.>
<AND WE'RE GOING TO DO SO MUCH GOOD.>
BOOM

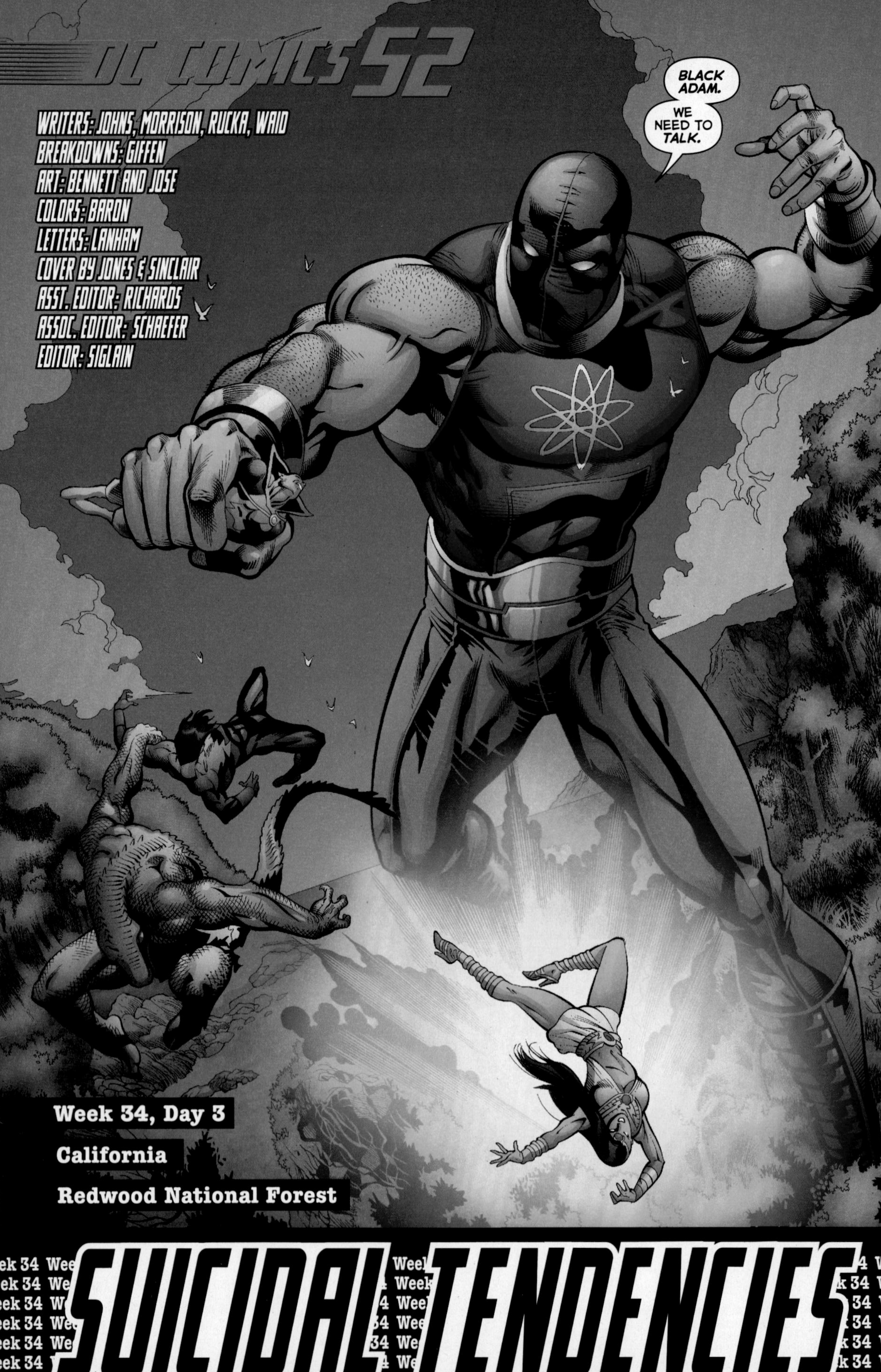
DC COMICS 52
WRITERS: JOHNS, MORRISON, RUCKA, WAID
BREAKDOWNS: GIFFEN
ART: BENNETT AND JOSE
COLORS: BARON
LETTERS: LANHAM
COVER BY JONES & SINCLAIR
ASST. EDITOR: RICHARDS
ASSOC. EDITOR: SCHAEFER
EDITOR: SIGLAIN
BLACK ADAM.
WE NEED TO TALK.
Week 34, Day 3
California
Redwood National Forest
SUICIDAL TENDENCIES

ATOM SMASHER?
WHAT ARE YOU DOING?
I'M DOING WHAT I HAVE TO. YOU CAN'T IGNORE WHAT YOU'VE DONE IN THE PAST.
YOU NEED TO TURN YOURSELF IN, ADAM.
THOOOM
I WILL NOT TURN MYSELF IN TO A HYPOCRITICAL GOVERNMENT TO BE JUDGED AS YOU HAVE. TO ROT IN A CELL WHILE THERE IS STILL SO MUCH WORK TO BE DONE.
MURDER IS A SIN THAT CAN'T BE WASHED AWAY.
I HAVE ALREADY ASKED FOR FORGIVENESS. IN SOME EYES THAT IS ENOUGH.
I DON'T WANT TO HURT YOU.
ALBERT--
--YOU WON'T.

THERE'S THE KID AND HIS MONSTER.
SUICIDE SQUAD'S JOB DOESN'T INCLUDE ANIMAL CONTROL.
KAZZATT
SO COOK THE CROC.
BOOOM
ATOM SMASHER?!
OH, #$@%.
BOOMERANG? ARE YOU ALL RIGHT?
IF YOU HAVE HURT THE BOY--

THE TREES ARE CRYING OUT.
YOU SOME KIND OF GREEN PEACE FANATIC?
BOOM
KKAAZZ
THE FIRE. AND THAT AXE. IT IS RADIOACTIVE. IT IS POISONING THE AIR AROUND US.
BUT THE ROOTS OF THESE REDWOODS WILL BURY IT FAR BELOW THE EARTH WHERE IT CAN DO NO HARM.
YOUR WORLD'S SPINNING AND SPINNING AND SPINNING.
Nnnf.
MY DEAR PRINCESS. THE CAMERAS DON'T DO YOU JUSTICE.
YOU TRULY ARE LOVELY.
BACK OFF, COUNT!
SLASHH
THE TREE HUGGER IS MINE.

THEY WANTED YOU ALL ALIVE.
FWASHHHT

CHOOM
TITANS, THIS IS OSIRIS. I NEED HELP!

AAAAIIIEEE!

AAAAIIIEEE!
ADRIANNA!

BUT $%#@ IT.
THIS IS TOO MUCH FUN.

<LEAVE MY SISTER ALONE!>

BWAATCHH
Ungh!
<OH, DEAR.>

<YOU SHOULD'VE...>
<YOU SHOULD'VE LEFT MY SISTER *ALONE!*>
<I...I WANT TO DO GOOD.>
<I WANT TO DO GOOD.>
<AMON.>
<I AM SORRY.>
KRAKOOOOM
<LET'S GO HOME.>
<BUT...>
<BEFORE ANYONE ELSE GETS HURT.>

KRAKKOMMMM
PLASTIQUE AND ELECTROCUTIONER ARE REGROUPING. DO YOU WANT US TO--
THAT'S ALL RIGHT, VERTIGO. I NEVER EXPECTED THE SUICIDE SQUAD TO ACTUALLY BRING THEM IN. I GOT WHAT I REALLY NEEDED.
VIDEO FEEDS WERE LIVE AND RECORDED.
WE PUSHED THE BLACK MARVELS--
--AND THEY PUSHED BACK.
ALL THESE SUPER-POWERED TEENAGERS ARE THE SAME.

Week 34, Day 4

Metropolis

WAIT A MINUTE, ISN'T THAT--
OMIGOD! OMIGOD, IT'S THEM--
--ONES FROM *INFINITY, INC.*, THE *HOT* ONES--
DINAH, WHAT'VE YOU *GOT?*
--SIGN THIS FOR ME? I'M YOUR *BIGGEST*--
--ABOUT YOU AND *SKYMAN*, IS IT *TRUE*--
...BETTER KISSER, NUKLON OR FURY?
--IT OUT TO BRIAN, UHM...HE'S MY *BROTHER*...
LIGHT COVERAGE, LOOKS LIKE ONLY *GRAVES* CAME WITH THEM...
...I'M THINKING *NOW* MIGHT BE THE MOMENT, BABS.
I'LL LET OUR FRIEND *KNOW*. IT'LL TAKE HIM AT *LEAST* THIRTY MINUTES TO GET INTO *POSITION*...
...WAIT FOR MY *SIGNAL* BEFORE RUNNING *INTERFERENCE*.
...CLOSED *THREE* WHOLE FLOORS FOR THEM, DID YOU HEAR?
I'M *COUNTING* THE SECONDS.

...OUGHT TO TRY THIS ONE. I GUARANTEE YOU IT'LL MAKE JAKE SIT UP AND BARK.
SIERRA! DO YOU EVEN KNOW HOW OLD I AM?
SERIOUSLY. JUST BECAUSE YOU DRESS LIKE A WHORE DOESN'T MEAN NATASHA HAS TO.
YEAH? WELL, THIS WHORE IS TRACKING HIGHER WITH MALES FOURTEEN TO TWENTY-FOUR THAN THE TWO OF YOU PUT TOGETHER.
WAS THAT BEFORE OR AFTER WORLD'S FINEST RAN THOSE NUDE QUOTE-UNQUOTE ART PICTURES OF YOU LAST MONTH?
GUYS, LET'S GO HIT DOMINIC'S...
...I STILL NEED TO GET A GOWN FOR THE NEW YEAR'S EVE PARTY.
COOL YOUR JETS, YOU THREE DON'T GO ANYWHERE WITHOUT ME.
I'M SORRY, THIS CARD'S BEEN DECLINED.
WHAT?
IT'S BEEN DECLINED.
I WORK FOR LEX LUTHOR, YOU INSIPID WAGE-SLAVE, THERE'S NO WAY IT'S BEEN DECLINED.
I KNOW WHO YOU ARE, MA'AM, AND I'M SORRY, BUT THE COMPUTER SAYS THE CARD'S STOLEN...
...I'M AFRAID SECURITY IS GOING TO HAVE TO DETAIN YOU UNTIL THE POLICE ARRIVE AND THIS GETS SORTED OUT.
THIS IS A SET-UP.
FINE...
...BUT I WANT THE THREE OF THEM ESCORTED BACK TO THE LIMO, AND I WANT IT RIGHT NOW.
BUT I STILL NEED--

YOU'RE GOING BACK TO THE DORMS.
DISPATCH, POST FOUR, WE'RE WITH THE VIPS. WE NEED SUPPORT FOR A ROUTE OUT.
CONFIRMED. THE CROWD OUTSIDE HAS GOTTEN PRETTY LARGE, INCLUDING PAPARAZZI...
...RECOMMEND TAKING EACH OF THEM VIA SEPARATE ROUTES.
I'M DISPATCHING AN ADDITIONAL ESCORT TO MEET YOU IN THE SOUTH SIX STAIRWELL...
VOICE MODULATION ENGAGED
...SHOULD BE THERE ANY SECOND.
WE'RE SPLITTING UP? WHY ARE WE SPLITTING UP?
IT'S CALLED SECURITY, STUPID. YOU HEARD THE RADIO, THE PRESS IS OUTSIDE.
DISPATCH...
...I'M WITH THE VIPS, BEGINNING ESCORT.
CONFIRMED.
IF YOU'LL COME WITH ME, MS. IRONS.
WE'RE GOING DOWN?
JUST ONE FLOOR, THEN WE'LL CUT ACROSS. DON'T WORRY, MS. IRONS...
...YOU'RE IN GOOD HANDS.

HELLO, NATASHA.
NICE PLAY, BLACK CANARY. THOUGHT I RECOGNIZED YOU.
WHAT'S THIS ABOUT, UNCLE JOHN? YOU CAN'T JUST TEXT MESSAGE ME ANOTHER HUNDRED TIMES?
WITHOUT LUTHOR KNOWING ABOUT IT? NO.
I NEEDED TO TALK TO YOU ALONE. WITHOUT ANY OF HIS PEOPLE LISTENING.
IF THIS IS ANOTHER WARNING--
LOOK AT ME, NAT. LOOK AT MY SKIN.
IT'S BACK TO NORMAL. CONGRATS, YOU FOUND YOURSELF A CURE OR WHATEVER.
NO. I DIDN'T DO THIS. IT ENDED ON ITS OWN.
WHAT'S YOUR POINT?
YOUR FRIEND BLOCKBUSTER KILLED ELIZA HARMON, TRAJECTORY.
HOW DID A SLUG LIKE BLOCKBUSTER MANAGE TO GRAB SOMEONE WHO COULD MOVE THAT FAST?
HOW DID HE MOVE FAST ENOUGH TO SNAP HER NECK?
YOU'RE A SCIENTIST, NAT, THAT'S WHAT YOU TOLD ME.
JUST LOOK AT THE FACTS...
...DRAW YOUR OWN CONCLUSIONS....

Week 34, Day 5
Metropolis
SODIUM PENTOTHAL? YOU'RE MIRED IN THE PAST, MR. KENT.
HIGHLY EXPERIMENTAL AS TRUTH SERUMS GO, BUT THEN, WE HAVE ONLY ONE QUESTION FOR YOU.
ONE TO WHICH YOU WILL CERTAINLY KNOW THE ANSWER...
FFFFF
THIS IS GAEAMYTAL. IT'S AS CLOSE AS MODERN CHEMISTRY CAN COME TO SYNTHESIZING THE ATOMIC STRUCTURE OF WONDER WOMAN'S LASSO.
...BECAUSE IT REGARDS SUPERMAN'S SECRET IDENTITY.
TELL ME, MR. KENT...
...WHY IS THE MAN OF STEEL MASQUERADING AS SUPERNOVA?
Heh
OH, HO, HO, HO...
WE'RE QUITE SERIOUS, MR. KENT.
THAT'S WHAT MAKES IT FUNNY. GENTLEMEN, I HAVE NO IDEA WHO'S UNDER THAT MASK, BUT THE ONE THING I DO KNOW FOR CERTAIN IS THIS:
HE'S NOT SUPERMAN.

This is the *death* watch, now.

Week 34, Day 7

Gotham City

St. Luke's Hospital Emergency Bay

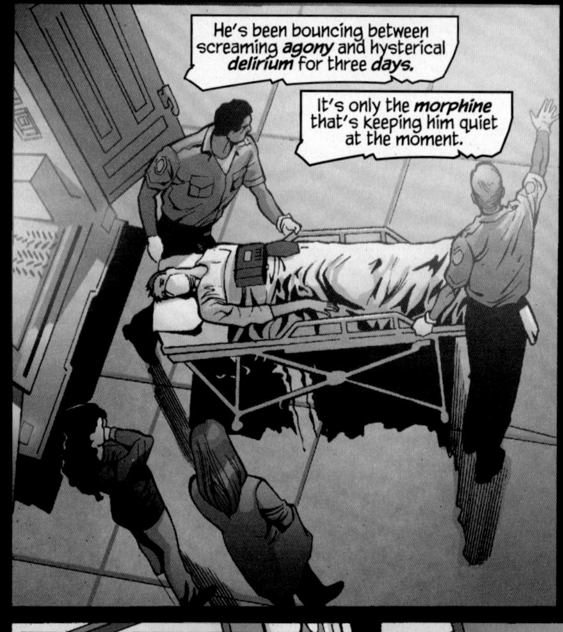

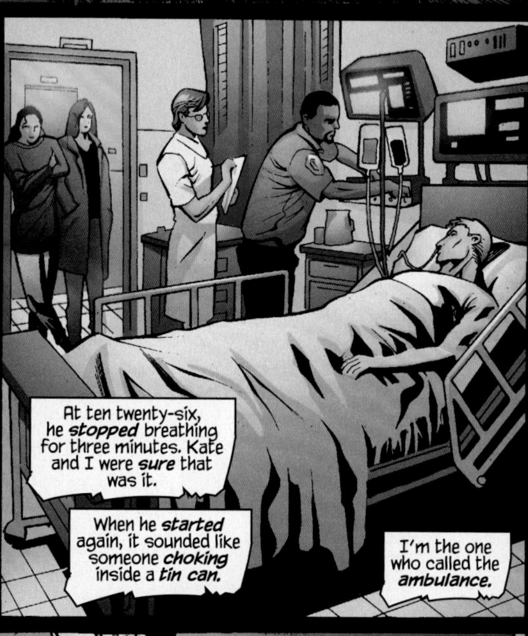

...putting him out of his misery once and for all.
But I know what he'd say if I told him what I was thinking.
He'd say *don't.*
...the pipes, the pipes are calling...

It's the *last* big question for him.
He wouldn't want to *miss* that.
--IVE FROM METROPOLIS'S REBUILT LEXCORP CIRCLE WITH A ROCKIN', HERO-FILLED NEW YEAR'S PARTY!
...from glen to glen and down the mountainside...
And I wouldn't want to take it from him.

NEUROSENSORS VERIFY KENT'S NOT *LYING,* MR. LUTHOR.
THE *DAILY PLANET* HAS BEEN USING KENT TO GET *EXCLUSIVE COVERAGE* ON SUPERNOVA. THERE'S NO BETTER SOURCE OF *INFORMATION.*
IF *HE* DOESN'T KNOW WHO'S UNDER THE MASK, THEN--

DRUG MR. KENT, TAKE HIM BACK HOME, AND LET HIM BELIEVE HE WAS INTERROGATED BY THE *YAKUZA.* HE'S OF NO FURTHER USE TO ME.
YOU WERE SO *SURE...*
AND GET OUT.

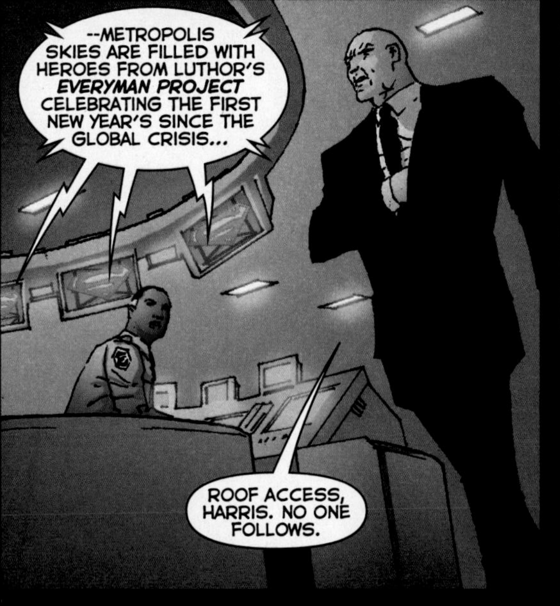
--METROPOLIS SKIES ARE FILLED WITH HEROES FROM LUTHOR'S EVERYMAN PROJECT CELEBRATING THE FIRST NEW YEAR'S SINCE THE GLOBAL CRISIS...
ROOF ACCESS, HARRIS. NO ONE FOLLOWS.

Test Subject: Lex Luthor
Results of Adaptive Mutant Genegraft: NEGATIVE
Subject's body continues to reject Everyman Treatment. Further experimentation could be fatal to

HAPPY NEW YEAR!

THIS IS IT! THE COUNTDOWN IS ABOUT TO START!
...summer's gone and all the leaves are turnin'...
IT'S NEW YEAR'S, CHARLIE...

WHOEVER YOU ARE, SUPERNOVA, THIS CITY ISN'T YOURS. IT'S MINE. AND YOU'RE WINNING TOO MANY HEARTS.
TEN!

now you
NINE!
must go
EIGHT!
away
SEVEN!
and I

IT'S TIME YOU FAILED...
...IN THE FACE OF A REAL CHALLENGE.
2007
must
THREE!
must
FOUR!
HAPPY NEW YEAR!
and I
FIVE!
SIX!

bide...
TWO!
...ONE...
ZERO.
NEXT IN
LOOK! UP IN THE SKY!

WEEK THIRTY-FOUR NOTES

GREG RUCKA

A lot to comment on, so I'll try to hit fast and hard. Geoff wrote the Suicide Squad sequences. They are, to me, devastatingly effective, and an example of great skill in both writing and plotting. It's not easy to give characters with such immense power, like Isis, Osiris, and Black Adam, a conflict that actually threatens them without raising the opposing force to a similar level. Superpower escalation, the bad guys have to have even more power than the good guys.

But the most powerful person in those first ten pages? The chunky black woman back at Belle Reve. Amanda Waller, ladies and gentlemen. Don't piss her off.

Then there's Steel, finally able to speak to Natasha in a way that Natasha will listen. Not by telling her what she can do, or what she can't, but by appealing to her as an adult. "Draw your own conclusions." Well, she pretty much damn well has to after he says that, doesn't she?

One page, Clark Kent at Lex Luthor's mercy. Clark Kent without any of Superman's powers. Clark Kent, about to be broken. If only Lex had known what question to ask.

Speaking of Questions...a lot of people read the end of the issue, in concert with its very grim cover, as the death of Charlie, something that was still a few weeks off at this point. In retrospect, I wish we hadn't used this cover for this issue, as I still think that it, more than anything that actually happens within, is what led to that conclusion. I could be wrong.

Charlie singing "Danny Boy" was yet another nod to Denny's QUESTION, a song he used in the very first arc of the series to indicate an impending death.

...the pipes, the pipes are calling...

The double-page spread leading to the last page was a pain in the rear to write, and required multiple go-rounds with Mark, Steve, Mike, and myself, to break down properly. One of the most effective moments of cross-cutting of the series, I think.

MARK WAID

Kudos once more to editor Steve Wacker and layout artist Keith Giffen. Due to some miscommunication, Greg and I, independent of one another, had written both the Luthor scene and the Montoya scene as the closing scene in the issue. Steve and Keith figured out how to show them as happening simultaneously.

THE PROCESS

BREAKING DOWN WEEK THIRTY-FOUR — PAGE EIGHT (COMPARE WITH PAGE 171)

Original Script

PANEL ONE (splash)
OSIRIS flies right through PERSUADER, fists first. Keith, not sure how you can make this look "acceptable" but this should be horrifying.

SFX: BWAATCHHH!!

PANEL TWO
On OSIRIS as a fountain of blood splatters on his face and golden emblem. His eyes wide with horror.

PANEL THREE
From a distance, COUNT VERTIGO watches it all happen.

PANEL FOUR
OSIRIS stops, paralyzed with fear. The PERSUADER'S remains all around him and unrecognizable. FIRE, like Hell, burns all around him.

PANEL FIVE
OSIRIS looks back towards ISIS. SOBEK looks at the gore around him.

SOBEK: < Oh, dear. >

Breakdown by Keith Giffen

Pencils by Joe Bennett

Final Page

DC COMICS 52
WRITERS: JOHNS, MORRISON, RUCKA, WAID

BREAKDOWNS: GIFFEN PENCILS: JIMENEZ, JURGENS

INKS: LANNING, RAPMUND COLORS: HI-FI LETTERS: LANHAM

ASST. ED: RICHARDS ASSOC. ED: SCHAEFER

EDITOR: SIGLAIN COVER: JONES & SINCLAIR

YEAR!
Södei Co
Week 35, Day 1
New Year's Day, 12:00:01 A.M.
Downtown Metropolis
RAIN OF THE

SUPERMEN
35 Week

THEY'RE FALLING OUT OF THE SKY...
OHMYGOD OHMYGOD GEORGE WHAT'S HAPPENING--?
LEE, GET BACK! THIS IS MY MOMENT, BABY! THIS IS WHAT WE TOOK THAT EVERYMAN LOAN OUT FOR!
GEORGE CALDERON CAN'T SAVE THESE GUYS--
--BUT LEVIATHAN CAN!
?
WAIT-- I'M NOT GROWING! WHY AM I NOT--
GEORRRGE!
GRAVITY NULL GRAVITY NULL GRAVITY NULL IT'S NOT WORKING--!
RUN! RUNNNN!
THEY'RE STILL FALLING!
WHOOOM
AAAAHH!
HELP!
SOMEBODY CALL 911!
WHAT'S HAPPENING?
SMASSH

BREEET
BREEET

YES, DENNIS. YES, I'M WATCHING RIGHT NOW. UTTERLY HORRIFYING. OUR EVERYMEN, DROPPING LIKE ANVILS. SOMETHING SEEMS TO HAVE--
--HOLD ON.

SOMETHING SEEMS TO HAVE NEGATED THEIR POWERS RIGHT AT THE STROKE OF MIDNIGHT.

NO, I CAN'T IMAGINE HOW THAT COULD HAVE HAPPENED...

--ONLY SECONDS AGO, LOLA. EVERYMAN HEROES ARE...MALFUNCTIONING, CAUSING MASS PANIC IN METROPOLIS SQUARE...
...WHERE HUNDREDS OF THOUSANDS ARE GATHERED TO MARK THE NEW YEAR--
--PRAYING THAT THEY'LL LIVE TO SEE IT!
LUTHOR--!
I KNOW! I'M SHOCKED! APPALLED! GOSH, IF ONLY METROPOLIS HAD A SUPERMAN WHO COULD STOP THIS CHAOS!
OH, WELL.

LOLA, THE FREE-FALLS SEEM TO HAVE TAPERED OFF, BUT THE TERROR HAS NOT!
OH, DEAR GOD!
THE ENTIRETY OF FIFTH AVENUE IS SURGING WILDLY IN ALL DIRECTIONS! PEOPLE ARE BEING CRUSHED-- TRAMPLED AND--
DAVID, IS THERE A GAS MAIN BELOW--? THERE IS?
LOLA, THE GAS MAIN BELOW FIFTH HAS ERUPTED--
--BUT NO ONE CAN STOP THE PUSH OF THE CROWD!

WAIT! I SEE *SUPERNOVA* APPROACHING! DAVID, KEEP YOUR CAMERA *ON HIM!*
THAT *LIGHT--!*
THIS REPORTER FEELS LIKE SHE'S STARING INTO THE *SUN!* SUPERNOVA IS BLANKETING THE MOB *BELOW* IN SOME SORT OF *ENERGY-BURST,* AND...
...AND...
Cola
...NO... NO, NO, *NO...*
ONE WAY
READ THE Daily Planet
USA TODAY
...WHAT HAS HE *DONE?*

SUPERNOVA, AMI SOON, CHANNEL FIVE! IS THAT YOUR IDEA OF SAVING THE CITY--VAPORIZING TEN THOUSAND INNOCENT BYSTANDERS?
2007
DON'T BE ABSURD.
RIGHT NOW, THOSE ARE THE SAFEST PEOPLE IN TOWN--
"--OR, RATHER--"
WELCOME TO METROPOLIS HOME OF SUPERMAN, THE MAN OF STEEL!
"--OUT OF TOWN."
WELCOME TO METROPOLIS HOME OF SUPERMAN, THE MAN OF STEEL!

LOOK! IT'S INFINITY INC.!
I NEED HELP HERE!
--NOTHER ONE, OMIGOD PLEASE SOMEBODY DO SOMETHING--
AHHH!!
--HURTS AHHH IT HURTS!!!

--NOT WATER, BUT IT'LL GET THE FIRE OUT.
THE MAINS ARE OUT BETWEEN HERE AND MIDTOWN.
NOTHING LIKE THE SMELL OF BURNT MILK.
SMILIN' BESS MILK
WHATEVER WORKS, JAKE, THAT'S ALL THAT MATTERS. ANY WAY WE CAN HELP.

HURRY, JADE--I CAN'T HOLD THIS MUCH LONGER!
GOT HIM!

CHOOM
NO!

NUKLON--YOU ALL RIGHT?
UNGH! SURE, NOW YOU ASK...
...LUCKY THING WE'VE STILL GOT OUR POWERS...

I DON'T THINK IT'S LUCK--

--IT'S MORE LIKE...
NAT?

HE WAS RIGHT...
C'MON! WE'VE GOT TO HELP THESE PEOPLE!

EVERYONE CLEAR A PATH!
ONE SIDE! WE'VE GOT WOUNDED HERE!

THIS MAN NEEDS IMMEDIATE MEDICAL ATTENTION!
Week 35, Day 2
Saint Camillus Hospital

ERNIE? ERNIE?!

WHAT HAPPENED TO MY SON?
PLASTIC MAN?
OFFSPRING WAS IN METROPOLIS WHEN ALL OF LUTHOR'S SELF-MADE HEROES STARTED FALLING OUT OF THE SKY.

HE SAVED OVER TWENTY OF THEM, MR. O'BRIEN.
HE STRETCHED HIMSELF SO THIN HE NEARLY SNAPPED.
HEY, DAD.
HEY, PAL.

THERE ARE DOZENS DEAD, RAVEN. MORE DYING BY THE MINUTE.
NOT ANY LONGER, GARFIELD.
HE DID THIS.

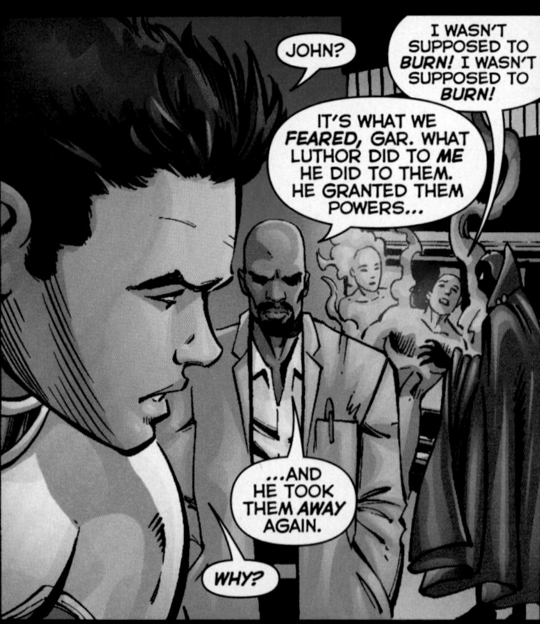
JOHN?
I WASN'T SUPPOSED TO BURN! I WASN'T SUPPOSED TO BURN!
IT'S WHAT WE FEARED, GAR. WHAT LUTHOR DID TO ME HE DID TO THEM. HE GRANTED THEM POWERS...
...AND HE TOOK THEM AWAY AGAIN.
WHY?

WE'RE GOING TO FIND OUT.
GET THE TITANS TOGETHER.

Week 35, Day 3
...TO DETERMINE WHAT WENT WRONG THAT CAUSED SO MANY PARTICIPANTS TO SPONTANEOUSLY REJECT THEIR ENHANCEMENTS.
NOW THAT WE'VE ISOLATED THE ERRANT GENE-SEQUENCE, WE'VE INSTITUTED MANDATORY SCREENING FOR IT.
INFINITY INC.'S SAFETY IS A PERSONAL PRIORITY, WHICH IS WHY I HAD DENNIS HERE RUN YOUR TESTS AS SOON AS WAS POSSIBLE.
FOR THOSE OF YOU WONDERING WHERE EVERYMAN IS...
...HANNIBAL WAS SCREENED THIS MORNING. HIS RESULTS WERE INCONCLUSIVE.
HE'S DOWNSTAIRS UNDERGOING FURTHER TESTING AS WE SPEAK.
I NOW HAVE YOUR RESULTS.
PLEASE GOD OH PLEASE...
YOU'RE ALL CLEAN.

DAMN, I WAS *SCARED* THERE, I DON'T MIND *TELLIN'* YOU...

YES!!

NAT?

LEX! I COULD *LICK* YOU!

THAT WON'T BE *NECESSARY,* SIERRA.

BELIEVE ME, I AM AS *RELIEVED* AS YOU ARE BY THIS.

BUT WE'RE LEFT WITH YET *ANOTHER* PROBLEM.

BECAUSE OF THIS *HORRIBLE* TRAGEDY, THE EVERYMAN PROJECT HAS LOST THE PUBLIC *TRUST.*

I'M GOING TO *NEED* YOUR *HELP* TO GET IT *BACK.*

YOU *TELL* US WHAT TO *DO,* BOSS, WE'LL DO IT.

EVERYTHING WE *HAVE,* WE OWE IT TO *YOU.*

WHAT NUKLON SAYS, LEX. ***ABSOLUTELY.***

THERE YOU ARE, I WONDERED WHERE YOU WENT...

...HANNIBAL CHECKED OUT **CLEAN,** SO LUTHOR WANTS **ALL** OF US TO SUIT UP AND JOIN HIM FOR THE **PRESS CONFERENCE...**

...ARE YOU OKAY, NAT?

NO, JAKE.

NOT AT **ALL.**

HE WAS TRYING TO **WARN** ME ALL ALONG.

AND I WAS TOO **STUPID** AND TOO **SELFISH** AND TOO...**IMPATIENT** TO LISTEN.

I'M LOST, HERE. WHO'S BEEN WARNING YOU WHAT?

WE CAN'T TRUST LUTHOR, JAKE. WE CAN'T TRUST ANYTHING HE SAYS, ANYTHING HE DOES.
WHAT HAPPENED ON NEW YEAR'S...I THINK HE'S RESPONSIBLE FOR IT...
...I THINK HE DID IT ON PURPOSE.
LIKE HE DID TO TRAJECTORY.

LIKE HE CAN DO TO THE REST OF US.
NATASHA... YOU'RE SCARING ME, HERE, YOU'RE SCARING ME A LOT--
GOOD, BECAUSE I NEED YOUR HELP, JAKE.
WE HAVE TO FIND PROOF. WE HAVE TO GET IT TO MY UNCLE.
YOU'VE GOT TO HELP ME, JAKE. THERE'S NOBODY ELSE HERE I CAN TRUST.
OF COURSE I'LL HELP YOU...

...I LOVE YOU NATASHA...
...I WON'T LET ANYTHING HAPPEN TO YOU....

THIS WAS PLANET VARTU--STANDARD TYPE 2 CIVILIZATION...
WORLD OF BEAUTY...AND PROMISE...
Umm, IS THAT A GREEN LANTERN SUIT?
I THOUGHT THOSE GUYS WERE PRETTY HARDCORE...
Week 35, Day 6

THIS IS WHERE THAT AWFUL TELEPATHIC MESSAGE FROM CAPTAIN COMET CAME FROM...
THE STYGIAN HORDE DID THIS.
AND THERE ARE BILLIONS OF THEM, HEADED TOWARD OUR HOMES...
WHERE DO WE START?
NOT TRUST LOBO.
SAYS THE GUY MISSING AN EYE...
LOOK ON THE BRIGHT SIDE, HUH?
I FINALLY REALIZED I COULD ADAPT FISHY'S POWER TO FLY IN SPACE UNAIDED.
SOMETIMES I MISS THE OBVIOUS...
YA GOTTA UNDERSTAND MY PREDICAMENT, FISHY.
TH' MAIN MAN NEVER BREAKS HIS WORD!
WE HAFTA DITCH THE EMERALD HEAD BEFORE HE TRIES TO GET HIS EYE BACK.
YOUR HOLINESS, I...

LOBO.
YOU KNOW WE DON'T HAVE A PRAYER OUT THERE.
THREE OF US AGAINST A WAR MACHINE WITH THE FIREPOWER TO FLATTEN WHOLE STAR SYSTEMS?

IT'S SUICIDE FER SURE.
I'D HELP YA OUT, STRANGE, BUT I GOTTA GET THIS EYE BACK TA TH' TRIPLE FISH GOD AN' I'VE TAKEN A VOW OF NON-VIOLENCE...
YEAH?
TELL THAT TO DEVILANCE THE PURSUER.
ANOTHER BOUNTY HUNTER LIKE YOU, AND HE JUST HAPPENS TO WALK INTO A TRAP, LEAVING YOU WITH THE SPOILS?

I MEAN, WHAT IF YOU BROUGHT US ALL THIS WAY TO CLAIM THAT BOUNTY FOR YOURSELF?
YOUR HOLINESS, SURELY NOT...
WHAT ARE YOU INSINUATIN'?
THREE LITTLE PEOPLE COULD DO A HELL OF A LOT OF DAMAGE... FROM INSIDE THE MACHINE.

HEH.

HE'S COMING BACK.
SOMETHING'S WRONG.
TRIED TO WARN YOU.

ADAM?
WHAT'S UP?
CHANGE OF PLAN.

I THINK LOBO HAS SOMETHING TO TELL US.
LADY STYX PUT A BOUNTY ON YER HEADS, YA KNOW THAT.
SO THERE AIN'T NO NEED TO FIGURE OUT HOW YER GONNA FIGHT...
...'CAUSE I'M TAKING YA STRAIGHT TO HER.
NEXT IN

WEEK THIRTY-FIVE NOTES

MARK WAID

Man alive, did Phil Jimenez and Dan Jurgens hit this one out of the park.

The title of this story — one of the few titles I contributed, because I'm very, very bad at story titles — is a callback to the 1993 DC storyline "Reign of the Supermen," which was itself a reference to a 1933 prose story written by Superman creator Jerry Siegel called "Reign of the Superman," and since I can see your eyes starting to glaze over, I'll stop for now with the history lessons. Greg still thinks the title is in poor taste given the gravity (har) of the opening sequence. Maybe he's right. Greg doesn't get enough credit for being the writing team's moral barometer.

Solicited Cover

Plastic Man's son, Offspring, is a character I created with Frank Quitely ten years ago for a story from which, I swear to you, he was the only good thing to emerge. (Offspring, not Quitely, although...). I'm flattered that Geoff and others have since picked up on the kid for use in TEEN TITANS.

MICHAEL SIGLAIN

Let's talk about the cover. J.G. Jones and Alex Sinclair did yet another outstanding job when they depicted Lex watching the "rain of the Supermen" from his lofty office window (and Mark's right, there was a big debate over the title of this issue). However, since this was the cover that we were going to use for solicits, the writers were at odds whether we should show the heroes falling from the sky. Yes, it's a very striking cover, but does it give away too much? Well, at the end of the day, we decided that it did, and Alex turned all of the falling heroes into giant balls of fire. If you look closely at the solicit cover (pictured above) you can just barely make out some of the people behind the flames.

Also: a quick shout-out to our new **52** colorists is also in order. Brian and Kristy Miller of Hi-Fi Design came on board to lend a helping hand, and not only did they do an amazing job, but they also contributed some great little bits to the issue, such as the shadow that falls over Lex Luthor on page 215, panel 3. It's black humor at its finest. You can see more of Hi-Fi's renowned coloring in week Thirty-Eight (their snowstorm effects are particularly enjoyable). Give it a gander!

THE PROCESS

PAGES 188-189 BREAKDOWNS BY **KEITH GIFFEN**

PENCILS & INKS BY **PHIL JIMENEZ & ANDY LANNING**

DC COMICS 52

Week 36, Day 3

WRITTEN BY GEOFF JOHNS, GRANT MORRISON, GREG RUCKA, MARK WAID

ART BREAKDOWNS BY KEITH GIFFEN • PENCILS BY JAMAL IGLE • INKS BY KEITH CHAMPAGNE
COLORS BY DAVID BARON • LETTERING BY PAT BROSSEAU • ASSISTANT EDITOR HARVEY RICHARDS
ASSOCIATE EDITOR JEANINE SCHAEFER • EDITED BY MICHAEL SIGLAIN • COVER BY J. G. JONES & ALEX SINCLAIR

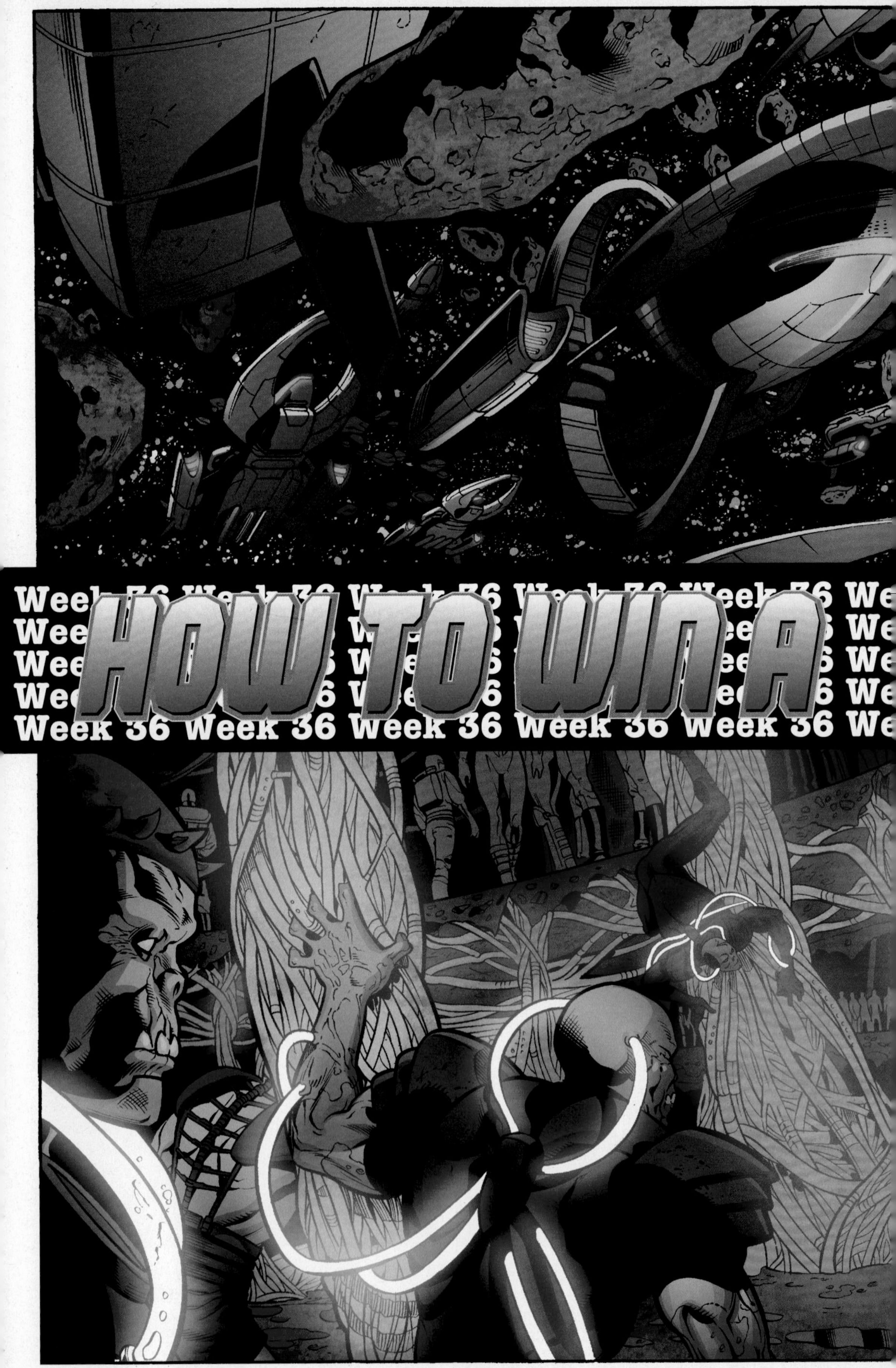

Week 36 Week 36 Week 36 Week 36 Week 36 Week 36 Week 36 Week 36 Week 36 Week 36 We

HOW TO WIN A

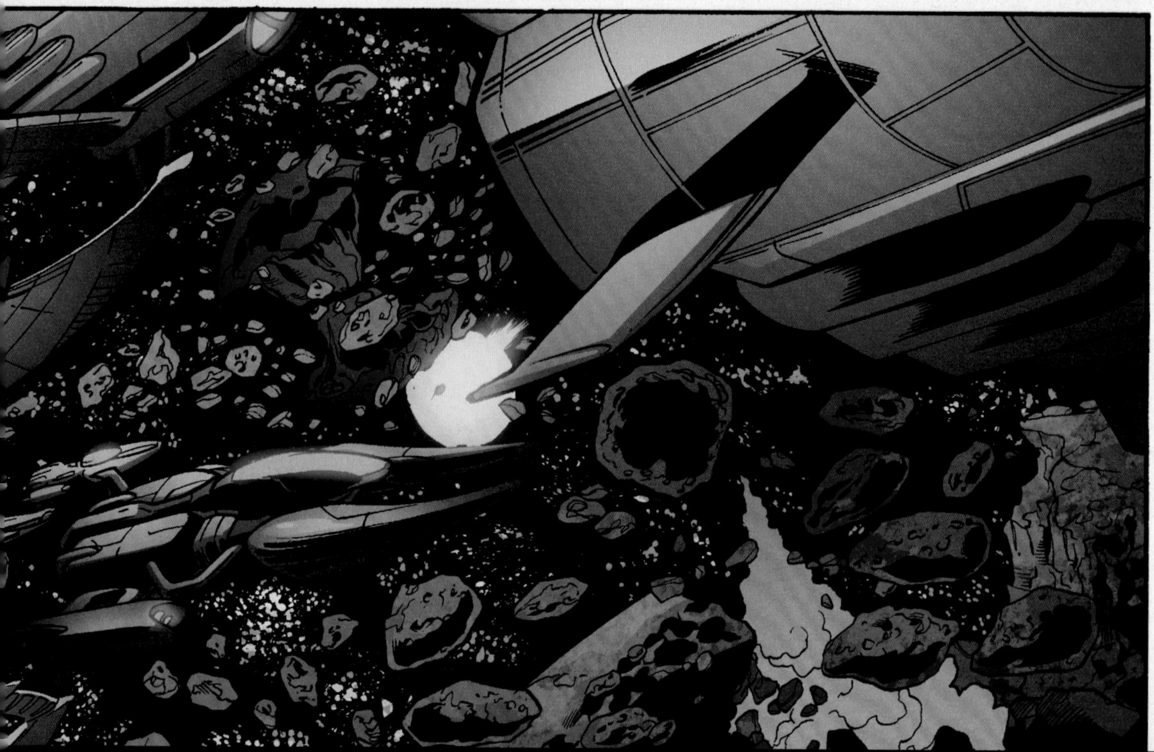

36 Week 36 Week 36 Week 36 Week 36 Week 36

WAR IN SPACE

SEE?

I TOLDJA I COULD GET YA PAST SECURITY.

I REALLY HOPE THIS WORKS.

YER LADYSHIP?

I BROUGHT YA TH' PRIZ'NERS.
WHAT ABOUT MY BOUNTY?
WHAT'S SHE *SAYIN'*, FISHY?

THE LADY STYX SAYS THERE... THERE IS NO BOUNTY, YOUR WORSHIP.
WE... WE'RE ALL TO BE BROKEN DOWN INTO BIO-MASS TO SERVE HER NEEDS.
SHE'LL TAKE THE INFORMATION SHE NEEDS DIRECTLY FROM THEIR NERVOUS SYSTEMS.

OH, YEAH?
WHAT ABOUT MY BOUNTY!
ALL SHE HAS TO GIVE IS DEATH, SHE SAYS.
PLEASE... TAKE YOUR FILL!

OH NO.
BELIEVE IN HER.
BELIEVE IN HER.
BELIEVE IN HER.
BELIEVE IN HER.

THIS ISN'T WORKING OUT, LOBO!
RELEASE US!
BELIEVE IN HER.
BELIEVE IN HER.
BELIEVE IN HER.
BELIEVE IN HER.

KORY, NO!
LOBO, IT'S ALL GOING WRONG!
WE NEED YOUR HELP!
GZZ!

I BOUGHT YA HERE, I DID WHAT YA WANTED.
BUT I CAN'T FIGHT YER BATTLES FOR YA, ANIMAL GUY...
YOUR GRACE...
SHE... SHE SAYS.. SHE SAYS YOU CAN'T FIGHT AT ALL.
...I THINK SHE'S CALLING YOU A COWARD, YOUR GRACE.

LOBO, FOR GOD'S SAKE!
SHE SAYS WHAT?
BELIEVE IN HER.
YES... AND... SHE SAYS ONLY A TRULY PATHETIC COWARD WOULD SO WHOLEHEARTEDLY EMBRACE DOCTRINES OF UNIVERSAL PEACE AS A WAY...A WAY TO AVOID A SLAPPING.
BELIEVE IN HER.
BELIEVE IN HER.
BELIEVE IN HER.

IN FACT, IT'S...WELL, IT'S A COMPLETE U-TURN SHE SAYS, A...A CHEESY BETRAYAL OF THE LOBO BRAND AND EVERYTHING IT STANDS FOR...OH DEAR...
A COWARD AND A SELL-OUT! SHE SAYS!
GHHNN
VOWS!
GRAAAA
REMEMBER YOUR VOWS, YOUR HOLINESS!

AND SHE SAYS...SHE SAYS THE CHURCH OF THE TRIPLE FISH GOD IS...IS THE SUBECT OF M-M-MOCKERY THE UNIVERSE OVER AS A HAVEN FOR BIG COWARDS WHO LIKE TO ACT TOUGH BUT NEVER WANT TO PROVE IT!
GNNNNAAA!
AND THAT'S NOT ALL.

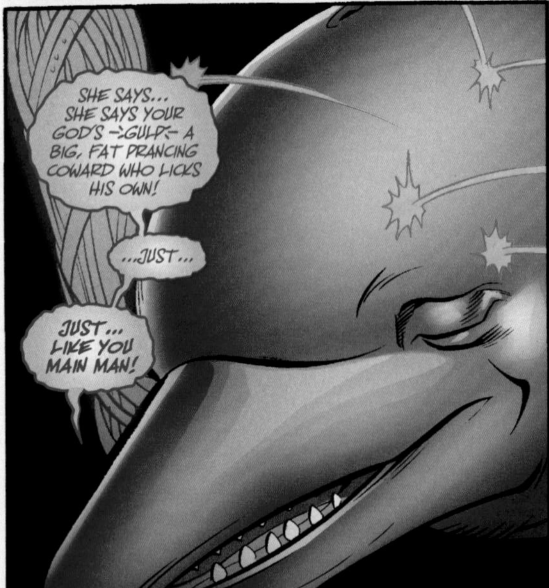
SHE SAYS... SHE SAYS YOUR GOD'S -GULP- A BIG, FAT PRANCING COWARD WHO LICKS HIS OWN!
...JUST...
JUST... LIKE YOU MAIN MAN!

IKKT
FORGIVE ME.

NOW SEE WHAT YOU MADE ME DO.
I KILLED EVERY LIVING THING ON CZARNIA FER FUN. I KILLED SANTA CLAUS AND THE EASTER BUNNY AN' THINGS THAT DON'T EVEN EXIST, AN', SO HELP ME, I TRIED TA FOLLOW TH' TRIPLE-FOLD PATH O' PEACE.
I TRIED MY BEST...

...BUT FRAG ME FOR A BASTICH, EVEN I GOT LIMITS!

SHHRRIPP

BELIEVE IN HER.
BELIEVE IN HER.

OVER HERE!
DON'T LOOK TOWARDS EARTH!
LOOK AT ME!
YOU WANNA KNOW WHAT I BELIEVE IN?
BELIEVE IN HER.
BELIEVE IN HER.

THIS IS WHAT I BELIEVE IN!
ADAM!
A LITTLE TO YOUR LEFT, MAN!

CHOOM!

TODAY'S LESSON--
--PACIFISTS GOT A LOT OF PENT-UP AGGRESSION.
AN' THERE'S A GOOD REASON I WAITED 'TILL TH' *SUN-EATERS* STARTED THEIR MIGRATION.

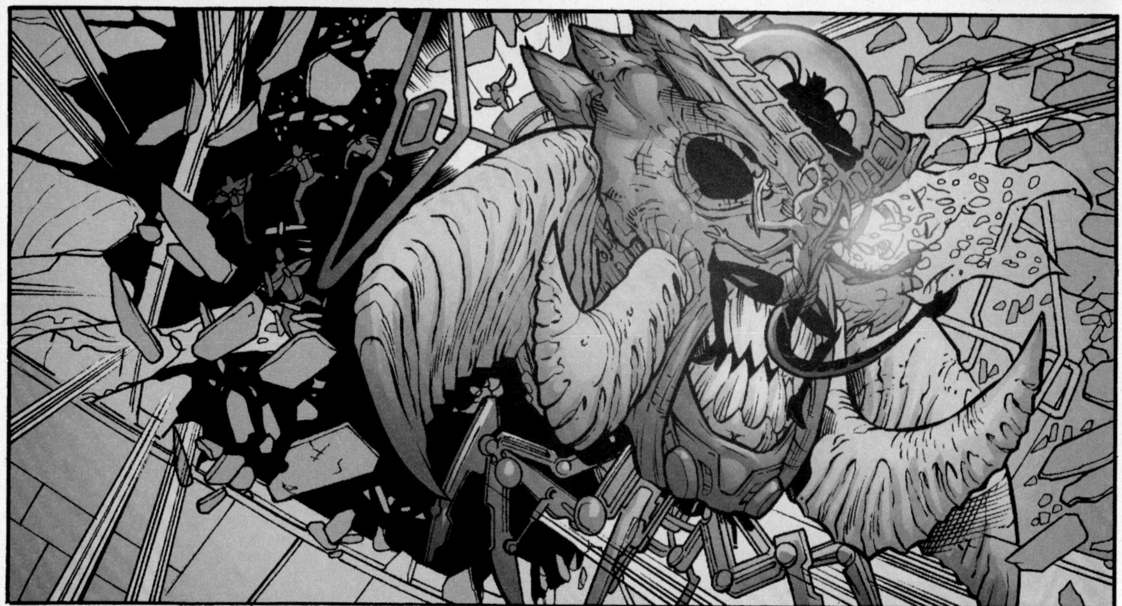

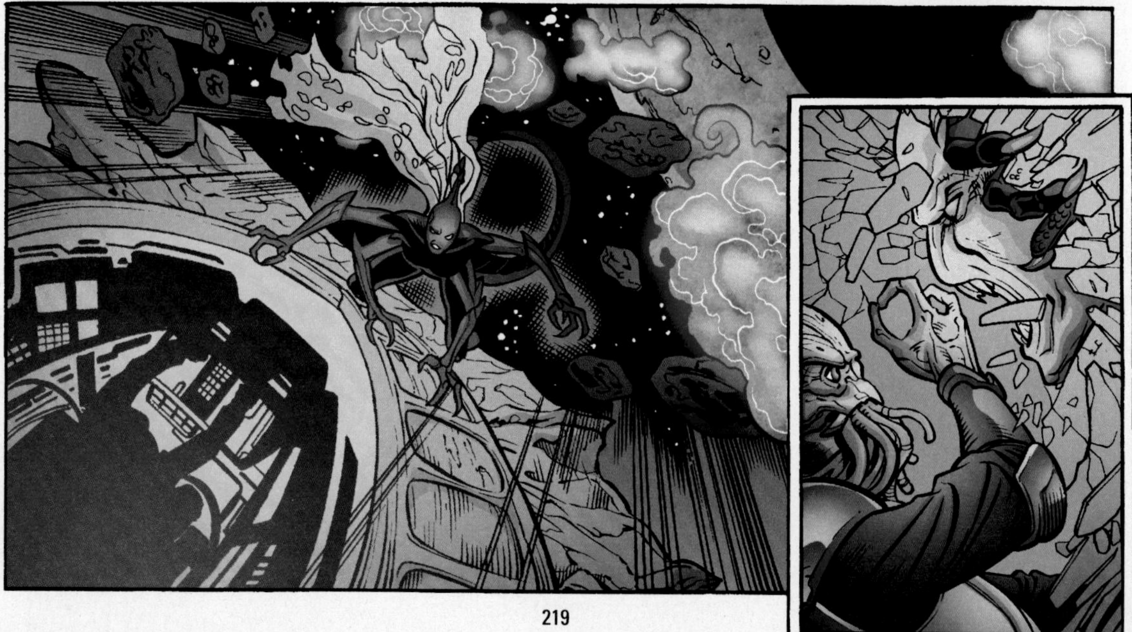

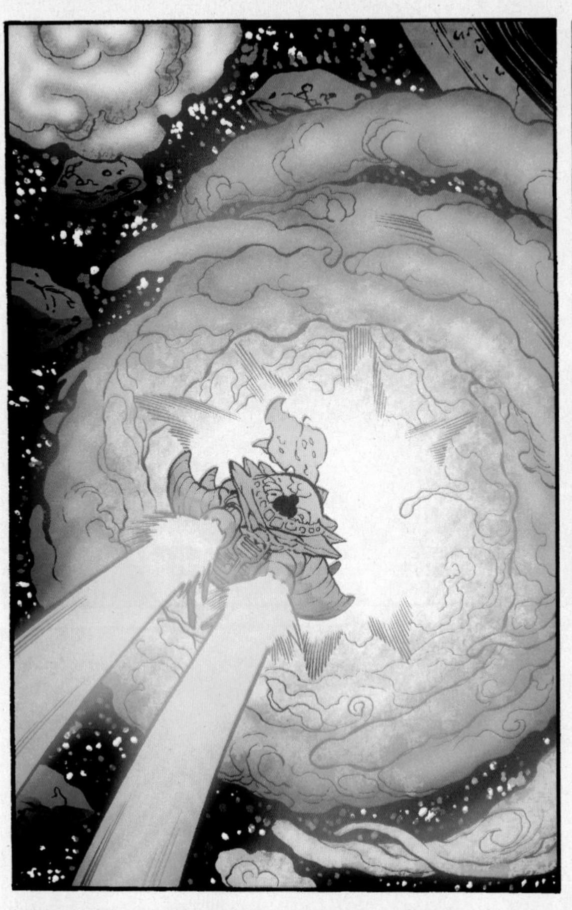

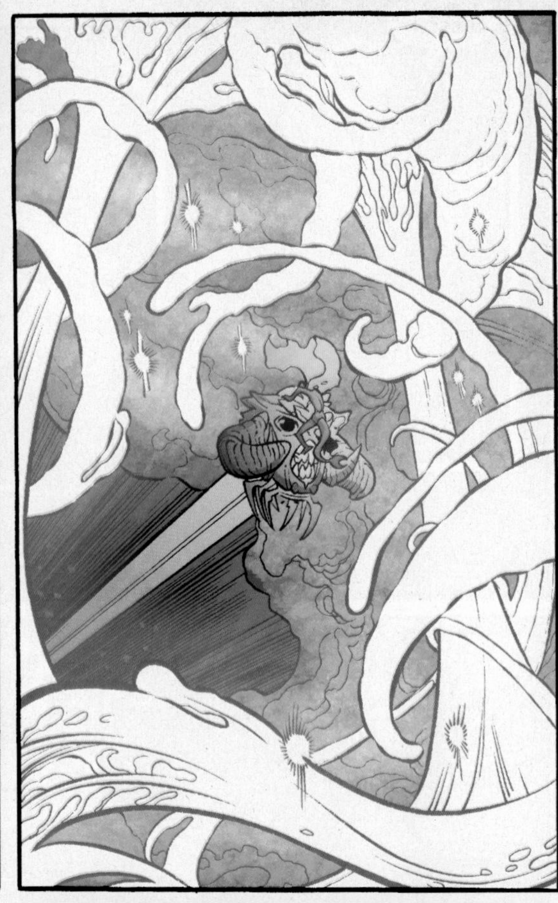

LIVE THROUGH BEIN' DIGESTED!
TALK ABOUT KILLIN' TWO BIRDS WITH ONE STONE.
YOUR HOLINESS, PLEASE...
...THE ANIMAL MAN...

BUDDY, STAY WITH US!
WHAT'S HAPPENING?
NECRO-TOXIN--THEY SHOT HIM.
IT'S OKAY.

BUDDY!
USE YOUR POWERS!
THEY KNOW HOW MUCH I LOVE THEM.
YOU WON'T...WON'T EVEN HAVE T-T-TO TELL 'EM, KORY...

LOOK... CAN YOU SEE?
THEY'RE... CH--CHEERING US ON...I TOLDJA...
TOLDJA THE UNIVERSE... GNNN...LIKES ME...

NNN
KORY!
KORY... PROMISE YOU WON'T LET ME COME BACK AS A ZOMBIE...

NO.
HKKT

OH DEAR.

San Diego, Earth

MOM?

A month ago he was Vic Sage. He was *Charlie.*

SAID TAKE *FIVE* FREDDIE FREELOADER, SAID... SAID...

A month ago he was at once *cheerfully* vague and hungrily *curious.*

...THAT'S NOT THE CHEESE, IZZY, THAT'S... NO, I'M DOING... ALL RIGHT...

...BABY BABY BABY BLUES IN GREEN...

He was *funny.* He was *smart.* He was a royal *pain* in my *ass.*

He was my best friend in the world.

CONGO BILL

Week 36, Day 5

St. Luke's Hospital—Gotham City

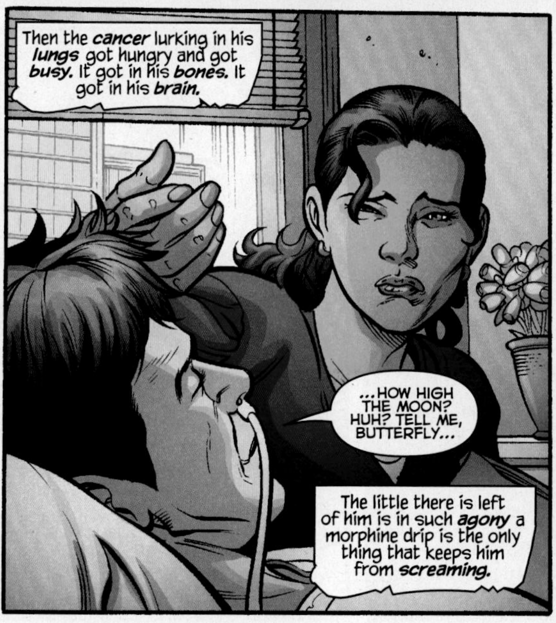

Then the *cancer* lurking in his *lungs* got hungry and got *busy.* It got in his *bones.* It got in his *brain.*
...HOW HIGH THE MOON? HUH? TELL ME, BUTTERFLY...
The little there is left of him is in such *agony* a morphine drip is the only thing that keeps him from *screaming.*

To say it's not *fair* is like saying rain is *wet.*
Absolutely *obvious* and entirely *unhelpful.*

He deserves better than this.
Better than to die in a Gotham hospital stinking of urine and bleach and antiseptic.

He deserves to live.
But he's not going to.

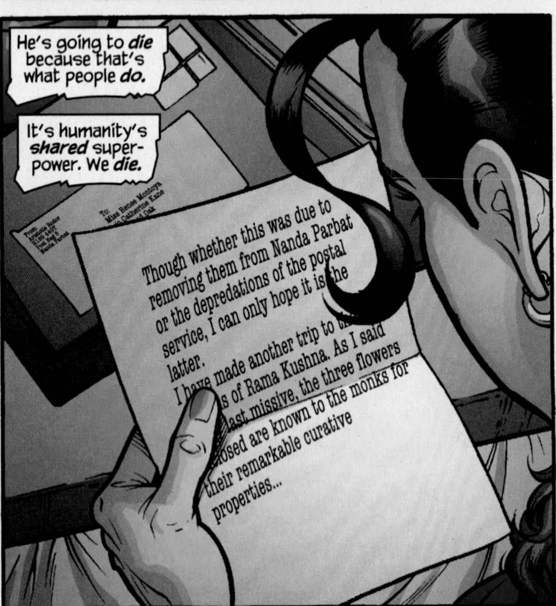
He's going to die because that's what people do.
It's humanity's shared super-power. We die.
Though whether this was due to
removing them from Nanda Parbat
or the depredations of the postal
service, I can only hope it is the
latter.
I have made another trip to
of Rama Kushna. As I said
last missive, the three flowers
are known to the monks for
their remarkable curative
properties...

And it doesn't matter how many radiation treatments he undergoes.
Like the flowers Tot keeps sending in vain, hoping they will survive long enough to do Charlie some good.

But they don't. Outside of Nanda Parbat, they can't.
Outside of Nanda Parbat, their days are numbered...

...outside of Nanda Parbat...

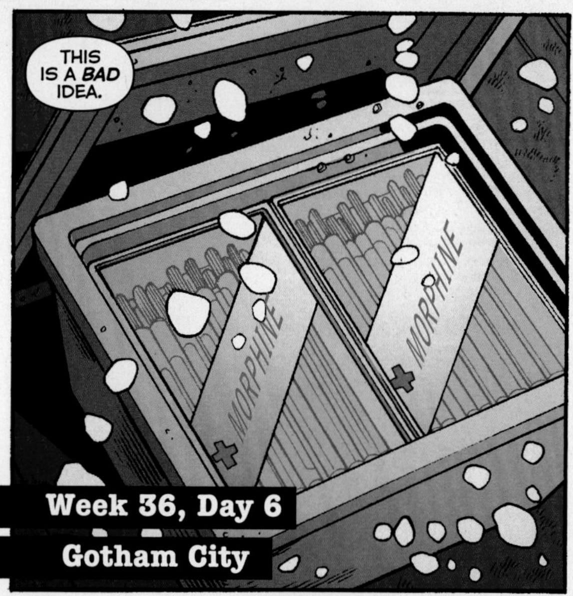
THIS IS A BAD IDEA.
MORPHINE
MORPHINE
Week 36, Day 6
Gotham City

CHARLIE'S ALMOST DEAD AS IT IS, KATE. THERE'S NOT A HELL OF A LOT I CAN DO TO MAKE THAT WORSE, IS THERE?
NO QUESTION.
BUT I'M NOT TALKING ABOUT HIM, I'M TALKING ABOUT YOU...

...AND I'M THINKING THIS LOOKS AN AWFUL LOT LIKE DENIAL.
NO. NOT DENIAL.

DEFIANCE.

I'VE LOST TOO MANY PEOPLE, KATE.
THE JET WILL ONLY TAKE YOU SO FAR! THERE'RE NO FLIGHTS WHERE YOU'RE GOING! NO ROADS!
YOU CAN'T HIKE A DYING MAN UP THE HIMALAYAS IN THE MIDDLE OF WINTER!

THE WEATHER ALONE COULD KILL YOU BOTH!

RENEE, PLEASE! STAY HERE, STAY WITH ME, HELP ME FIGHT MANNHEIM!
I JUST GOT YOU BACK IN MY LIFE, I DON'T WANT YOU WALKING *OUT* AGAIN!
I KNOW.

HE SAVED ME, KATE.
HE PULLED ME OUT OF SELF-PITY AND DESPAIR AND I *OWE* HIM MY *LIFE*...

...AND IF THERE'S EVEN A *CHANCE* THAT GETTING CHARLIE BACK TO *NANDA PARBAT* WILL SAVE *HIS*, THEN I'LL DO IT...

...OR I'LL DIE TRYING.

GOODBYE.

Kahndaq
KAHNDAQ NEWS
English Edition
OSIRIS--MURDERER!
TEEN TITANS REACT
<OSIRIS?>

<I DON'T WANT TO TALK, SOBEK.>
<DO YOU W-WANT SOMETHING TO EAT? I PICKED THESE WONDERFUL APPLES FROM A TREE IN YOUR SISTER'S GARDEN.>
<THEY ARE AS SWEET AS HONEY!>

<BLACK ADAM SAID IT WAS AN AMBUSH. HE SAID SOMEONE SENT THOSE SUPER-VILLAINS TO TRY TO PROVOKE US.>
<HE SAID SOMEONE WANTED TO DO TO US WHAT THEY DID TO WONDER WOMAN WHEN SHE KILLED MAXWELL LORD!>
TEEN TITANS REACT
<THEY WANTED TO TRY TO LIE TO THE WORLD AND TELL THEM WE WERE NOTHING MORE THAN A "DARK" FAMILY OF SADISTIC MURDERERS!>

<WHO WOULD DO SOMETHING SO MEAN?!>
<THE TEEN TITANS SAID IF I CAME BACK TO THE TOWER THEY'D HAVE TO ARREST ME.>
<BUT ISIS SAYS THE PEOPLE EVENTUALLY SAW THE TRUTH ABOUT WHAT WONDER WOMAN DID. WONDER WOMAN ACTED IN SELF-DEFENSE. YOU DID TOO!>
<BUT EVERYONE LOVED WONDER WOMAN BEFORE IT HAPPENED.>
<THEY HATE US, SOBEK. AND NO MATTER WHAT WE EVER DO, THE ENTIRE WORLD WILL ALWAYS HATE US!>

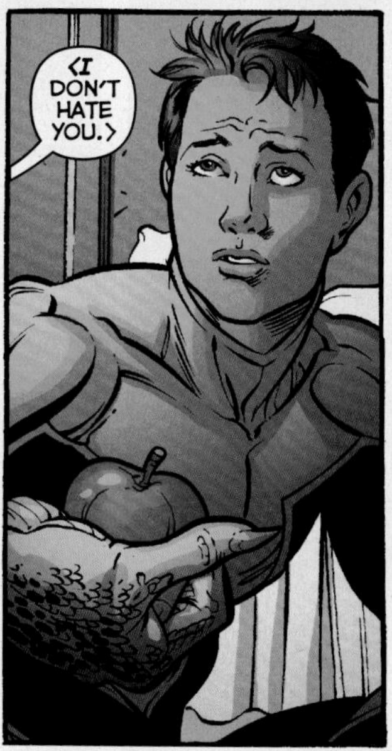
<I DON'T HATE YOU.>

<THANK YOU, SOBEK.>

Week 36, Day 7
BROKEN! IS TIME!
FIND CAN'T THE RIGHT POWER SOURCE FOR CHRONOSPHERE THE!
I'VE BROUGHT EVERYTHING YOU'VE ASKED FOR--

--THE STAFFS OF THE STARMEN, LUTHOR'S KRYPTONITE GAUNTLET, SHADOW THIEF'S DIMENSIOMETER AND MORE. CAN'T YOU MAKE SOMETHING OUT OF THEM?

S'GNIHTON WORKING!
RIP, CALM DOWN! IT'S TOUGH ENOUGH UNDERSTANDING YOU WHEN YOU'RE LINEAR!

YOU'RE THGIR. I APO...LO...LO...GGGGIZE.
BUT WE. CAN'T FFFIGHT. HIM YET. WHAT IF. HE SDNIF--FINDS US. BEFORE WE'RE RRRREADY?
YOU'RE RIP HUNTER. YOU'RE THE TIME MASTER. I WON'T WORRY ABOUT DEADLINES IF YOU CAN STAY FOCUSED.

I REALIZE SKEETS HAS BEEN *SEARCHING* FOR YOU.

HE KNOWS YOU NEED ACCESS TO THIS LEVEL OF *TECHNOLOGY,* BUT WE'RE IN THE LAST PLACE HE'D THINK TO *LOOK*--IF HE EVEN KNOWS IT *EXISTS.*

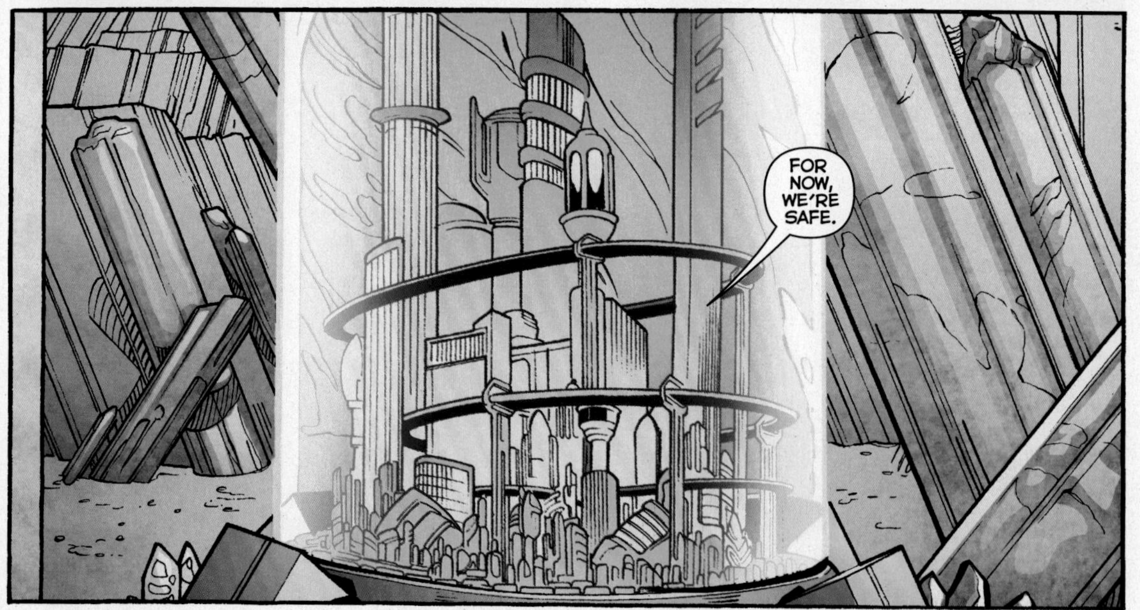
FOR NOW, WE'RE SAFE.

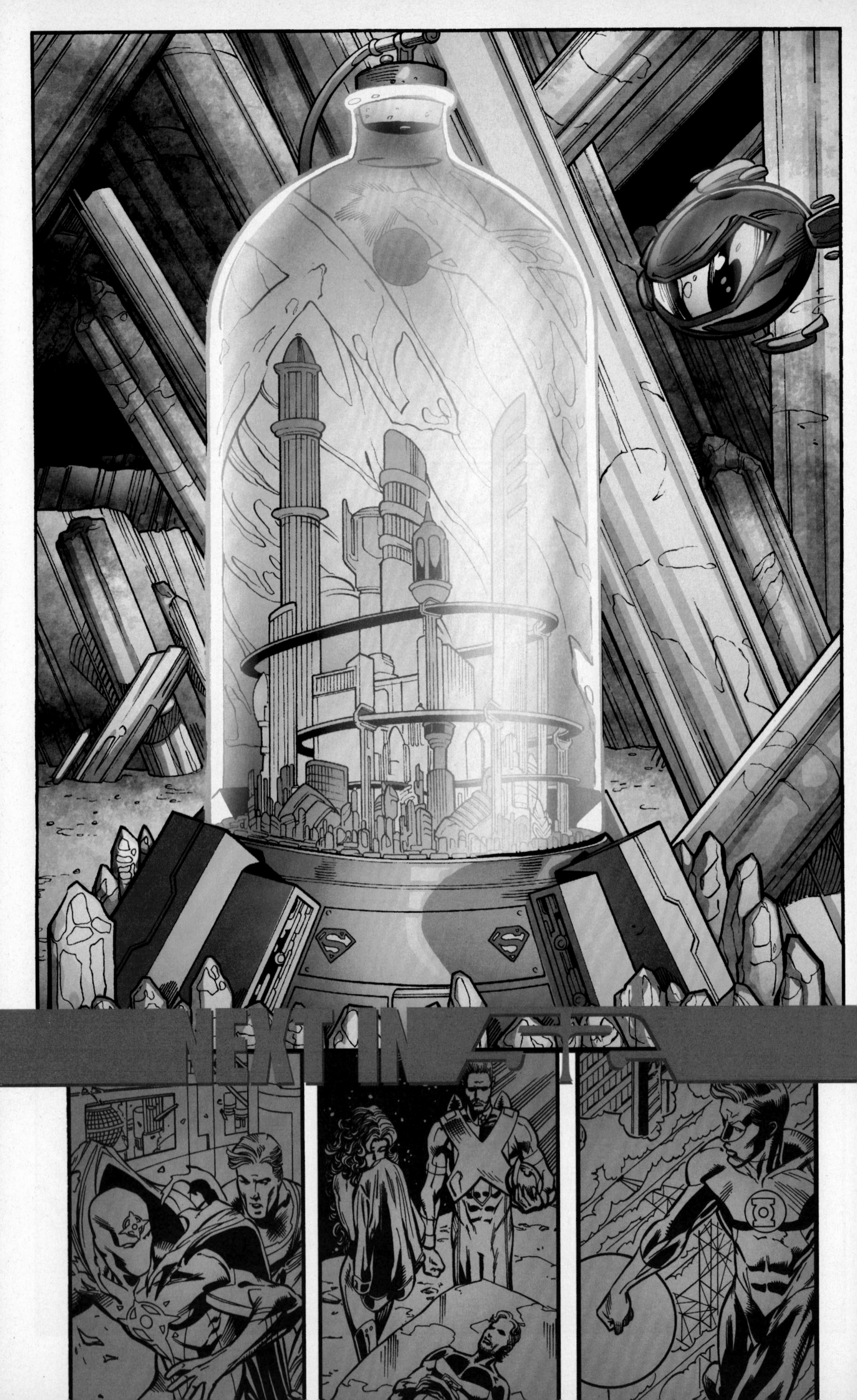
NEXT IN JLA

KEITH GIFFEN

I wish we'd had more pages.

An odd wish considering the workload that was **52**, but that's the way I felt and still do. Lobo, after months of pent-up frustration, finally reverting to form (after a hilarious space dolphin as questionable translator sequence)...I wish I'd had more room to play out the mayhem. If I remember correctly, Grant had called for something like fourteen or sixteen small panels that would act as shutter click images, a Grand Guignol strobe of Lobo in blood-drenched action.

---

52 WEEK 36 PAGE SEVEN

The top 2/3rds of the page is divided into sixteen identical squares. In each a shot of carnage — as Lobo slices and dices his way through to Lady Styx.

Uh huh.

Here's the deal. I knew what Grant wanted but had no idea how to pull it off without it looking like bad MTV vidiot editing. So...I opted for an impact shot and hoped it would play out. I think it did. Barely.

My bad.

I fared better on the rest of the issue; Montoya makes the decision that would change her life irrevocably, a nice interlude with Buddy's family, Osiris gets pointed in the direction of the event I'd been most anticipating (I hated that kid!) and Rip Hunter shows up in, of all places, the bottle city of Kandor.

Did I mention that Animal Man kinda, sorta died? Well, he did. So, for that matter, did Lady Styx. I was in the minority when it came to Lady Styx dying. Didn't like it then, don't now. Hey, y' can't like 'em all.

Oh, and we had a new hand at the editorial helm. Michael Siglain. Talk about your battlefield promotions. One day an assistant editor, the next the editor of **52**. That the transition from Wacker to Siglain went so smoothly is a testament to the questionable efficiency of the machine Wacker built to keep the book up and running and Siglain's John Dorian (a *Scrubs* reference no less) affability and his willingness to admit to feeling like a deer caught in the headlights of an oncoming semi.

As for Jamal Igle, his schedule precluded any return visits to **52**. Our loss.

SCRIPT EXCERPT

(COMPARE WITH PAGE 221 OF THIS COLLECTION)

52 WEEK THIRTY-SIX PAGE ELEVEN

PANEL ONE
Kory kneels by Buddy, gathering him up. He's shaking. Adam lands. Fishy swims towards him, trying to help.

KORY: Buddy, stay with us! What's happening?

FISHY: Necro-toxin — They shot him.

BUDDY: It's okay.

PANEL TWO
Adam rushes to him. Fishy concerned...

ADAM: Buddy! Use your powers!

BUDDY: They know how much I love them. You won't...won't even have t-t-to tell 'em. Kory...

PANEL THREE
They turn to look past us where Buddy's looking — Buddy looks straight at us, as if he can see us. He's shuddering, frothing green at the mouth, lifting a hand to point at us.

BUDDY: Look...can you see? They're...ch-cheering us on...I toldja... Toldja the universe...gnnn...likes me

PANEL FOUR
Buddy close. He can't even see us now.

BUDDY: NNN

BUDDY: Kory! Kory...promise you won't let me come back as a zombie...

PANEL FIVE
Starfire looks up, anguished, as Buddy dies in her arms. His head lolls away. Froth from his mouth.

STARFIRE: NO.

BUDDY: HKKT

PANEL SIX
Long shot. Buddy dead in Kory's arms. A mournful grouping in the wrecked ship. Fishy's tail hangs.

FISHY: Oh dear.

DC COMICS 52

WRITTEN BY GEOFF JOHNS, GRANT MORRISON, GREG RUCKA, MARK WAID

BREAKDOWNS BY KEITH GIFFEN • PENCILS BY PAT OLLIFFE • INKS BY DREW GERACI

SECRET IDENTITIES

Week 37

COLORS BY ALEX SINCLAIR • LETTERS BY TRAVIS LANHAM
ASSISTANT EDITED BY HARVEY RICHARDS • ASSOCIATE EDITED BY JEANINE SCHAEFER

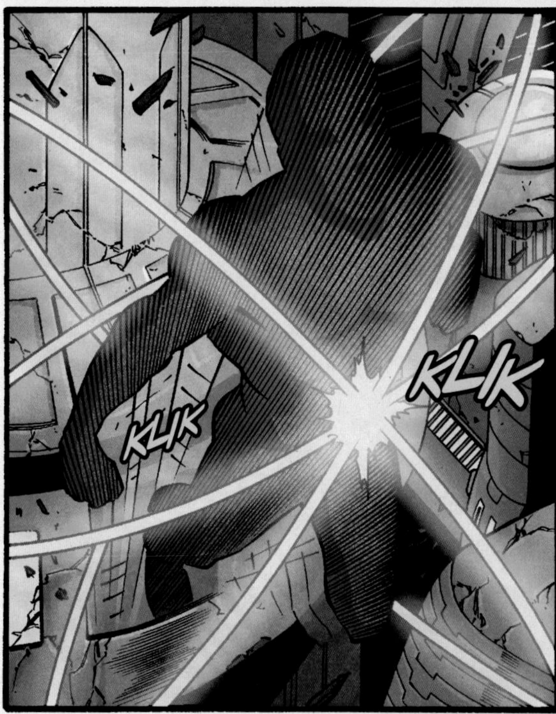

EDITED BY MICHAEL SIGLAIN
COVER BY J.G. JONES & ALEX SINCLAIR

--I AM.
MICHAEL?
KANDOR

DNA SCAN:
MICHAEL JON CARTER
100% MATCH
IT...
...IT *IS* YOU. HOW--?

TELL HIM *EVERYTHING*, BOOSTER. IT'LL BUY ME SOME TIME, AND HE'LL KNOW SOON ENOUGH ANYWAY.

JUST KEEP *TALKING.*
I'VE KNOWN WHAT'S UP WITH YOU FOR *WEEKS* NOW.

"WHEN I WENT INTO RIP'S LAB, THE CLUES WERE EVERYWHERE. I WAS STUNNED, CONFUSED. I ALMOST *ASKED* YOU ABOUT IT--

"--BUT RIP SHOWED UP TO *STOP* ME.

"I TOLD YOU RIP WASN'T IN THE LAB...THE FIRST OF *MANY, MANY LIES* I'D LEARN TO SPIN.
"CLOAKED FROM YOU IN A CHRONAL FIELD, HE TOLD ME THE *TRUTH* ABOUT YOU--AND WE MADE A *PLAN.*"

FIRST OFF, I HAD TO PLAY DUMB.
AND IF YOU WERE REALLY YOURSELF, SKEETS, YOU'D BE HAVING A FIELD DAY WITH THAT STATEMENT.

RIP KNEW HE WAS DESTINED TO FACE OFF AGAINST YOU, SO HE NEEDED WEAPONS-- BUT HE HAD TO STAY HIDDEN UNTIL HE WAS PREPARED TO FIGHT.
IT WAS MY JOB TO GATHER AN ARSENAL--
--AND THERE WAS NO WAY TO DO THAT UNDER YOUR 24/7 OBSERVATION. I HAD TO GET TOTALLY OFF YOUR RADAR SOMEHOW.

"SO WE PULLED A FAST ONE. RIP EXPLAINED HOW I COULD BE IN TWO PLACES AT ONCE--

"--WITH THE HELP OF TIME TRAVEL. RIP FAKED MY DEATH--

"--YANKING ME OUT OF THE TIMESTREAM AT A CRUCIAL MOMENT AND REPLACING ME WITH MY OWN FUTURE CORPSE--
"--SOMETHING I WOULD REALLY RATHER NOT DWELL ON, BY THE WAY."

"SUDDENLY, I WAS TWELVE WEEKS BACK IN TIME--CO-EXISTING BOTH AS BOOSTER AND UNDER A NEW, HUMBLE, VIRTUOUS IDENTITY THAT WOULD, FRANKLY, BE THE LAST PLACE ANYBODY'D LOOK FOR ME.
BOOSTER GOLD SAVES CITY
NEWS 9
LIVE

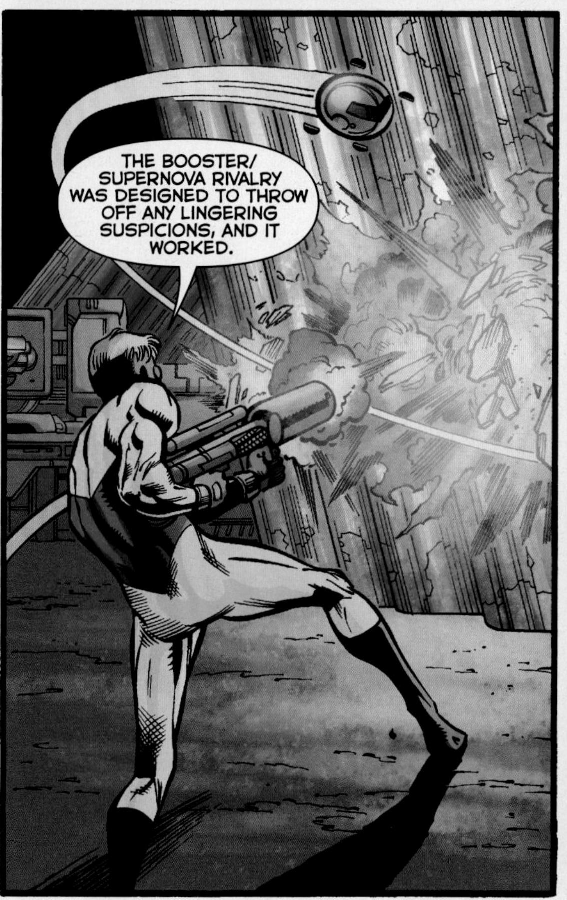
THE BOOSTER/ SUPERNOVA RIVALRY WAS DESIGNED TO THROW OFF ANY LINGERING SUSPICIONS, AND IT WORKED.

MEANWHILE, RIP--WHO HAD ME LIFT THE ATOM'S SIZE-CHANGING BELT AND GLOVES FROM JLA STORAGE--
--HE TOOK ADVANTAGE OF THE SUPER-SCIENCE IN THE BOTTLE CITY OF KANDOR.
THAT'S IT...ALMOST THERE...

AS SUPERNOVA, I BROUGHT HIM EVERY SUPER-WEAPON I COULD FIND, FROM LUTHOR'S KRYPTONITE GLOVE TO HAWKGIRL'S NTH METAL--
YEEOW!
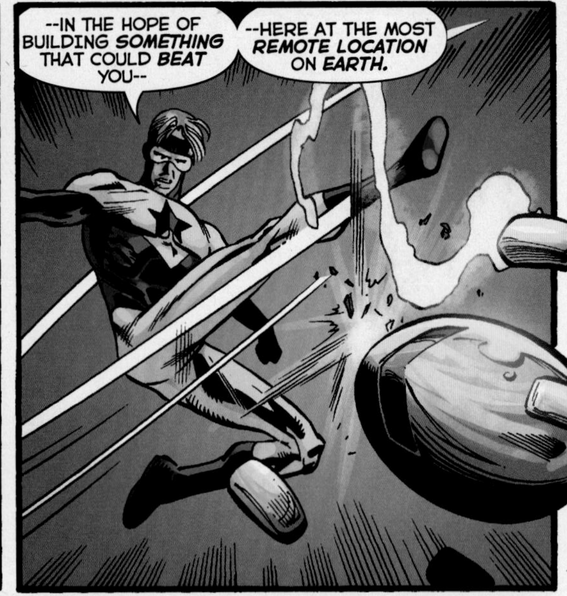
--IN THE HOPE OF BUILDING SOMETHING THAT COULD BEAT YOU--
--HERE AT THE MOST REMOTE LOCATION ON EARTH.

"THAT'S RIGHT, BUDDY. WE OPERATED OUT OF THE FORTRESS OF SOLITUDE."
EVEN LEVELED AND ABANDONED, IT'S SUBLEVELS WERE STILL INTACT.

AND DON'T THINK WE DIDN'T PLUNDER IT.

WHERE DO YOU THINK WE FOUND THE PARTS AND POWERS FOR THE NEW SUIT?

KEEP HIM DISTRACTED, BOOSTER. I'M ON MY WAY!
KLIK

THINK BACK. EVERYTHING I DID AS SUPERNOVA--EVERYTHING--WAS BASED ON UNEARTHLY LIGHTS AND APPLIED TELEPORTATION.

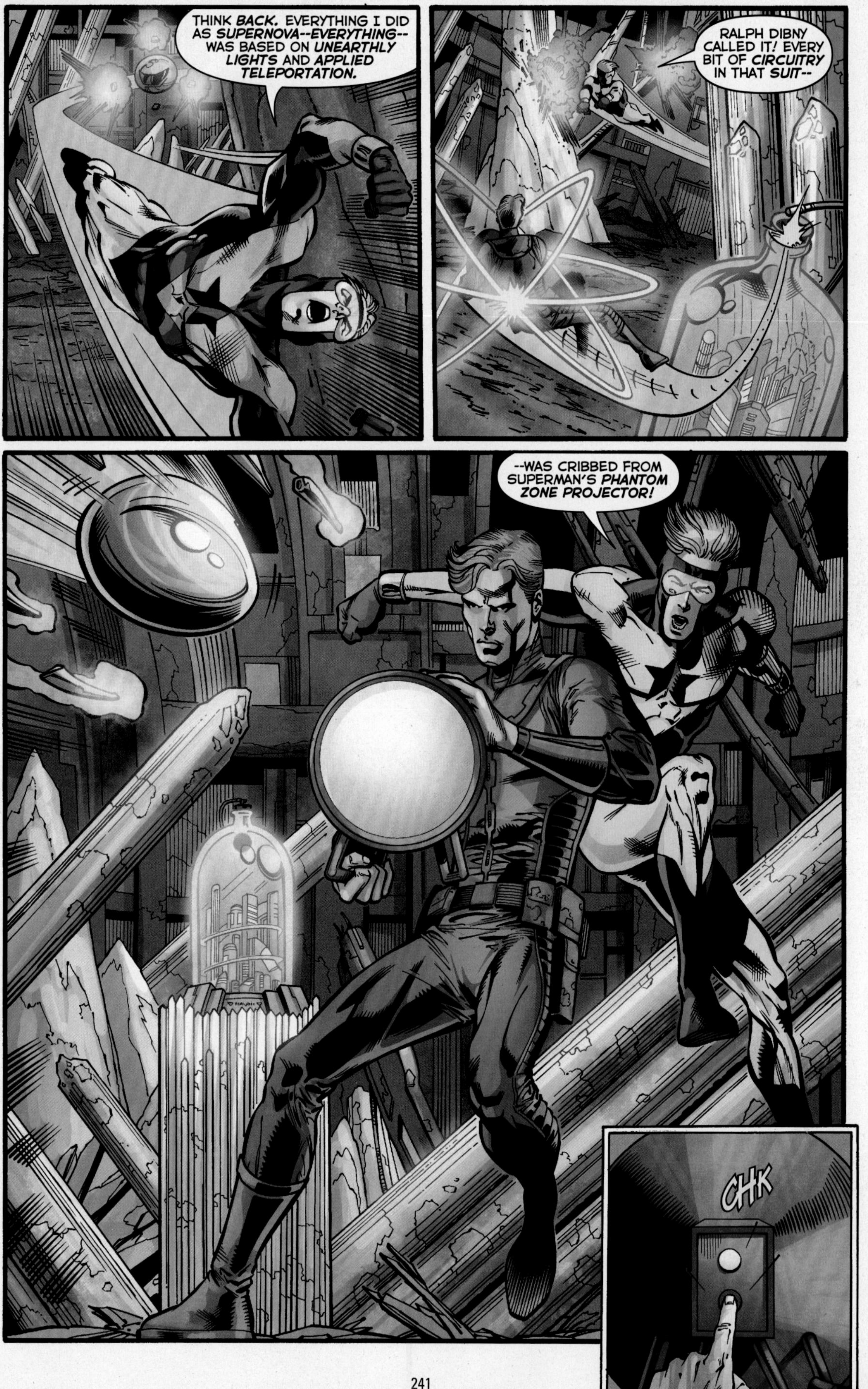

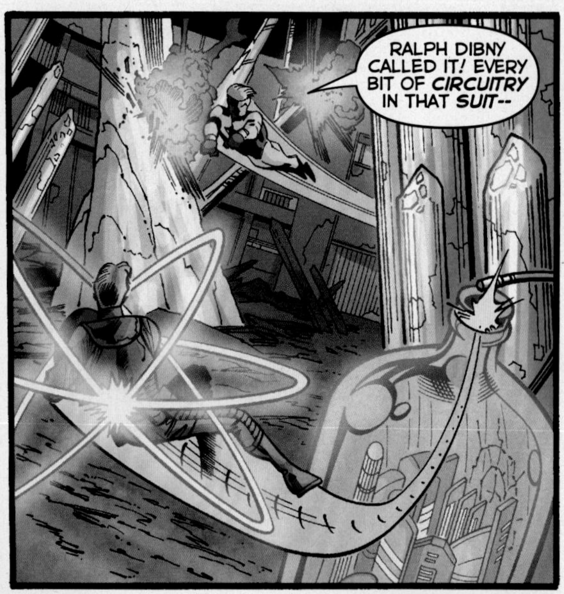

RALPH DIBNY CALLED IT! EVERY BIT OF CIRCUITRY IN THAT SUIT--

--WAS CRIBBED FROM SUPERMAN'S PHANTOM ZONE PROJECTOR!

CHK

NOOOO!
THAT'S IT! CRANK IT UP!
IT'S NOT A GUITAR AMP, BOOSTER! IT'S A PRISON PORTAL--
--WHAT THE HELL IS HE--

--AND SKEETS IS HOLDING ON FOR DEAR LIFE!
RIP, WHAT'S HE--
OH, DEAR GOD--

I'LL GO YOU ONE WORSE. IT'S NOT A MEAL FOR HIM.

IT'S JUST AN APPETIZER.

BUT IT BOUGHT US A RETREAT. ARE YOU READY?

READY?
READY FOR WHAT--?
FIFTY-TWO...FIFTY-ONE...

OH, NO, NO.

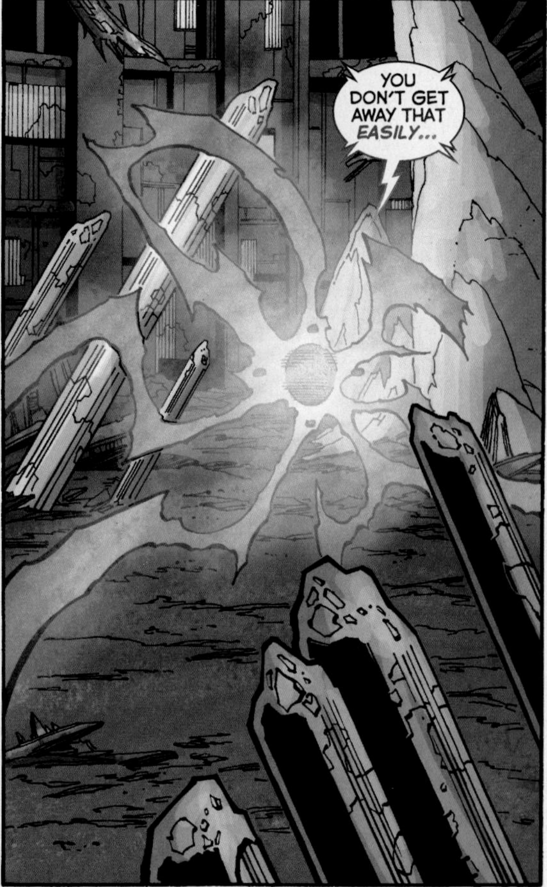
YOU DON'T GET AWAY THAT EASILY...

"ANYBODY SEEN *HAL?*"

Week 37, Day 4

Star City

OVER *THERE.*
WHEN HE SAW FIRST-HAND WHAT A *SINKHOLE* THIS CITY HAS BECOME, HE TOOK IT UPON THAT GREEN LANTERN *RING* OF HIS TO AT LEAST RESTORE SOME *BASIC SERVICES.*
I'D PUT HIM ON THE *PAYROLL* IF I HADN'T MADE *SELF-RELIANCE* A *PLATFORM ISSUE.*

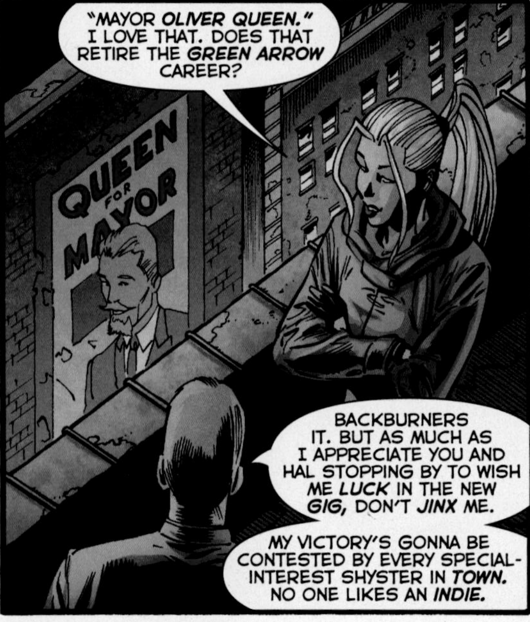

"MAYOR *OLIVER QUEEN.*" I LOVE THAT. DOES THAT RETIRE THE *GREEN ARROW* CAREER?
QUEEN FOR MAYOR
BACKBURNERS IT. BUT AS MUCH AS I APPRECIATE YOU AND HAL STOPPING BY TO WISH *ME LUCK* IN THE NEW *GIG,* DON'T *JINX* ME.
MY VICTORY'S GONNA BE CONTESTED BY EVERY SPECIAL-INTEREST SHYSTER IN *TOWN.* NO ONE LIKES AN *INDIE.*

YOU'LL WIN. YOU DON'T KNOW HOW NOT TO.
WHAT ABOUT YOU? WHAT'S BLACK CANARY BEEN UP TO SINCE THE WORLD WENT TO HELL?
YOU STILL WITH BARBARA'S "BIRDS OF PREY" OUTFIT?

YES AND NO. SABBATICAL. YOU REMEMBER A GIRL NAMED GYPSY?
SHAPECHANGER, RIGHT?
CAMOUFLAGE, ACTUALLY. SHE'LL FILL IN FOR ME WHILE I LEARN SOME NEW SKILLS OUT EAST. YOU WANNA COME WITH?
ONLY IF WE CAN STOP ON THE WAY TO FIND SOMEBODY.

OLLIE, I'VE ALREADY TOLD YOU, WE'VE ALL BEEN LOOKING HIGH AND LOW FOR RALPH.
EVERYONE WHO EVER PUT ON A CAPE OR A MASK HAS BEEN ASKED TO REPORT ANY SIGHTING WHATSOEVER.

HE'S UNSTABLE, DINAH. WHEN WE LOST HIM, HE WAS SEARCHING FOR A WAY TO BRING HIS WIFE BACK.
DON'T MISTAKE PASSION FOR INSANITY, OLLIE. RALPH JUST LOVED SUE TOO MUCH TO EVER, EVER LET HER GO.

HOW DOES THAT WORK...?

...HE WAS A FEISTY LITTLE BASTICH AND NO MISTAKE.
MAY THE BLESSINGS OF THE TRIPLE FISH GOD BE UPON HIS PASSING AND GRACE HIM WITH PEACE ON THE TRIPLEFOLD PATH.
NOW LET'S GET GOIN'.
AYYYY-MEN.
Week 37, Day 5

THIS IS WHERE WE PART COMPANY.
ALPHA CENTAURI'S THAT WAY.
I CAN SLINGSHOT YA ROUND TH' BINARY SYSTEM UP AHEAD IF YA NEED THE BOOST... MAYBE YOU CAN HOOK UP WITH ONE OF THEM GREEN LANTERN PARTORLS.

LET'S GO, FISHY.
ON TA TH' SEVEN GOLDEN PLANETS WITH THE EMERALD EYE!
SO WHAT DIDJA SEE OUT THERE ANYWAY THAT EVERYBODY WANTS TA KNOW?

I DON'T KNOW.
GIANT HANDS AND... AND...SOMETHING ELSE...I CAN'T REMEMBER.
LOBO, LOOK... WE JUST WANT TO THANK YOU FOR GETTING US THROUGH THIS...

YA CAN THANK ME BY NEVER CROSSIN' MY PATH AGAIN, STRANGE, HOW 'BOUT THAT?
GIANT HANDS.
FIGGERED IT HADTA BE SOMETHIN STOOPID.

PRINCESS.

I KNOW.
BUT WE CAN'T TAKE THE CHANCE THAT HIS BODY'S BEEN CONTAMINATED.
WE HAVE TO GO.

NO.

DON'T LEAVE ME!!!

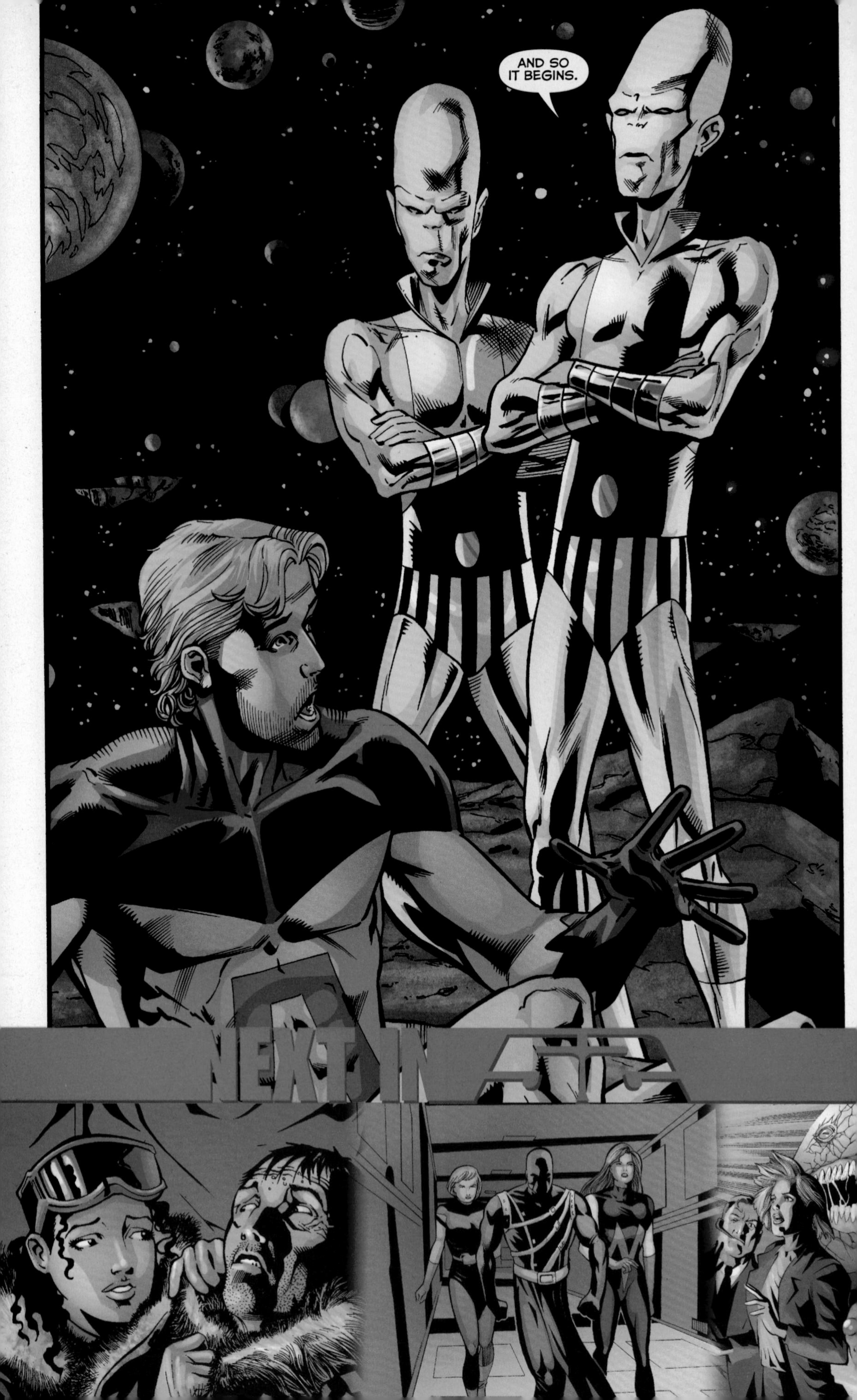
AND SO IT BEGINS.
NEXT IN

WEEK THIRTY-SEVEN NOTES

MARK WAID

At last, Supernova's identity is revealed. A lot of online fans had theorized Supernova was Ray Palmer, the Atom, but I promise you that it was only after we'd decided to hide him and Rip Hunter in Kandor that we realized how perfectly we were playing into that expectation. That's why, at the last minute, we added the "klik-klik" and atomic radiants to Supernova on page 235 — those were the Atom's trademarks.

And now that you know who's under the mask, I can talk about a moment of heart-break back during week 15, where I was overruled on something.

One of my favorite episodes of *The Simpsons* introduces the Springfield nuclear power plant's newest employee, the ultra-capable polymath Frank Grimes. Frank is gradually driven to insanity because no matter what he does to prove that he's a genius and that Homer Simpson is an atomic disaster waiting to happen, people ignore him and embrace Homer. In the end, faced with the madness of the Springfield community's unspoken mutual suicide pact, Frank snaps. And that was exactly the note I wanted to hit during Booster's week fifteen "death," because that's how I saw the Booster/Supernova relationship — Booster was Frank Grimes. Here's Booster's final speech as originally written:

SCRIPT EXCERPT

WEEK FIFTEEN PAGE EIGHTEEN

PANEL ONE

BOOSTER (big): HEY, METROPOLIS! You want a big, shiny STAR to light your SKIES? Well, HERE I AM!

PANEL TWO

BOOSTER (big): That's RIGHT, everydamnBODY! OOH! LOOK AT ME! I'M a big MYSTERYMAN who tries to make Booster Gold look like a JERK!

PANEL THREE

BOOSTER (big): OOH, I'M the city's BIG SENSATION in my wavy, blue CAPE! I'M everybody's new FAAAAAVORITE!

WEEK FIFTEEN PAGE NINETEEN

BOOSTER (huge): LOOK AT ME, I'M SUPERNOV—

[BOOM]

(CONTINUED)

WEEK THIRTY-SEVEN NOTES

MARK WAID (cont.)

I was particularly proud of that last line, not just because it was the truth, but because it reinforced my ironclad conviction that Booster's ego would never allow him not to eventually break down and take public credit for Supernova's acts of heroism. I was outvoted on the "stealth reveal," and bowing to peer pressure, I rewrote the scene under protest. Only time will tell if I was right or if I'm simply being bitter and stubborn, but I'll warn you right now, if my own personal history has taught us anything, it's to place your money on the latter.

Also of note: as recently established by Richard Donner and Geoff Johns in ACTION COMICS, all inhabitants of the Phantom Zone wear protective goggles. That information didn't get communicated to artist Pat Olliffe properly, which is why all the Zone inhabitants are shown wearing eyeglasses. If I were a less honest man, I would claim that the glasses were a deliberate clue to Skeets's true martinet.

Ralph Dibny on Supernova's real identity, week 31: "Superman being out of the picture was the key. One of two keys, if you want to be cute about it." Page 8, panel 3, week 37: lying in the rubble is the key to Superman's Fortress.

THE ORIGINAL ENDING FOR WEEK THIRTY-SEVEN WAS SCRAPPED WHEN THE STORY TOOK A NEW DIRECTION. HERE'S A SNEAK-PEEK INTO WHAT MIGHT HAVE BEEN:

Original Script

PANEL ONE (splash)
Rip and Booster — disheveled, bruised, costumes torn, clearly having been in a major fight — rematerialize elsewhere. We're super-tight on them.

DATESTAMP: Week 51, Day 7.

RIP (fades in): ...one...

PANEL TWO (BIG)
We pull way, way back to see that they're standing atop the Daily Planet Globe, all right — but the Globe lies embedded in the pavement, shattered, and Metropolis has been annihilated on a nuclear-blast level. There is no skyline, just rubble, and most of what is there is on fire. Strewn about are the corpses of numerous super-heroes.

PANEL THREE
Rip and Booster wince and shield their eyes from a brilliant blast of light from up and off.

RIP (fades in): ...zero

Art by Pat Olliffe & Drew Geraci

I'm not crazy.
HnNHnnKkk
KAFF KAFF
nyhh--
I'm not.
--HHARhnn
HNnnHAAAA--
--Aanngg ghnn HURTS hnnnn hnnnn...
I KNOW, CHARLIE. I KNOW IT DOES.
I'm trying to save his life.
...nhnm hnn KAFF khnk...
DO ANY OF YOU KNOW THE WAY TO NANDA PARBAT?
DO ANY OF YOU SPEAK ENGLISH? PLEASE...
He's dying and I'm trying to save him.
I can save him.
...I HAVE TO GET MY FRIEND TO NANDA PARBAT...
WRITTEN BY JOHNS, MORRISON, RUCKA, WAID
BREAKDOWNS BY GIFFEN • ART BY BENNETT & JADSON
COLORS BY HI-FI • LETTERS BY LEIGH
ASSIST. EDITOR RICHARDS • ASSOC. EDITOR SCHAEFER
EDITOR SIGLAIN • COVER BY JONES & SINCLAIR
Week 38, Day 1

If I can even *find* Nanda Parbat.
rrhhsss
rhhkkk
KAFF KAFF
KAFF
If I can get him there in time.
HKkkk
shhh POISON
hrkkk POISON
hkSHh
Then he won't die.
PLEASE, CHARLIE. JUST A SIP.
cCkckkSsh
POISON
KAFF
He'll be safe.
PLEASE, BABY, YOU GOTTA KEEP YOUR STRENGTH UP.
YOU hshhh THINK I DON'T rRrcKkk KNOW--
He'll be saved.
--STUPID cRKkrs GIRL
KAFF KAFF KAFF
I can save him.
hrm
heh
Please God...
STUPID GIRL...
...let me save him...
DC COMICS 52
BREATHLESS
Week 38

WHO ORDERED THREE HUNDRED THERMOMETERS?
Week 38, Day 2
Oolong Island
IT...IT MIGHT HAVE BEEN ME...
I HAVEN'T BEEN FEELING AT ALL WELL SINCE THAT DOCTOR DEATH TALKED ME INTO A CRACK ADDICTION...
LEAD SHIELDING'S MINE!
AND THE BEANS.
...AND I'LL TAKE THE THERMOMETERS IF NOBODY WANTS 'EM.
A WORD IN YOUR EAR, WILLIAM.
PROFESSOR MORROW!
COME ON IN!
I'M JUST HAVING DINNER.
A FAN OF THE COLD BEAN, I SEE.
THE DOWNFALL OF MANY A LONELY MAN OF SCIENCE.
err...
I SEE YOUR CONTRIBUTION TO THE WAR EFFORT IS FINALLY SHOWING SIGNS OF PROGRESS; I TOLD THEM YOU COULD DO IT, MY BOY.

NASTY.
I'M ONLY DOING IT TO PROVE I CAN DO IT RIGHT THIS TIME.
THE FIRST PLUTONIUM MAN TURNED OUT A DISASTER BECAUSE I WAS MENTALLY ILL!

err... YES.
YOU CERTAINLY SEEM A LOT MORE...PERKY, SHALL WE SAY, SINCE THEY TOOK AWAY YOUR MEDICATION...
NO... munnch... YOU WERE RIGHT!
I WAS HALF-ALIVE ON THOSE PILLS, PROFESSOR!
LOST IN A WORLD OF FOG AND BOREDOM.

TERRIFIED OF MY OWN IDEAS!
ANYWAY... YOU WERE SAYING, ABOUT THE WAR...
AGAINST WHOM EXACTLY? I KEEP MISSING THAT BIT...

STEADY, WILL!
YOU'VE BEEN SO RECLUSIVE RECENTLY I WANTED TO MAKE SURE YOU'D BE THERE TONIGHT TO WITNESS THE RIDE OF THE FOUR HORSEMEN.
HISTORY IN THE MAKING.

WAIT UNTIL YOU SEE WHAT THE GREATEST CYBERNETICS EXPERTS, TERATO-BIOLOGISTS AND GERM WARFARE SPECIALISTS CAN DREAM INTO LIFE GIVEN UNLIMITED RESOURCES.
IMAGINE THE UNIFICATION OF SCIENCE AND RELIGION, IN THE FORM OF UNSTOPPABLE DEATH MACHINES...

THE SOUL CODE YOU GAVE ME--I CAN IMPROVE ON IT...
HISTORY.
IT'S NOT SOMETHING YOU SEE EVERY DAY, WILL...
A NEW WORLD ORDER BEING BORN IN FIRE.

THE REVELATION OF APOKOLIPS, BOOK 10, CHAPTER SEVEN OF THE BIBLE OF CRIME.
"THERE WERE FOUR AGES OF DREAD APOKOLIPS IN ITS ANGUISHED, BLOODY MORNING."

"THE AGE OF HUNGER, RULED BY YURRD THE UNKNOWN, IN FORMLESS TIME BEFORE TIME..."
THRILLING, ISN'T IT?
NOT THAT I BELIEVE ANY OF THIS IRRATIONALIST NONSENSE, BUT CHANG TZU HAS SUCH A WONDERFUL READING VOICE.

"THE AGE OF WAR, WHEN ROGGRA SAT ON A THRONE OF SKULLS AND THE RIVERS RAN HOT AND RED WITH BLOOD.
"LORD OF THE AGE OF FEVERS WAS ZORRM."

WHAT HAVE WE MADE?

"THEN CAME AZRAEUZ, SILENT KING OF THE AGE OF DEATH, WHO RODE A PALE STEED ACROSS A DESERT OF ASH AND BONE AT THE BLACK DAWN OF THE FOURTH WORLD."

"BEFORE GODS, BEFORE NEW GODS, THESE TITANS RULED THE VOID.
"NO FLESH CAN BEAR THEIR PRESENCE, BUT CERTAIN MIGHTY FORMS ARE TO BE CONSTRUCTED THROUGH WHICH THE KINGS MAY EXPRESS THEIR SHATTERING COSMIC JUDGMENT!

"ONLY BODIES OF STONE AND STEEL AND STORM CAN CARRY SUCH RIDERS, AND HEREIN IS WRITTEN HOW SUCH VESSELS WILL BE MADE..."
INDEED.
NO ONE IN HISTORY HAS EVER HAD THE MONEY, THE GENIUS, OR THE RESOURCES TO DARE WHAT CHANG TZU'S SCIENCE-SQUAD HAS DONE!

THEY HAVE RISEN!!! THEY HAVE COME AGAIN!!!
THE EYES ARE BASED ON MY DEATH LENS DESIGNS.
THAT WAS MY IDEA.
WHAT D'YOU WANT, CYCLOPS? A CERTIFICATE?
Shh!

BLAKK
AH-DUMM

WHAT HAPPENED TO THE FOURTH HORSEMAN?
YURRD THE UNKNOWN, THE...THE HUNGER-LORD RODE OUT BEFORE THE OTHERS.
...OH GOD, WHAT HAVE WE MADE?

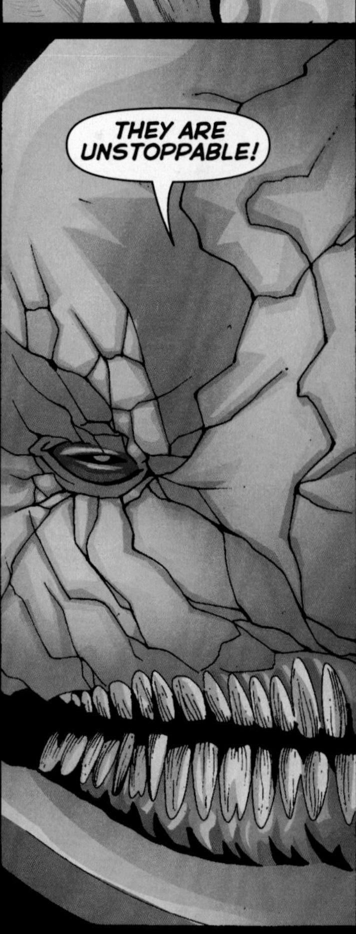
THEY ARE UNSTOPPABLE!

Week 38, Day 3
WH-WH-WHO
nffgg D-D-DO
YOU THINK YOU
ARE?

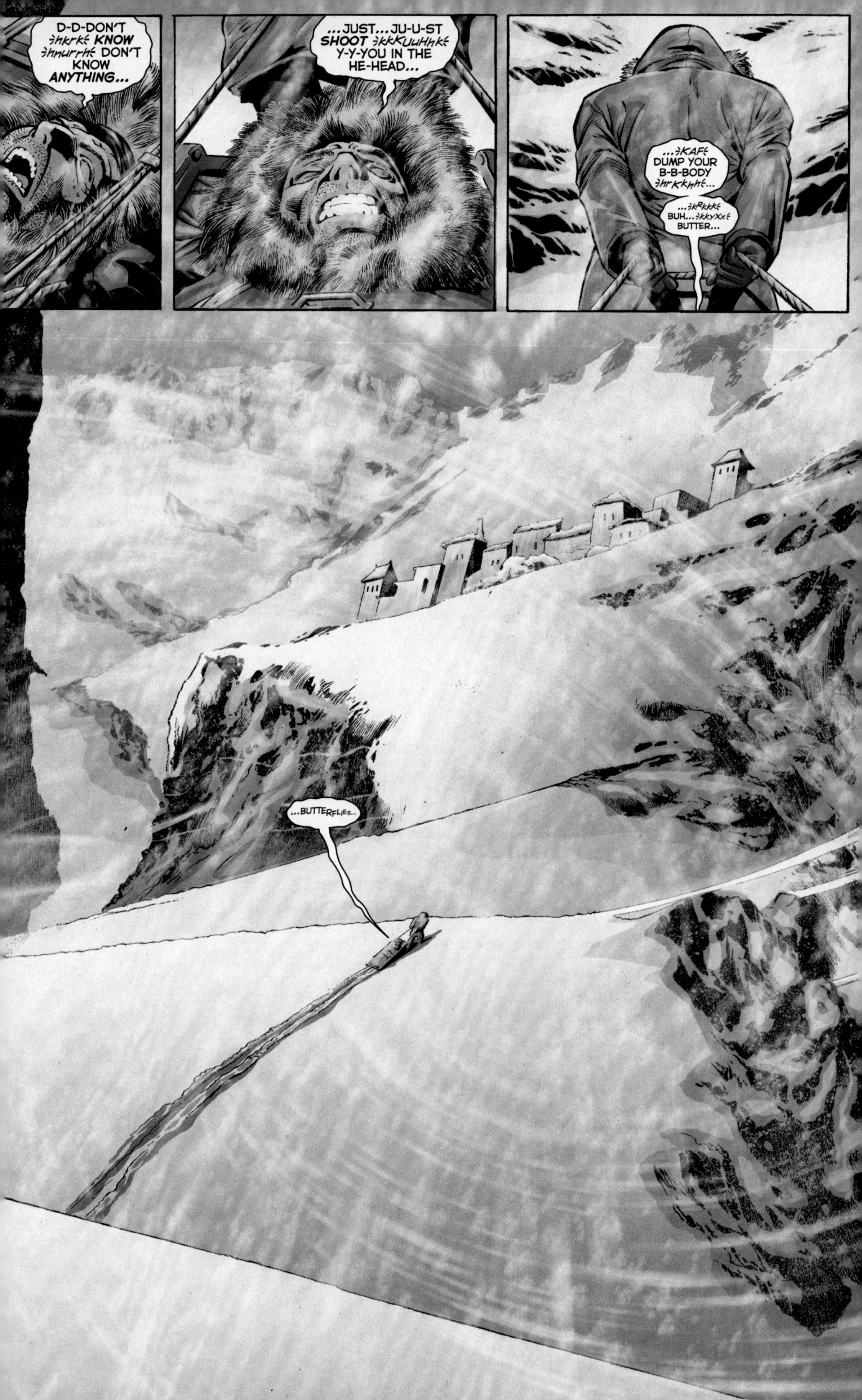
D-D-DON'T
hkrk KNOW
hnurrh DON'T KNOW ANYTHING...
...JUST...JU-U-ST SHOOT kkkuuhhk Y-Y-YOU IN THE HE-HEAD...
...KAF DUMP YOUR B-B-BODY hrkkhh...
...kRkkk BUH...kkyxx BUTTER...
...BUTTERFLIES...

I'm *not* crazy.

Week 38, Day 4

...another *friend*...
YOU...

...I've lost *so* many friends...
...YOU HAVE TO *HELP* ME...

...IT'S OKAY, WE'RE GOING TO NANDA PARBAT, THEY KNOW US THERE.
...I don't want to lose you, too, Charlie...

BUT I...I DON'T KNOW WHICH *TRAIL* TO TAKE...
...we're in this together, remember? You said we were in this together...

...I COULD USE SOME *HELP,* SOME *DIRECTIONS*...

...I'm afraid of who I'll become *without* you....
...WHICH WAY DO I GO?

"RAIN OF THE SUPERMEN"?
WHAT DO YOU EXPECT, JOHN? THE DAILY STAR'S A RAG THAT'S BEEN KISSING LUTHOR'S ASS FOR YEARS.
YOU HAVE TO STOP LEX LUTHOR.
WE'RE WORKING ON IT, GABE.
I KNEW THIS ONE, JOHN. HIS NAME WAS BRIAN. WE WERE IN THE SAME ROTATION WHEN WE WERE INDUCTED INTO LEX LUTHOR'S EVERYMAN PROJECT.
THAT BALD BASTARD GAVE HIM POWER OVER MAGNETISM. HE GAVE IT TO HIM AND HE TOOK IT AWAY AND IT KILLED HIM.
Week 38, Day 4
Steelworks
HE WAS HOLDING UP A COLLAPSING STEEL BEAM WHEN THEY STARTED FALLING. FROM WHAT I UNDERSTOOD, HIS POWERS DIDN'T FADE AS FAST AS THE OTHERS.
RESIDUAL MAGNETIC FIELD HELD IT, DR. MID-NITE.
OR A DESIRE TO SAVE LIVES. THE POWER OF FAITH CAN'T BE UNDERESTIMATED, KALA.
EVEN BY A SCIENTIST.
YOU NEED TO STOP HIM, JOHN.
WE NEED MORE INFORMATION. THERE'S NO TELLING WHAT'S IN THAT COMPLEX OF HIS. AND IF BEAST BOY AND THE TITANS STORM IN...
...WHO'S TO SAY HE DOESN'T SHUT OFF THEIR POWERS TOO?
MAYBE THAT'S HIS ULTIMATE GOAL. TO GROUND EVERY SINGLE ONE OF US.
THAT'S WHAT I'M GOING TO FIND OUT.
WHAT?! WHO'S THERE?!

NATASHA?
NAT, IS THAT YOU?
YEAH.
THIS IS A BUG. OR ONE OF MY BUGS ANYWAY. I BUILT IT.
THEY HAVE THE PHONES TAPPED. THEY'RE WATCHING ME ALMOST EVERY SECOND OF THE DAY.
I KNOW SOMETHING'S WRONG, UNCLE JOHN. I...
...I'M GOING TO GET EVERYTHING I CAN ON LUTHOR'S RESEARCH AND I'LL SEND IT OVER AS SOON AS I CAN.
THERE'S A HIDDEN ROOM OFF HIS OFFICE I SAW HIM GO INTO A FEW TIMES. I'M GOING TO TRY AND GET INSIDE.
HE'S GOT SOMETHING HE DOESN'T WANT ANYONE ELSE TO SEE.
NATASHA. JUST LEAVE. LEAVE RIGHT NOW AND COME HOME.
I CAN'T. TOO MANY PEOPLE HAVE DIED BECAUSE OF...OF THIS.
IF LUTHOR CATCHES YOU--
HE WON'T.
I'M SORRY. FOR EVERYTHING.
GOODBYE, UNCLE JOHN.

Week 38, Day 5
I hate the *noise* you're making, Charlie.
uuuuuuuuu
The sound of you trying to *breathe.*
uuuuuu uuu
The pain of it.
uuuu uuuuu
WE'RE *ALMOST* THERE, CHARLIE...
You've got to stay with me.
...IT'S NOT FAR NOW...
uuuu uhhh huhhhh
Please stay with me.
...WE'RE ALMOST THERE...

uuuuuuuu
Almost there.
Week 38, Day 6
uuuuuuuu
Almost there.
Almost--
uuuuuuuu
SHUT UP ALREADY!!!
uh--
I'M SORRY, CHARLIE.
I'M SO SORRY...

I think...
...NOTHING LEFT TO KEEP YOU WARM...
...I think I made a mistake, Charlie.
...ONLY THIS THING...
I think maybe...
...PROVIDE SOME INSULATION, AT LEAST...
...HOW D'YOU...?
KLIK
...just maybe...
...I've gotten us both killed.

I don't know where I am anymore.
I don't know which way to go.
hHHuuuhh
I'm lost.
You're my sense of direction, Charlie.
uhhhkkk-kkk-kkk
I don't know who I am without you.
CHARLIE!!
kkhsssss
Don't leave me...
kkkhhhsss
...please not again...
OH GOD, OH GOD, CHARLIE, HOLD ON...
...HOLD ON, PLEASE HOLD ON, I'M HERE, I'VE GOT YOU...

...I can't do this again...
...PLEASE--
YOU NEVER ANSWERED MY QUESTION.
AAHH!!
CH-CHARLIE?
GET THIS *KAFF KOFF* THING OFF MY FACE.
HARD ENOUGH TO BREATHE AS IT IS.
WHAT THE HELL *KAFF* ARE YOU DOING, RENEE?
TRYING... TRYING TO GET US TO NANDA PARBAT.
TRYING TO SAVE YOU, CHARLIE.

BUT YOU CAN'T.
I TOLD YOU...
...SOME THINGS YOU HAVE TO ACCEPT--
I CAN'T! I CAN'T! I NEED YOU--
--I DON'T KNOW WHO I AM WITHOUT YOU!
IT'S A TRICK QUESTION, RENEE...
...NOT WHO ARE YOU *KAFF*...
...BUT WHO ARE YOU GOING TO BECOME?
TIME TO CHANGE...

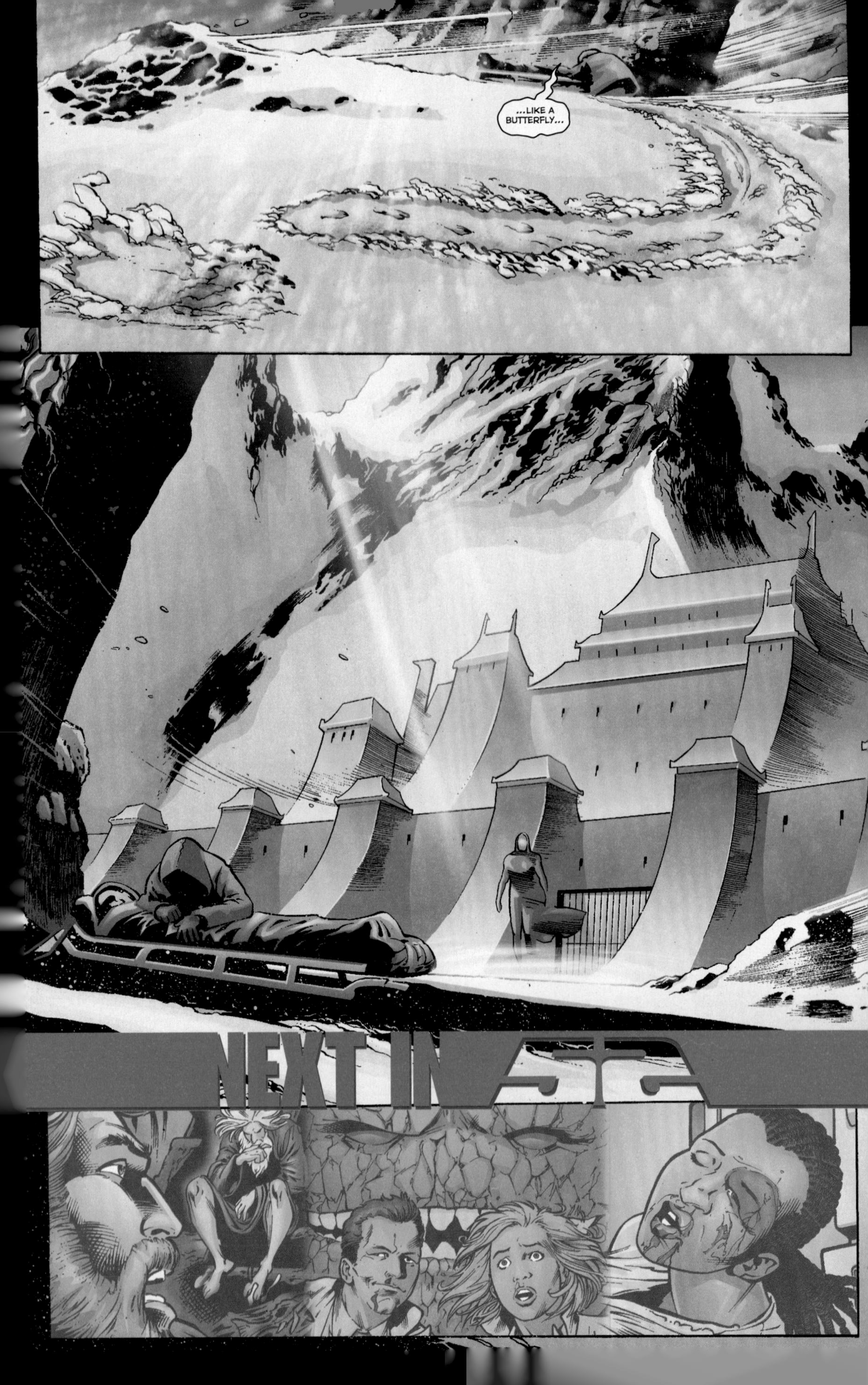
...LIKE A BUTTERFLY...
NEXT IN 52

WEEK THIRTY-EIGHT NOTES

GREG RUCKA

Morphine is a wonderful, terrible drug. It steals the pain and it replaces it with euphoria. It is, essentially, heroin in a medicinal form. It's addictive. It can kill you. But for people living with chronic pain, or dying with chronic pain, it is mercy in a syringe.

Four Horsemen arrive. Well, three of them. The Fourth, we're told, already rode out before the others. The amusement park fun ride that is Oolong Island back in Week Twenty-Three has become something altogether different; we've passed funny, we're onto Evil now. Really, the stakes change here, and it's through Veronica Cale that we know it, her horror at what she's become a part of. The look Will gives her as she says "...oh God, what have we made?" is another beautifully subtle bit of storytelling, and confirms what we're coming to suspect: those 300 thermometers were no mistake.

Week Thirty-Eight, Day 3 was a page I'd had in my mind's eye since the start, and, unlike most pages I hold in my mind's eye, executed in reality far more elegantly than I'd ever imagined.

"Butterflies." I wish I could say more about this here, but for the moment, all I can say is that some things honestly write themselves. We couldn't have planned it better if we'd tried.

Keith Giffen, for all of his cantankerous crotchety you-young-whippersnappers-don't-know-how-lucky-you-have-it manner, is a brilliant *writer*. He is as responsible as I or anyone for the emotional strength of this issue. In the build-up to writing Week Thirty-Eight, I'd been keeping pretty quiet about how I planned to execute Charlie's passing. It was Keith, more even than Wacker or Siglain, who I discussed the story with, and it was Keith, more than anyone, who made this story work. The weeks of dementia pay off in a moment of final lucidity. The blood-stained mask and the question mark in the snow. These were all Keith's ideas.

A lot of people don't realize, but when Denny gave Vic a birth name, he was naming him, in part, after Thomas Stephen Szasz, a prominent academic and psychiatrist. Szasz is best known, perhaps, for his book *The Myth of Mental Illness*, in which he argues (and I grossly simplify here) that mental illness is used by society to define and marginalize those behaviors it deems inappropriate or finds uncomfortable. Renee's declaration that she's "not crazy" was written in honor of that – she's dragging a dying man up a mountain in the hope of reaching a miracle, and that makes perfect sense to her, that is a rational, reasonable course of action to her at this time, even if everyone and everything around her is screaming otherwise.

The "uuuuuuuuuu" sound that Charlie is making for several pages comes from personal experience. It is a distinct sound, and those who have heard it will never forget it. It's the sound of a body preparing to stop, a vocalization made by the dying, and it is a truly awful, endless noise, so horrible and painful that when it does, finally and literally terminate, one is almost grateful for the silence.

These were some of the most difficult pages I have ever had to write.

(COMPARE WITH PAGES 273 AND 274 OF THIS COLLECTION)

52 WEEK THIRTY-EIGHT PAGE NINETEEN

PANEL ONE
MONTOYA carefully taking VIC in her arms. VIC is weak — he's on his last seconds, and maybe he knows it — but he is also lucid and he knows this is the last chance he has to connect with Renee, to make her see.

VIC (hoarse): But you CAN'T. I told you...

PANEL TWO
On MONTOYA, really starting to cry.

VIC (hoarse): ...some things you have to ACCEPT—

MONTOYA: I CAN'T! I can't! I need you—

PANEL THREE
MONTOYA holding VIC against her, pleading with him. VIC is beginning to fade. VIC bringing a hand up to touch MONTOYA'S CHEEK as she sobs.

MONTOYA: — I don't know who I am without you!

VIC (hoarse/small): It's a TRICK question, Renee...
VIC (hoarse/small/linked): ...NOT who ARE you *kaff*...

PANEL FOUR
Begin pulling out, as VIC starts to fall back in MONTOYA'S arms.

VIC (hoarse/small): ...but who are you going to BECOME?

PANEL FIVE
Continue the pull-back, so we're looking down at an angle on MONTOYA, now sobbing inconsolably. Holding VIC. VIC is dropping back, on his last breath.

VIC (hoarse/smaller): Time to change...

52 WEEK THIRTY-EIGHT PAGE TWENTY

PANEL ONE
The big panel, revealing the QUESTION MARK SHAPE that's been dragged in the snow, mixed and marred by Vic's blood. MONTOYA holds VIC in her arms, weeping silently. The last of the storm is ending.

The storm has ended.

VIC (smallest): ...like a butterfly....

Week 39, Day 1
Metropolis

DENNIS KNOWS SOMETHING.

HE KNOWS HIS *EVERYMAN* PROJECT FAILED AND SUPERHEROES FELL OUTTA THE SKY LIKE *MORTARS.*
PROBABLY FEELS LIKE *OPPENHATTER* DID WHEN HIS A-BOMB NUKED *TOKYO.*

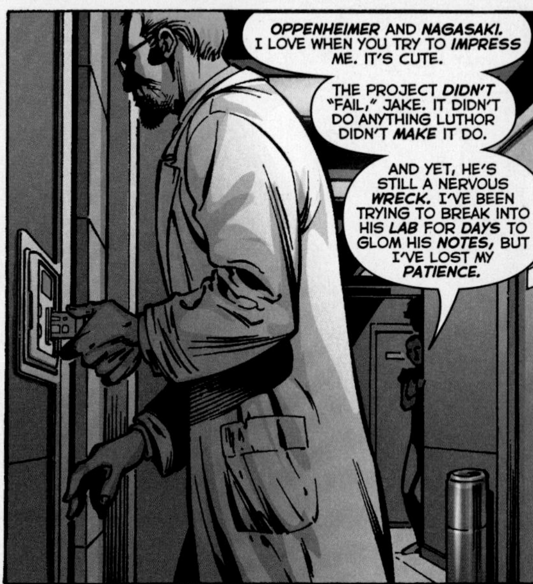
OPPENHEIMER AND *NAGASAKI.* I LOVE WHEN YOU TRY TO *IMPRESS* ME. IT'S CUTE.
THE PROJECT *DIDN'T* "FAIL," JAKE. IT DIDN'T DO ANYTHING LUTHOR DIDN'T *MAKE* IT DO.
AND YET, HE'S STILL A NERVOUS *WRECK.* I'VE BEEN TRYING TO BREAK INTO HIS *LAB* FOR *DAYS* TO GLOM HIS *NOTES,* BUT I'VE LOST MY *PATIENCE.*

I SAY WE FOLLOW HIM *IN.*

OH, NO, *NO*... OH, *JESUS*... WHAT ARE YOU--?

GET OUT! GET THE *HELL OUT* OF--

BOOOM

DC COMICS 52

POWERS & ABILITIES

Week 39

WRITTEN BY GEOFF JOHNS, GRANT MORRISON, GREG RUCKA, MARK WAID

BREAKDOWNS BY KEITH GIFFEN • PENCILS BY ANDY SMITH • INKS BY RAY SNYDER • COLORS BY ALEX SINCLAIR • LETTERS BY ROB LEIGH

ASST. EDITOR HARVEY RICHARDS • ASSOC. EDITOR JEANINE SCHAEFER • EDITOR MICHAEL SIGLAIN • COVER BY J.G. JONES & ALEX SINCLAIR

koff
YOU OKAY?
FINE. HE BOMBED HIS OWN-*koff*-LAB? HOW COME?
SAME REASON HE JAMMED THE SPRINKLERS AND EMPTIED THE FIRE EXTINGUISHERS! HE'S BURNING EVERYTHING!
GET SOME WATER IN HERE--
--AND I'LL SALVAGE WHAT I CAN!
IN HERE! HURRY!
Uh-oh...

NO RESPONSE FROM THE FIRE ALARMS, MS. GRAVES! I'LL CALL 911--
NO! THIS LAB IS SHIELDED. IT WON'T SPREAD!
DR. LAUGHLIN! ARE YOU IN HERE? DENNIS!
FOUND HIM...

...WELL, SOME OF HIM.
THIS WAS A THERMOEXPLOSIVE JOB. LOOKS LIKE HE SET IT HIMSELF.

MS. GRAVES, WE NEED TO PULL BACK AND LET THIS BURN OUT.
...

NO. I WANT THIS LAB CLEARED. EVERYTHING SALVAGEABLE, I DON'T CARE HOW SMALL. EVERY HARD DRIVE, EVERY SAMPLE, EVERY SCRAP OF PAPER.
NOW!

OH, DENNIS...

...YOU DUMB, DUMB BASTARD...

ATLANTIS. THE BIRTHPLACE OF MAGIC ON EARTH... NOW A *WASTELAND* CRUSHED BENEATH THE BOOTHEEL OF A VENGEFUL *SPECTRE*.
THE ATLANTIS *I* REMEMBER WAS BUSTLING WITH *LIFE*. *AQUAMAN* PROTECTED IT *FIERCELY*.
HE WOULD NEVER HAVE LET THIS HAPPEN UNLESS HE...

Week 39, Day 3

The Ruins of Atlantis

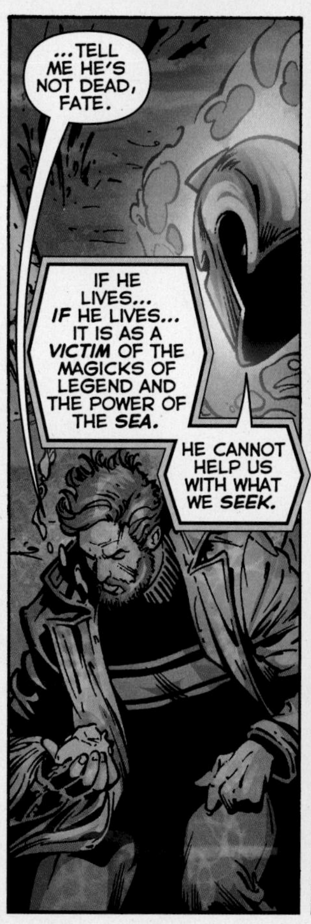
...TELL ME HE'S NOT DEAD, FATE.
IF HE LIVES... *IF* HE LIVES... IT IS AS A *VICTIM* OF THE MAGICKS OF LEGEND AND THE POWER OF THE *SEA*.
HE CANNOT HELP US WITH WHAT WE *SEEK*.

PERHAPS...
...PERHAPS *I* CAN ASSIST YOU...
AQUAMAN...?

THERE *IS*... NO AQUAMAN. HE IS GONE... HE WILL *COME*... I THINK...
HE SAVED... THE *CITY* BUT... LOST HIS *HOME*...? I...CAN'T *REMEMBER*...
THEN WHAT DO YOU KNOW, MAGICIAN, ABOUT THE *SHACKLES OF ARION*? WHERE CAN WE *FIND* THEM?
WE ARE IN DESPERATE NEED OF A *WARDED LINK* FROM ITS *ENCHANTED CHAIN*.

THE SHACKLES. YES. THEY ARE IN A CAVERN A HALF-DAY'S SWIM FROM HERE.
"...FOR BREAKING THE CHAIN FREES THE ANCIENT BEAST IT CONTAINS."
EASIER SAID...
I WARN YOU, THOUGH...NO ONE HAS EVER OBTAINED A LINK AND LIVED TO TELL THE TALE...
AND YET, FOR WHAT WE MUST DO, IT IS AN ABSOLUTE NECESSITY.

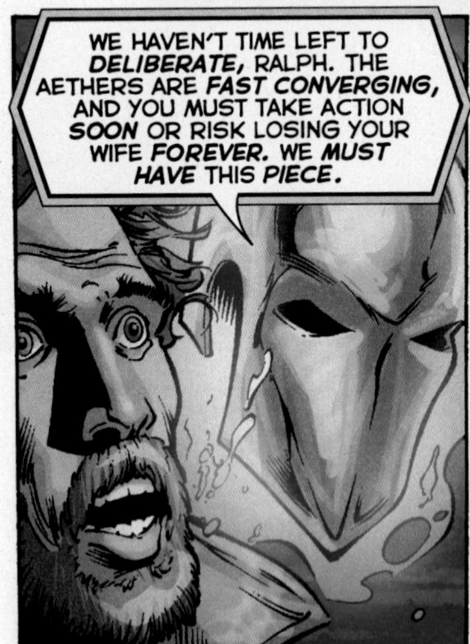
WE HAVEN'T TIME LEFT TO DELIBERATE, RALPH. THE AETHERS ARE FAST CONVERGING, AND YOU MUST TAKE ACTION SOON OR RISK LOSING YOUR WIFE FOREVER. WE MUST HAVE THIS PIECE.

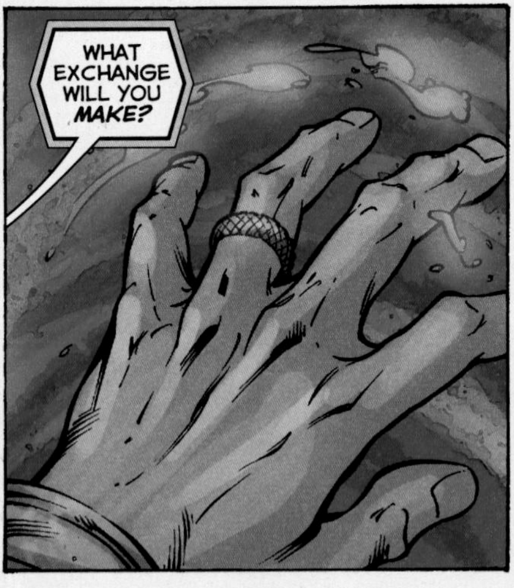
WHAT EXCHANGE WILL YOU MAKE?

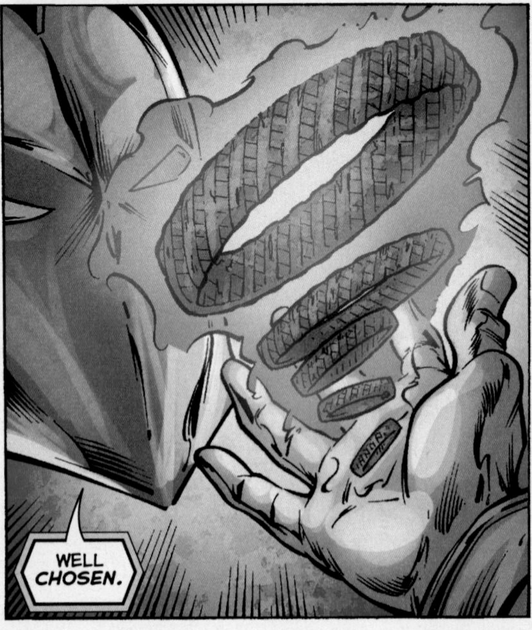
WELL CHOSEN.

WE HAVE VERY LITTLE LEFT TO GATHER, DON'T WE? WE'RE ALMOST DONE.
ALMOST.

Week 39, Day 6
Oolong Island
ACTIVATE SPACE WARP.

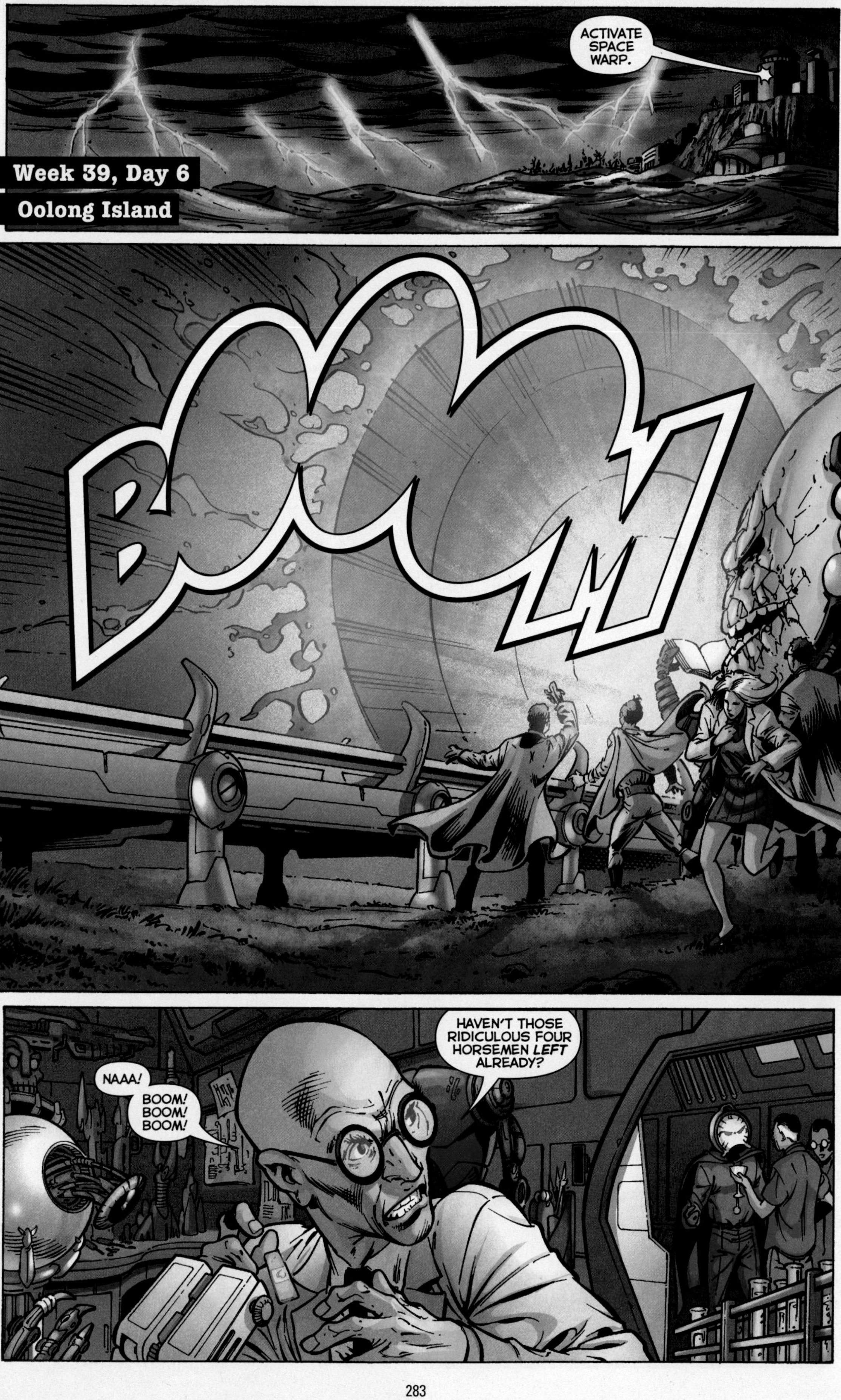

BOOM

NAAA!
BOOM! BOOM! BOOM!
HAVEN'T THOSE RIDICULOUS FOUR HORSEMEN *LEFT* ALREADY?

YOU KNOW WHAT'S RIDICULOUS? THEY CANCELLED THE HIGH CHAPPARAL REVIVAL AFTER ONE SEASON!
THE CIA KNOWS THAT'S MY FAVORITE SHOW!
SO, HAS THE GREAT DOCTOR SIVANA FOUND ANY SIGN OF MY MISSING 52 SECONDS?
I WASN'T EVEN LOOKING.

BUT I DID FIND A WORLD OF MICROSCOPIC, NAKED AMAZONS WHO WORSHIP YOU AS A GOD!

WHAT, REALLY?
LET ME SEE!
I KNEW THERE HAD TO BE A WORLD OUT THERE SOMEWHERE THAT VALUES THE WORK OF DOCTOR TYME...
WHAT ARE YOU? AN IDIOT?
I'M LOOKING AT A GREATER MYSTERY THAN ANY YOU'LL EVER COMPREHEND.

ARTIFICIAL TIME.
IN PARTICLE FORM.
I CALL IT SUSPENDIUM.

Hmm.
YOU NEVER DID TELL US WHAT HAPPENED TO POOR LITTLE MISTER MIND, THADDEUS.
SHOULDN'T HE BE HERE WITH US?
I'D FORGOTTEN ALL ABOUT HIM.
WE'RE TALKING ABOUT AN ALIEN MUTANT CATERPILLAR TRAPPED IN A LARVAL STAGE, DENIED HIS FULL POTENTIAL.

I JUST WANTED TO SEE WHAT WOULD HAPPEN IF I BOMBARDED THE SLIMY LITTLE CREEP WITH SUSPENDIUM RADIATION, WITHOUT HIS CONSENT.
I HAVE NO IDEA WHERE HE WOUND UP AFTER THEY BROUGHT ME HERE, BUT THE SUSPENDIUM'S BEEN ACTING VERY STRANGELY...
SAY NO MORE, THADDEUS, SAY NO MORE!
WE'RE ALL BORED ALREADY!

BOOOOM
WILLIAM!
THE SOONER THEY'RE *GONE*, THE BETTER.

IT IS DONE.

TIN CANS, *MERCURY* THERMOMETERS, A MISSING *GOLD* WATCH, *LEAD* SHIELDING...
YOU'LL HAVE TO TAKE CARE PEOPLE DON'T GET *SUSPICIOUS*, MY BOY.
AND YOU'VE BEEN TALKING TO YOURSELF.
SUSPICIOUS?
MAYBE IT'S JUST A SUBCONSCIOUS THING...

I CAN SEE THAT, IT'S JUST... PEOPLE GOSSIP...
THERE ARE NO...SECRET PROJECTS, I HOPE, WILL?
I'D NEED A LOT MORE THAN THAT TO REBUILD MY METAL MEN, IF THAT'S WHAT YOU'RE GETTING AT, PROFESSOR MORROW.
AND I'M BEING WATCHED CONSTANTLY.

Hmmmm.
I SUPPOSE...
I JUST FOUND SOMETHING THAT MIGHT INTEREST YOU.
REMEMBER YOU TOLD ME HOW THE RED TORNADO VANISHED IN SPACE?
WELL, I WAS WATCHING THE NEWS FROM AUSTRALIA AND, WELL...

AUSSIE ARTIST KICKS UP STORM WITH PROVOCATIVE NEW SHOW
DOES THIS LOOK FAMILIAR?

I SENT YOU THE LINK.
GOOD LORD, WILL! IT'S HIM!
I HAVE TO LOOK INTO THIS IMMEDIATELY.
EXCUSE ME.

I REALLY MUST DASH.
SURE.

LOOK, I DON'T WANT TO HAVE TO TELL YOU AGAIN.
PLEASE STAY OUT OF SIGHT, MERCURY.

OH SURE.
LIKE I EVER LISTENED TO A WORD YOU CAME OUT WITH!

SAY, DOC, DID I EVER TELL YOU I WAS THE ONLY METAL THAT'S LIQUID AT ROOM TEMPERATURE?

Week 39, Day 6
Shiruta, Kahndaq
The Gardens of Isis
<OSIRIS STILL HAS NOT LEFT HIS ROOM. HE STILL WILL NOT TALK TO BLACK ADAM OR MYSELF ABOUT IT.>
<YOUR BROTHER HAS TALKED TO *ME* ABOUT IT, ISIS. HE'S MY F-FRIEND.>

<AND WHAT DOES OSIRIS SAY, SOBEK? PERHAPS IF I SHOULD ATTEMPT TO SPEAK WITH HIM AGAIN-->
<I THINK A VISIT FROM YOU WOULD ONLY H-HURT RIGHT NOW. OSIRIS BELIEVES...>
<WHAT? WHAT DOES HE BELIEVE?>
<HE BELIEVES THE POWER INSIDE HIM M-M-MADE HIM KILL.>
<THAT HE IS ***C-CURSED.*** THAT ALL OF US ARE C-CURSED.>

<THAT'S ABSURD.>
<HE IS A BOY, ADAM. HE IS TRYING TO RATIONALIZE SOMETHING HE DID. SOMETHING HE FEELS INCREDIBLY *GUILTY* FOR.>
<I UNDERSTAND THAT, ISIS, BUT MY POWERS DID NOT MAKE HIM *KILL*. HE HAS THE WISDOM OF ZEHUTI TO TELL HIM THAT. HOW CAN HE BELIEVE SUCH MYTH?>

BOOOOM

KRAAKOOOM
<RAIN? THERE WERE NO CLOUDS IN THE SKY MOMENTS AGO.>
<ISIS? DID YOU--?>
<NO.>
<THE GARDENS! WHAT'S HAPPENING TO OUR BEAUTIFUL GARDENS?!>
<THEY'RE DYING!>

TIGHTEN THAT UP, YOU DON'T WANT THAT COMING LOOSE...

...AT FIVE POINT TWO MICRONS, ALTERNATING...

... CLEAR THE CHAMBER BEFORE PROCESS ACTIVATION...

...AMPLIFICATION AT THE THIRD AND AGAIN AT THE NINTH SEQUENCE...

DID WE SECURE THAT? IS THAT LEAD SECURE?

...REATTACHING THE RELAY INHIBITOR ON THE DORSAL SIDE...

Week 39, Day 5

GENTLEMEN AND LADIES...

DAMMIT, JAKE! YOU NEARLY MADE MY HEART STOP!
WHAT'RE YOU DOING? SECURITY'S MAKING ROUNDS, THEY'LL BE HERE ANY SECOND!

LUTHOR'S DOING SOMETHING IN THE ALPHA LAB!
I CAN ONLY GET A VISUAL FROM MY BUG IF I'M WITHIN FIFTY METERS. I HAVE TO STAY CLOSE!

ALL RIGHT...

...FOLLOW ME, I FOUND SOMETHING I WANT TO SHOW YOU.
IT'S NOT TOO FAR, SO YOU SHOULD STILL HAVE A SIGNAL, AND IT'S SAFE FROM SECURITY.
I DON'T UNDERSTAND WHAT'S GOING ON ANYMORE, JAKE.

IT'S LIKE THE WHOLE PROJECT HAS COME OFF THE RAILS.
WHY DID DOCTOR LAUGHLIN KILL HIMSELF? AND WHAT'S GOING ON IN THE ALPHA LAB?

IF THEY'RE PREPPING IT FOR TREATMENT, WHO'S THE SUBJECT?
NONE OF THIS IS MAKING SENSE ANYMORE!
I TOLD YOU, I FOUND SOMETHING...

...I THINK IT WILL EXPLAIN A LOT.

JAKE!!!

JAKE...
YOU'RE A GOOD *KISSER,* Y'KNOW THAT, BABY?
WANT TO HEAR SOMETHING *FUNNY?* I DON'T ACTUALLY NEED TO EAT THAT *MUCH* IN ORDER TO STEAL A THING'S *SHAPE...*
...JUST A *TINY* BIT WILL DO IT. I DID JAKE THERE OFF A *FINGERNAIL* CLIPPING.
...HANNIBAL... PLEASE...
THING IS, I JUST *LOVE* HOW IT *TASTES.* I CAN'T GET *ENOUGH* OF IT.

...EAT THIS!!!
GHHHNNN!!!

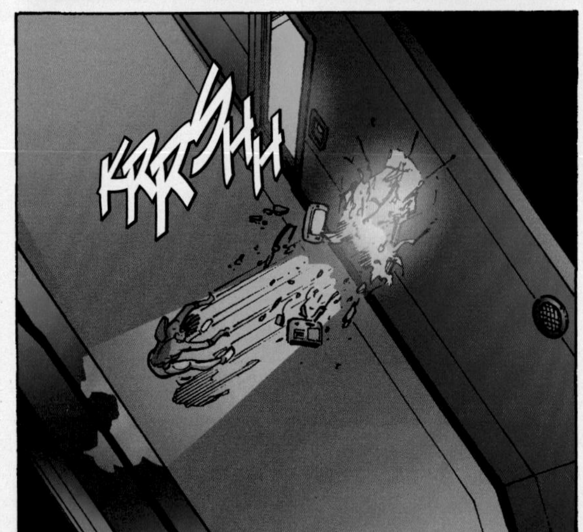
KRRSHH

YOU SICK DOG! YOU ANIMAL!
HNNnNn

I'LL MAKE YOU PAY! YOU'RE GOING TO PAY--
GNn HnnGHhhh

--YOU'RE GOING TO GET WHAT YOU DESERVE--
Heh

--WHAT YOU'VE EARNED--
YOU'RE CERTAINLY ONE TO TALK.

TELL ME, NATASHA...
...DID YOU EARN THE POWERS I GAVE YOU?

THE POWERS THAT I'M ABOUT...

CLIK
...TO TAKE AWAY?

YOU...THE PROCEDURE WAS FOR YOU?
BUT YOU--YOU WERE INCOMPATIBLE!

nhnn
YOU'VE ALWAYS BEEN A SMART GIRL, NATASHA.
DENNIS LIED.
ALL THOSE TIMES HE REPORTED BACK...

...HE LIED.

SUBJEC
Luthor, Lex.
RESULT:
ELIGIBLE FOR
TREATMENT

YOU'RE AS MUCH AN *ANIMAL* AS EVERYMAN.

WRONG.

nhh

TO BE CONTINUED IN 52 VOLUME FOUR

WEEK THIRTY-NINE NOTES

MICHAEL SIGLAIN

Originally — and this is a spoiler alert for those of you who decided to miss the weekly bandwagon and wait for the trade — a major **52** player was supposed to die in this issue, but there was just too much ground to cover, and too many other stories to touch upon, so his death scene was pushed back to a later week. While this character's ultimate death is certainly the goriest moment of the series, week 39 is no slouch either.

52 has had its share of gruesome moments (after all, Black Adam rips a villain in half way back in week three), and in this issue we learn what really happened to Jake, as Hannibal reveals his Lecter-like taste for human flesh. This page was originally colored nice and bright — to go for the shock effect — but we decided to go for a darker, creepier feel, which makes the scene all that more horrifying. The red and white checkered tablecloth and the glass of wine are two nice little morsels of black humor that balance out the shock and terror of seeing a bloody dead body lying on an operating table. And, yes, everyone involved in **52** is a little twisted. That's what happens when you work on a weekly book.

Let's talk about the opening. It was during one of our weekly conference calls that the four writers came up with the last-minute idea that LexCorp Doctor Dennis Laughlin was withholding information about the Everyman Project from Lex Luthor. Everyone wanted Lex to gain powers (by artificial means, of course), but we had already stated that all of his attempts to alter his DNA came back negative. That's when the question was raised, "What if one of the LexCorp scientists was altering the results?" And then the light bulb popped on above all of our heads. By using a character that we already established, we could give Lex his powers, and also have the readers sympathize with the doctor who was trying to do the right thing, and who ultimately gave his life for the greater good. Plus, it allowed us to open this issue with a bang. Literally.

And in an extra little behind-the-scenes peek behind the curtain, the last page — which is the big dramatic splash of Luthor holding up Natasha — was actually drawn without the ripped "S-shield" on Lex's chest. Giving credit where credit is due, it was Keith Giffen who came up with the idea of having the shirt torn to reflect Superman's infamous S-shield. The design was in the layouts, but when it was drawn by the awesome Andy Smith, it was thought that it might be a little too convenient to have the shirt rip in exactly that way. Then, after seeing the page, we decided to go back to Giffen's layouts and have the tear resemble the S-shield, thanks to a last-minute tweak from colorist extraordinaire Alex Sinclair.

And as for the cover, well, you'll believe Lex Luthor can fly.

BREAKDOWNS

BY **KEITH GIFFEN**

Compare with the final version on page 288.

PENCILS

BY **ANDY SMITH**

PENCILLER ART OF ANDY SMITH INKER PAGE# 12
TITLE 52 ISSUE # 39 MONTH INTERIORS

DOUBLE PAGE SPREAD: CUT AS SHOWN, ABUT PAGE EDGES, TAPE ON BACK, DO NOT OVERLAP

Keith Giffen's breakdowns are used as a guide — but occasionally an artist (often instructed by the editor) will deviate from the layout slightly, when needed. In this example, more room was given for the panel showing Isis's reaction to the dying flower gardens.

COVER GALLERY

ART BY **J.G. JONES** WITH **ALEX SINCLAIR**

WEEK **TWENTY-SEVEN**

WEEK **TWENTY-EIGHT**

WEEK **TWENTY-NINE**

WEEK **THIRTY**

WEEK **THIRTY-ONE**

WEEK **THIRTY-TWO**

WEEK **THIRTY-THREE**

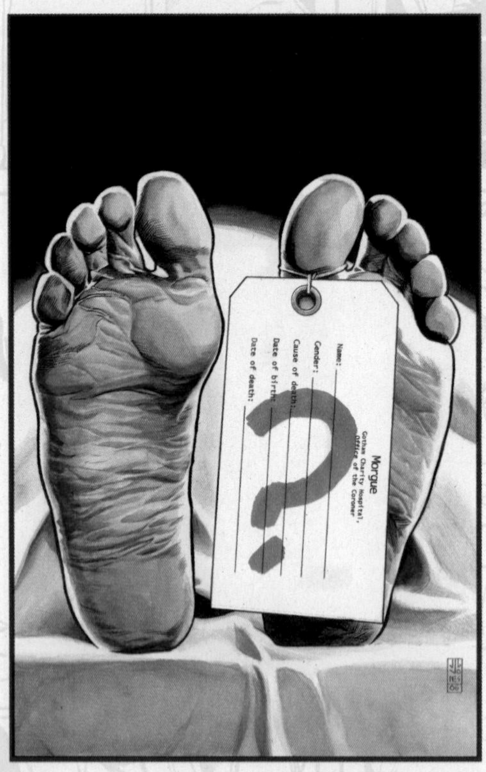

WEEK **THIRTY-FOUR**

WEEK **THIRTY-FIVE**

WEEK **THIRTY-SIX**

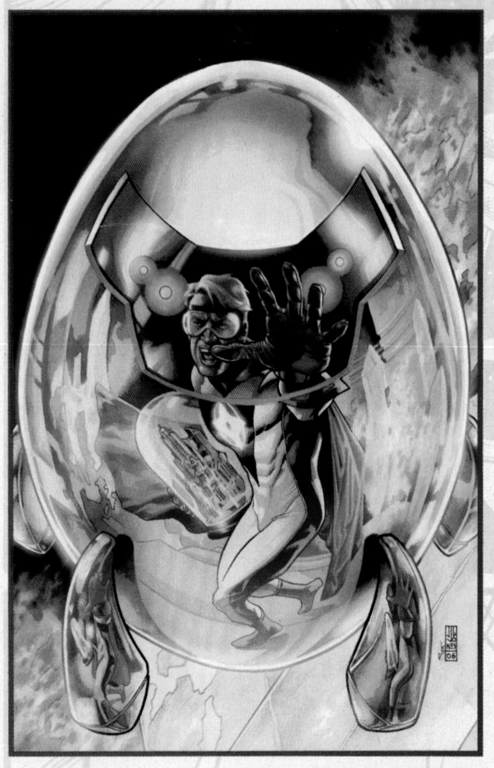

WEEK **THIRTY-SEVEN**

WEEK **THIRTY-EIGHT**

WEEK **THIRTY-NINE**